JURYMAN'S
TALE

THE JURYMAN'S TALE

Trevor Grove

BLOOMSBURY

The names of the jurors in the case
R v. Korkolis and Others have been changed

First published 1998

Copyright © 1998 by Trevor Grove
This edition first published 2000

The moral right of the author has been asserted

Bloomsbury Publishing Plc,
38 Soho Square, London WIV 5DF

A CIP catalogue record for this book
is available from the British Library

ISBN 0 7475 4558 8

10 9 8 7 6 5 4 3 2 1

Typeset by Hewer Text Ltd, Edinburgh
Printed in Great Britain by Clays Ltd, St Ives plc

CONTENTS

FOREWORD

by Lord Alexander of Weedon QC

Nothing in our law is more fundamental than the doing of justice in serious criminal cases. It is vital to victims of crime, to defendants, and to the confidence of society in our laws.

But we do not entrust this task to trained professional judges. Instead we ask twelve ordinary men and women, chosen at random, with widely varying intellects, education, interests and prejudices, all of whom are wholly untrained in the law, to undertake the awesome responsibility of deciding guilt and innocence. Jurors can give no reasons for their decisions, and they cannot talk afterwards about what took place as they discussed their verdict in the jury room. They are amateurs to the legal process, and inevitably they are sometimes fallible.

Yet for approaching eight hundred years we have favoured this system of justice. It is deeply embedded in our national psyche as a protection against unjust convictions or the pressures of an over-mighty state. Oliver Wendell Holmes, the great American jurist, said of trial by jury that it 'keeps the administration of the law in accord with the wishes and feelings of the community'. Why? Deep down we probably doubt the ability of judges to understand, let alone sympathise with, the accused in the dock. Judges can become 'case-hardened' or in other words just plain cynical.

Most criminal trials raise the fundamental issue of whether

the jury believes the victim, or whether it thinks that the defendant may possibly be right in protesting an alibi or the lack of criminal intent. Trevor Grove served as a juror in just such a trial. The charge was kidnapping. The hearing at the Old Bailey lasted some sixty-four days. But for all its length, for all the flummery and verbiage, there was one issue at the heart of the case. Was the victim genuinely kidnapped, or did he conspire with the defendants to fake a kidnapping so that he could get a ransom from his loving family and so settle his debts? The jury eventually reached its verdict, but only after long and anxious consideration. The conscientiousness with which they approached their role was highly impressive.

For all the importance of jury trials, we know little about what jurors experience and think during a case. What this book does is bring the experience of a jury to life through the pen of a gifted, witty and perceptive journalist. The majesty, gloom and tawdriness of the Old Bailey, the strengths and foibles of barristers, the changes of atmosphere as the trial meanders from November to March, the strain of delivering the verdict are all graphically sketched.

But fine and highly readable a story as this is, the effect and purpose of the book is ultimately serious and important. While Trevor Grove critically examines the jury system, the way it is shown to work gives one more vote of confidence that it is worthwhile. He also indicates ways in which the system can be improved. The role of the jury, and the essential law relating to the case, could be outlined by the judge at the start of the trial. Jurors could be encouraged to take notes from the outset, and get an explanation of when and how they can put any questions to the judge. Above all we are reminded that the present system for exemptions which enables people to get out of jury service favours the professional and affluent classes, who sadly often regard jury work as unworthy of their time. This could largely be

Foreword

redressed if people were to be given plentiful notice of jury service so that they had less excuse for avoiding it.

The author strikes a resounding chord when he reminds us of just how fundamental is the role of the juror to upholding a soundly based democracy. We are all the richer that he made no excuses, sought no exemption, did his duty and has told us his gripping tale.

March 1998

TRIED AND TESTED

OUT OF THE WOODS

In a democracy, law is made by the will of the people and obedience is given to it not primarily out of fear but from good will. The jury is the means by which the people play a direct part in the application of the law.

– Lord Devlin

The jury system puts a ban upon intelligence and honesty, and a premium upon ignorance, stupidity, and perjury.

– Mark Twain

I regard the jury as one of the great bastions of our liberty. I do so whatever its defects.

– Sir John Morris QC, former Attorney-General

In the spring of 1997 Stuart, Kate, Anna, Sophie, Eduardo, Keith, Magnus, Terrie, Bob, Pat, Daphne and I experienced one of the most extraordinary days of our lives. It was the culmination of sixty-four days of being at very close quarters with each other from ten every weekday morning until four o'clock every afternoon.

Back in November the previous year, when we first encountered each other, we were a group of strangers, with very little in common other than that we were all, give or take a few miles, Londoners.

Four months later, on a Wednesday evening in March, you might have seen us drinking in a pub not far from St

Paul's Cathedral, packed tightly around a single table. You would have judged that there was something odd about the mood of the group as we exchanged telephone numbers and addresses, a kind of stunned hilarity. We must have looked like the survivors of an air-crash.

We were in fact the survivors of an ordeal not much less stressful. We were the twelve members of a newly discharged Old Bailey jury. A few hours earlier, shortly after three in the afternoon, we had sent the last of many pencilled notes to the judge. We entered the jury box in Court 5 for the final time with every eye in the room fixed on us and our hearts thumping. In solemn tones the clerk of the court asked if we had reached a verdict. We had. And was this the verdict of a majority or was it the verdict of us all? It was the verdict of us all.

Such decisions are not reached easily or lightly. We were legal amateurs, after all: a dozen very ordinary men and women, including a postman, a Heathrow cleaner, a retired schools inspector and a Sainsbury's check-out lady. From the onset of the frosty winter of 1996 to the first days of the following spring, just as the 1997 general election was getting under way, our lives had been subjected to an immense upheaval. We had been frog-marched into a world we knew nothing of, speaking a language we sometimes barely understood, governed by regulations that made us feel we were back at school again. And when we got home from this topsy-turvy working day, we weren't even allowed to talk shop with our nearest and dearest.

For week after week we had been guided and misguided through a forest of bizarre criminal intrigue. It concerned a violent South American-style kidnap, heavy weapons, big-time gambling, blackmail, and allegations of a major police conspiracy. Our credulity was alternately appealed to and abused. Then, after four months of this, we had been abruptly abandoned and ordered to resolve our confusions as best we could on our own. We were like the befuddled lovers in *A Midsummer Night's Dream*, after Puck had scrambled their wits and left them sleeping on the forest floor. The judge's summing up was supposed to provide signposts towards the truth, which it did; but those that might have been of most use were subtly camouflaged in the legal undergrowth.

For nearly three and a half days we had sat deliberating: fifteen hours and fifty-five minutes, to be exact. We had had hundreds of hours of conflicting evidence to remember and resolve. Our jury room was submerged in stacks of ring-binders, documents in tottering heaps. There had been some eighty witnesses, a police video, scores of tape recordings and a hundred and three exhibits. They included a gun, an array of hypodermic syringes, a pair of handcuffs and a sinister leather mask with a zip across its mouth. Sheer weight of evidence, whatever its quality, can bamboozle the clearest mind.

Yet somehow we had found a road through the woods. And now, under the gaze of the whole court – the black-robed judge, the barristers in their horse-hair wigs, the ashen-faced prisoners, the police, the prison officers, the press – we had delivered our conclusion.

Anyone who has ever done jury service will recall the awesomeness of this moment and the intense feeling of relief once it is over. As the twelve of us walked out of the Old Bailey entrance into the bright March sunshine we felt a strong mixture of emotions. A sense of release was one of them. Another was a conviction that our small band of involuntary volunteers had done a demanding job well – maybe better than each of us had secretly expected. No wonder we marched across the road into McGovern's and ordered doubles all round.

THE SUMMONS

We had received our call to arms six months earlier.
Typically, my mail consists of a letter from an estate
agent beginning 'Dear Home Owner' and a sharp note
from the dental hygienist. But this October morning there
was a surprise. In one envelope there was a folded yellow
form and a sheaf of pamphlets. There was no question as
to what it was all about. The coat of arms and the words
at the head of the page were unambiguous: 'In the Central
Criminal Court at the Old Bailey,' it read. And underneath:
'Jury service'. I felt a small pop of apprehension.

There is no getting away from it: the yellow form is an
intimidating document. 'This is your jury summons,' it says
curtly. Your eye is drawn immediately to a shaded box:

Warning

You may have to pay a fine if:
you do not attend for jury service without a good reason
or you are not available to be a juror when your name
is called
or you are not fit to be a juror because of drink or drugs.

Although strewn with friendly get-out clauses for the
under- and over-privileged, the message to you and me
boils down to this: 'Turn up at such and such a court
on such and such a day at such and such a time. You may
be able to wriggle out of it. But if you do, we'll nail you
next time round, when it could be even less convenient.'

There are almost no occasions in the lifetime of the
modern Briton when the State intrudes in this peremptory
fashion. We grumble about bureaucracy. But how often are
ordinary citizens ordered to perform some disagreeable duty

which they have not brought upon themselves? A summons to appear before a magistrates' court for a motoring offence is seldom unexpected nor always undeserved. We must pay our taxes, educate our children and obey the law. Otherwise our civic duties are virtually nil compared with a country like Israel, say, or China, where you are ordered about as a matter of course. Even if you are Swiss you must spend weeks every year cycling around in uniform learning how to fend off invaders with a penknife. But as for the British, not since National Service was abandoned at the end of the 1950s have any of us been routinely compelled to lift a finger for Queen and Country. Even voting is non-compulsory.

Opening a summons for jury service must feel quite like it did to get one's call-up papers. Except that young men in those days at least knew roughly when to expect the buff envelope. Not so the prospective juror. The judicial tombola that picks out the names of some quarter of a million unsuspecting adults every year is as fickle as the giant finger of the National Lottery. It strikes out of the blue, without warning. Miss A may have been summoned three times in ten years while her neighbour Mr B will spend a lifetime wondering why he never has.

Naturally, if you are British, your first instinct on being ordered to do something by the authorities is to find a reason not to. In the case of jury service, Step One is to recollect whether you are at least 18, under 70 and on the electoral roll. You almost certainly are, or you would not have been summoned in the first place. So you proceed to Step Two. This is to scrutinise the list of exemptions. It is encouragingly long. It fills a page and a half of the yellow form. Those who are disqualified from doing jury service include the mentally ill, those with serious criminal records, anyone who has received a suspended sentence or a community service order in the last ten years, together with police and prison officers, lawyers, court officials of every description and, rather puzzlingly, clergymen. Less obviously, members of both Houses of Parliament, servicemen, doctors, dentists and vets are among those who may be automatically excused. You cannot be a juror if you are 'one of the Active Elder Brethren of the Corporation of Trinity House of Deptford Strond'. Who the Active Elder Brethren are is not explained, nor what it is they get up to in Deptford Strond.

At this point, the potential juryman will want to pause to enjoy a moment's indignation. Why on earth should peers and backbench politicians, among the most dispensable of working folk, be excused? Why should men and women in holy orders, who are surely – ayatollahs excepted – uniquely qualified to be fair-minded judges of their fellow men, be disqualified?

If MPs are too busy or too useful to take the oath, what about child-minders, pastry-cooks and bus drivers? If their lordships are too lofty or too loopy for the job, what about members of White's or believers in UFOs? As for lawyers, I have met several barristers who secretly yearn to experience the real-life drama of the jury room. I see no reason why they should not. In France, the judges join their jurors to deliberate on the verdict. Allowing counsel to experience a juror's lot from time to time – if only as a silent, non-participating observer – might be salutary.

In any event, short of taking holy orders or being elected an Active Elder Brother of the Corporation of Trinity House of Deptford Strond, I clearly had no claim to be excused. Was there another way out? This was not the first time Justice had caught me in her game of blind-man's-buff. I had done jury service before. I recalled that when the jury bailiff at Southwark Crown Court dismissed us after our fortnight's stint, he had added a parting shot about our being excused jury duty for another something years.

How many was something? It felt like only yesterday that the twelve of us had sat in our jury room on the south bank of the Thames, within ahoying distance of HMS *Belfast*, trying to decide whether a Covent Garden break dancer was guilty of a staggeringly minor drugs offence. (He was, but got off with probation: even so, when I saw him a few weeks later in the Piazza I hid my face, feeling like Judas.)

It was the year when Peter Carey's *Oscar and Lucinda* had not only won the Booker Prize but for once deserved to. I had read it in the longueurs while waiting to be assigned to a case. Crikey. That was 1987. Ten years ago. I checked the yellow form: 'If you have served on a jury within the last two years, you may ask for an automatic deferral . . .'

Blast. I cleared a fortnight's worth of pages in my 1996 diary, beginning on Monday 18 November. Had I been told then that it would not be until Wednesday 26 March, in my 1997 diary, that I would be able to write 'Verdict reached: trial ends', I might well have considered emigrating.

PEOPLE LIKE US

It was not just the conclusion of our long endurance test that we were celebrating that evening in McGovern's pub. Throughout the whole length of this trial our endeavours seemed to have been accompanied by an off-stage chorus querying the merits of the jury system. We had begun as the echoes of the two O.J. Simpson trials were still reverberating. We ended the week that two women jurors had been jailed for refusing to reach a verdict in a London court after a seventeen-day trial. In the middle of it all came the proposal by Michael Howard, then Home Secretary, to curtail the right of some defendants to opt for trial by jury. That was an opportunity for newspaper columnists such as Paul Johnson and Auberon Waugh to write witheringly about the jury system. Johnson argued that juries these days were over-peopled with the feckless, the grudge-bearing and the unemployed – partly thanks to the middle classes' reluctance to do their duty. Waugh was even more contemptuous. 'We know, as a nation, that we are no longer fit for jury service,' he wrote, echoing Mr Bumble in *Oliver Twist*: 'Juries is ineddicated, vulgar, grovelling wretches.'

(Just over a year later, Waugh was singing another tune. In the *Sunday Telegraph* of 25 January 1998 he congratulated a High Court jury for finding against Rupert Allason in a particularly footling libel case. The Tory MP had previously had a long run of successful libel actions: this was the first time he had appeared before a jury. The headline on the column was: 'For once the jury gets it right'. But that's another story . . .)

Up in the jury restaurant on the fifth floor of the Old Bailey, we began to feel like a species marked out for extinction: we were endangered not because of our glamorous hides or aphrodisiac horns but on grounds of ignorance and incompetence. Naturally we felt indignant. Anyone who has experienced the peculiar demands of being a juror can surmise that people like my friends Johnson and Waugh would be the jurymen from hell. Could any jury made up of men like themselves be anything but prejudiced, impatient and uncommon, in every sense of the word? That is a compliment to the vigour of their opinions. But if I were an out-of-work youth wearing an earring they would be the last people I would choose to appear before, accused of a crime I did not commit.

Opponents of the jury system argue that most jurors are too stupid to reach a reliable verdict. Perhaps very clever jurymen would be just as fallible. The composition of the jury is what makes us nervous, in other words. That is what much of the debate about the jury system boils down to. Those who passionately believe in it maintain that the principles it upholds outweigh its imperfections. Antagonists think the imperfections subvert the principles.

Here is an American academic, B. S. Oppenheimer, writing about juries in 1937:

We commonly strive to assemble twelve persons colossally ignorant of all practical matters, fill their vacuous heads with law which they cannot comprehend, obfuscate their . . . intellects with testimony which they are incompetent to analyse or unable to remember, permit partisan lawyers to bewilder them with their meaningless sophistry, then lock them up until the most obstinate of their number coerce the others into submission or drive them into open revolt.

And here is Lord Devlin's famous encomium in *Trial by Jury*, the book based on his 1956 Hamlyn Lecture:

The first object of any tyrant in Whitehall would be to make Parliament utterly subservient to his will; and the next to overthrow or diminish trial by jury, for no tyrant could afford to leave a subject's freedom in the hands of twelve of his countrymen. So that trial by jury is more than an instrument of justice and more than one wheel of the constitution: it is the lamp that shows that freedom lives.

My view is that even if Oppenheimer's invective is on target, which as a caricature of course it is, it does not extinguish Lord Devlin's lamp. In 1965 an independent committee under the chairmanship of Lord Morris of Borth-y-Gest, appointed by the Home Office to look into the jury system, had this to say:

Jury service is viewed by some as an onerous and unwelcome duty, and by others as a precious and inalienable right, but we have been told that those who start their service holding the former opinion often end up by holding the latter. While we do not wish to pronounce on whether jury service is a right as well as a duty, many of our witnesses have told us of the profound sense of responsibility with which jurors discharge their functions ... There may sometimes be doubts about the correctness of particular verdicts, but no witness has expressed the view that jurors act irresponsibly or perversely ...

Thirty years on, that still rings true.

John Mortimer QC, celebrated defence lawyer and creator of the immortal Rumpole, gave me a paper he had written some years ago.

Juries are not composed of perfect people – they are not meant to be. They are meant to be people like us, full of imperfections. Our peers. Those of us who appear in criminal trials are always impressed by the jury's care, attention and sense of responsibility, and by verdicts which show, when there are a number of charges to consider, an astute awareness of the strength of the evidence on various complicated counts.

The conviction of Louise Woodward by a Boston jury in October 1997 seemed at first to be a sickening blow to those who share John Mortimer's opinion. No one wanted to believe that this very ordinary 19 year old from Cheshire could have been capable of *murdering* little Matthew Eappen. The initial response on both sides of the Atlantic was that the jury's decision was incomprehensible. The tabloid press in Britain went into its usual chauvinistic mode on such occasions, jeering at the jury for perpetrating a miscarriage of justice. It was suggested that, as Bostonians, they were influenced by the city's historic anti-English prejudice. Louise Woodward's home village worked itself into a frenzy of outraged emotionalism, egged on by the media.

The overreaction was embarrassing. On cool reflection, it was plain that the trial had been meticulously conducted and what is more had been seen to be so, thanks to the very television coverage which had helped to whip up the controversy in the first place. Unlike most of their critics, the jury had listened to every word of the evidence and deliberated on it for three days. Judging by what a couple of them had to say afterwards, and the probings of Marcel Berlins on Radio 4's *Law in Action* programme, the real error was not theirs but the defence team's, in going for the flamboyant 'noose or loose' gambit. Had the nine women and three men been allowed to bring in a manslaughter verdict, there would not have been half the fuss, and Judge Hiller Zobel would not have had to do it on their behalf ten days later. His reconsideration of the verdict (which would have been impossible in most other states, just as it would in Britain) was to be applauded. The damage done to the standing of the jury system may take longer to mend, despite his exoneration of the jurors. He stated at the end of his ruling that 'neither they nor anyone else should interpret today's decision as in any way a criticism of them'.

The key point was that Judge Zobel did not exculpate Louise Woodward from having had a hand in the little boy's death, however unintentionally. Although the people of Elton seemed keen to disregard this fact as they partied uproariously to celebrate her release from prison, in that respect he supported the jury's finding.

I want to believe in the jury system because it seems to me not only a tolerably effective method of judging serious crimes but an inspired means of helping a society to believe in itself. Lord Bingham, the Lord Chief Justice, has expressed the view that jury trial is something that even a convicted defendant can live with, however much he may resent his conviction. Before he became New Labour's first Attorney-General, John (now Sir John) Morris QC said, 'It may well not be the perfect machine, but it is a system that has stood the test of time

. . . a system of which we can be proud. It has been exported across the common-law world . . .'

Its supporters throughout that common-law world, in the USA, Canada, Australia, New Zealand and other countries that still cling to it (plus some, like Russia, which aspire to it), would argue that to let justice rest in the hands of its own citizens is the highest expression of a mature, civilised, self-confident democracy. Whether one agrees or not, to undermine it or abandon it in this country, where it is so rooted in our history, would be catastrophically dispiriting. It would be to admit that as a people we no longer trusted ourselves.

Our case lasted long enough for me to form some strong and mainly favourable impressions of the jury system in action. This seemed a persuasive reason to try to write something in its defence, at a time when juries were so heavily under attack. Neither fiction nor faction would fit the bill. The difficulty was how to tell the story as authentically as possible without contravening or even appearing to challenge our very tough contempt of court laws – laws which I myself think are right and necessary.

Section 8 of the Contempt of Court Act 1981 forbids any disclosure of what occurs in the retiring room once a jury has been sent out to deliberate and reach a verdict. I saw no problem in sticking to this. As to what had occurred in court and corridor during the course of the preceding trial, here I would seek to abide by the spirit of Section 8, even where the letter of the law did not appear to apply.

To determine what this spirit might be, I looked up the House of Commons debates on Section 8, which took place in the first half of 1981. Most of the discussion focused on the desirability or otherwise of allowing some academic research into jury deliberations.

Despite the support of the Conservative Attorney-General of the day, the pro-researchers lost the argument. This was what the late Sir Michael Havers said: 'I should have liked an amendment that did not create the stupid, silly criminal offences arising, for example, from a discussion over the dinner table or a juror returning to his home and talking to his wife or to the neighbour over the fence. I should have liked to see some measure of research into juries taking place under strict control.'

The former Labour Attorney-General, Sam Silkin, was also in favour of allowing investigation of the jury system 'without breaching the secrecy of the jury room ... in a way which enables successive generations to see whether the system is working in the way that it should and, if it is not, put it right'.

John Morris, who was Mr Silkin's successor as Labour Attorney-General until 1999, spoke up passionately on behalf of both jurors and the jury system, 'warts and all'. Like many of the lawyers in both Houses he felt that research could imperil both them and it. However, he also championed an amendment which sought to avoid 'stupid and trivial prosecutions' by ensuring that prosecutions could only be brought with the consent of the Attorney-General.

He was questioned about this important safeguard by another Labour MP, Christopher Price, who recollected that 'folk as distinguished as Katharine Whitehorn, Simon Hoggart, Alan Coren and Graham Greene' had written about their experiences as jurors. 'Would a prosecution against someone of that kind ... come into the category of stupid and frivolous prosecution?'

Mr Morris replied: 'Certainly, reminiscences in the Graham Greene vein would not at first blush seem to me to be of a kind to be in contravention of the Bill. It would be for the Attorney-General of the day to ensure that there is both fairness and consistency and that the law is not brought into ridicule.'

Well, I was no Graham Greene. And unlike him, I preferred

not to disguise the case at issue, except by changing the names of my fellow jurors. On the other hand, I was encouraged by the words of the then Attorney-General, who took the view that the key amendment they were debating did not seem 'to exclude a journalist from saying afterwards that he did not think very much of counsel for the Crown or counsel for the defence; or that the judge was a bit dozy and did not seem to know the law; or that the usher was incompetent; or that the lunch was filthy; or that he had to wait for days before he was allowed to try a case.

'None of those interesting things,' he went on, 'which I think the bar, pupils, solicitors and everyone else could gain by, would be prevented by that amendment . . .'

So I decided to go ahead, though obviously with great care. In doing so, I did not pretend to myself that one juror's account of serving in one trial could amount to a clinching defence of the jury ideal. But the experience did reinforce my own belief in it. If I could convey why, it would be a worthwhile undertaking.

As a journalist I noted all sorts of aspects of those involved, such as class and education, to which in some quarters it is no longer considered politically correct to draw attention. But such matters are of great significance, for they form the blurred subtext of much of the debate about the jury system. Only two of our jury members had been to university. Few read a newspaper regularly. Our case was not a fraud trial, often claimed to be beyond the grasp of the average juror. Yet it lasted as long as some fraud trials do and was just as complex and document-laden as many of them are. If a jury such as ours could cope with this and reach the right conclusion, which we believe we did, then it seemed to me a jury such as ours could cope with almost anything.

TRIAL BY JURY

THE ARREST

At around nine o'clock on the evening of Tuesday 2 April 1996 two unmarked police cars drew up behind a rented green Rover saloon in the Golders Green area of north-west London. The driver of the Rover was a well-built, pale-faced Greek in his mid-twenties called Thanassis Zografos. Beside him in the passenger seat was an older, smaller man, also of southern European appearance. This was Constantinos Korkolis. A witness saw the two men laughing.

The next thing they knew was that the doors of their car were being pulled open and there were shouts of 'Police! Police!' Both men were hauled out on to the pavement. Neither of them put up any resistance. They were hustled out of sight of each other, searched, made to don police-issue paper overalls on top of their clothes, and driven off in separate cars.

Meantime a young woman detective constable who had arrived with the arresting officers spotted a mobile telephone on the car-seat vacated by Korkolis. WDC Hills saw that it was switched on, put it to her ear and spoke into it briefly. In the footwell in front of the passenger seat she noted an array of wires leading from the Rover's cigar lighter socket to what looked like two mobile-phone chargers placed side by side, in one of which sat another telephone. This did not strike her as odd at the time. Possibly she was too busy wondering about the short conversation she had just had on the mobile. Only seconds earlier, one of the arrested men had been speaking into it. Yet the voice at the other end was one she knew well. It belonged to Detective Inspector Peter Young of New Scotland Yard's Organised Crime Group, a specialist in hostage and kidnap operations.

About an hour and a half later, the residents of a quiet mews in Maida Vale might have noticed something unusual taking place. That is, if they were nosy, neighbourly types, which they were not. Hogan Mews is one of those incurious corners of London where people come and go without prying or asking questions. It is a stroll from the stuccoed mansions of Little Venice and just a spit away from what is nowadays the little Levant of the Edgware Road. On this particular April night, not a curtain in Hogan Mews twitched as a small group of police officers, some in plain clothes, sidled surreptitiously along the front of one of the houses, Number 5. One of the men rang the bell. There was no response. He tested the door gently to check that the mortice was not locked. Then, bracing himself against a colleague's shoulders, he kicked hard. The door gave. The police rushed in, stepping over a man lying crumpled in the narrow hallway. The door had evidently hit him in the face. One of the officers bundled him into the downstairs lavatory.

Like its neighbours, 5 Hogan Mews is a small, modern, unprepossessing town house. The kitchen/dining room is just a few strides from the front door. As the officers ran in, they could see this was no ordinary domestic household. A mattress lay propped against one wall. A coat was draped over the ceiling light. There were clothes in plastic bags hanging from a radiator. The kitchen surfaces were cluttered; among the bottles of mineral water, the washing-up liquid and several cartons of Malboros were one or two unusual items: a face mask, quantities of tranquilliser pills, and a pair of handcuffs.

A door led off the kitchen. It was unlocked. A uniformed officer opened it. Behind the door was a pitch-dark, windowless room not much larger than a cupboard, reeking of urine. The constable was joined by a detective. They peered in and saw a bedraggled middle-aged man wearing boxer shorts and a dressing gown. For a moment he looked startled. Then he fell on the necks of the two policemen. Detective Constable Graham Clemence, a dark, tough-looking police officer with a beetling brow, was slightly embarrassed when he came to tell the court what happened next. 'He grabbed me so tight as to cause me to feel pain,' said DC Clemence awkwardly. 'Then he kissed me on the cheek.'

The pale, unshaven man in the cupboard was George Fraghistas, a 43-year-old Greek who ran a thriving shipping agency in London. He was a member of a wealthy Athenian family which, if not quite in the Onassis class, figures prominently in the premier league of Greek shipping dynasties. Mr Fraghistas lived in a comfortable £600,000 house in West London. It was not far from Hogan Mews.

Nine days earlier, on 24 March, he had disappeared. Two women friends who had been expecting to have supper and play Scrabble with him that Sunday evening had grown alarmed when he failed to show up. He was a man of reliable habits. Mr Fraghistas's business partner, his family and the local police were informed. The next day, Monday, an apparently calm-sounding George made a couple of calls to his office. He spoke to Wendy, his secretary. He told her that he had bumped into an old girlfriend and was going away with her for a few days. He made some routine remarks about cancelling meetings and contacting the captain of a ship at sea. They failed to soothe his family's fears.

Then the ransom demands began. At first they were for £5,000,000. Then they dropped to $3,000,000 – just under £2,000,000. It was George himself who made the calls. He told his family that the sum was actually a debt. His brother Nicos and his sister Marily had by now flown to London from Athens to join his mother, Rhea Fraghistas, in her Kensington flat. They did not believe him. They were convinced he had been kidnapped. They called in Scotland Yard . . .

And now, nine days later, Scotland Yard had found him. George was almost incoherent with relief. Having kissed DC Clemence, he embraced Detective Sergeant Martin Hawkins, the man who had led the assault on 5 Hogan Mews and kicked in the door.

In the small hours of the following morning, 3 April, four men were charged with kidnap, false imprisonment and blackmail. They were Korkolis and Zografos and two Frenchmen. One was the man who had been knocked down as the police stormed Hogan Mews, Jean-Marc Mereu, a thick-set, bespectacled former Olympic wrestler. He was 36. The other was Djemel Moussaoui, 33, a dark-skinned, round-headed French-Algerian. He had been arrested in a phone box at the end of the mews minutes before the raid on the house. He had been making a call to his mother in Paris. From the moment they were charged until their trial in November the four men remained virtually silent – except that at one point Mereu blurted out to the police that he had been kind to George: he had brought him cigarettes and fruit.

It was all over Thursday's newspapers. The *Daily Telegraph* had a big story on the front page under the headline 'Kidnap victim is freed after nine days in cupboard'. On page two – 'Snatched shipping agent drugged' – there were more pictures, maps and a graphic showing a blindfolded man tied to a chair. A woman who lived next door to 5 Hogan Mews, Denise Bennett, was quoted as saying, 'There was constant banging in the house. I thought it might be the sound of internal doors, but now I think it may have been the poor fellow banging. I feel awful for not doing anything about it.'

The victim's solicitor praised the detective work that had led to Mr Fraghistas's release. His client, he said, was 'extraordinarily grateful for the way in which the police directed this operation . . .' The longest nine days any of the Fraghistas family had ever known were over. Their terror was at an end.

None of them knew very much about the English legal system or its adversarial court procedures. So they did not realise that only a few months later they would be living through that harrowing experience all over again as they took the stand, one after another, in a witness box at the Old Bailey. Only this time the ordeal would last not nine days but sixty-four.

INDUCTION DAY

My jury service was due to start on Monday 18 November 1996. On Friday 15 November I got into a dogfight. It was the dogs that were fighting; I was peacemaking. But I was the one who got injured. I did my back in. The idea of travelling into town and sitting in a jury box for five or six hours with my spine in spasm was intolerable.

The yellow form said to ring the jury bailiff if there was a problem, so I did. 'Look,' I said when he came on, 'I hurt my back this morning. It will probably be all right by Monday, but I just thought I ought to warn you that I might not be able to get in.'

There was silence on the line. Then a voice said indignantly, 'Why didn't you let us know sooner?' 'Well,' I said carefully, not wishing to get off on the wrong foot with the Old Bailey bailiff, 'I wasn't aware that I would have a bad back until I had it. Which was today. That's why I'm ringing you.' Another silence. I suppose people try this kind of thing on all the time, I thought. There was a sound of paper rustling. Perhaps he was looking up the Juries Act 1974 in *Archbold's Criminal Pleading, Evidence and Practice*. Eventually he spoke through what sounded like gritted teeth. 'If you can't come in Monday you must send us a doctor's certificate, first thing.'

There didn't seem any point in explaining that if I could not get out of bed on Monday morning I would not be able to get to the doctor's either, so I simply said I would do my best. In the event, I made it. At 9.30 a.m. on 18 November I hobbled up to the Old Bailey entrance clutching my jury summons.

There was a queue stretching a good way along the pavement. As we were to learn, there is a queue every Monday morning when the courts are sitting, as this is induction day for each new batch of jurors. There must have been fifty or more of us shuffling slowly past the glass-fronted noticeboard that lists the day's business in the Old Bailey's eighteen courtrooms. In one court, I noticed, half-a-dozen defendants, mostly with Irish surnames, were being tried together. Later we would learn that flak-jacketed policemen were an even surer sign that a terrorist trial was in progress.

The main entrance to the Old Bailey is a splendid example of Edwardian baroque: solid, dignified and slightly ludicrous. Seated stonily over the porch are the figures of three large women. The one in the middle is wearing a shawl over her head and staring gloomily into her lap. She is meant to be the Recording Angel although the sculptor, Frederick William Pomeroy, seems to have mislaid her wings, which could explain her despondency. On her right is Fortitude, in a sort of Lawrence of Arabia head-dress. She is holding a short, fat sword and looking intently up at the Recording Angel awaiting orders. On the other side lounges a young lady whose dress has tumbled to her waist, revealing her bosom. This is Truth. She must have been a beauty in her prime. Alas, she has lost her nose, which may be why, instead of gazing up at the Recording Angel like Fortitude, she is staring moodily into a hand-held mirror.

It would have lent to the drama of our first day as jurors had we been able to enter the building beneath the skirts of this allegorical trio. While we were waiting, we could also have studied the inscription carved above their heads: 'Defend the children of the poor & punish the wrongdoer.' That would have given us something to think about. It is from one of the Psalms but sounds more like a command from on high directed at faint-hearted jurors. Defend! Punish!

But the Grand Entrance is nowadays used only four times a year, when the Lord Mayor drops in ceremoniously. Otherwise, all the comings and goings of the court are via the squat doorway of the modern 1970s annexe, whose packed lobby I had now reached.

Even without the throng of first-day jurors, getting into the Old Bailey is a slow process. Once a uniformed officer has checked your credentials everyone has to go through a Perspex cylinder like an air-lock, one by one: Queen's Counsels must take their turn alongside defendants on bail and even common-or-garden jurors. Loose change and keys go into a plastic tray, bags through an X-ray machine and yourself through an airport-style metal detector.

On top of the X-ray machine there is always a fair-sized scrapheap consisting entirely of bunches of keys. There must be thirty or forty of them. These belong to people who have forgotten to collect them from the little trays after going through the metal detector. Do all these absent-minded barristers, witnesses and jurymen not notice they are missing something when they try to get into their homes in the evening? In the four months that I underwent this daily routine, the size of the pile never varied. The policeman lounging by the X-ray screen looked up from his copy of the *Sun* and agreed that it was rather droll, but did so in the weary tones of one who had seen everything and to whom no human foible came as a surprise. Staring at the X-rayed contents of people's briefcases all day can do this to a man.

We were told to take the lift to the fifth floor and assemble in the jury restaurant. The place looked like the waiting room of a fogbound provincial airport. It was packed. There must have been getting on for three hundred people. All the easy chairs were occupied. So were the rows of canteen-style tables. Those of us who could not find a seat milled about, queued at the coffee urn or read the security notices on the walls. There was a distinct feeling of apprehension in the air. Not many people were talking. Those who were, I guessed, were already on serving juries, waiting to be called down to court. They chatted or played cards, eyeing the rest of us with the disdain of war-weary veterans.

There was an airport-like ding-dong on the Tannoy. The bailiff had come into the room and was addressing the rookies. As soon as Adi opened his mouth I realised he was the fellow who had been so disgruntled about my call on Friday. We were to go down to Court 1 to be shown a video, he said bossily. And off we trooped, like overgrown children on our way to school assembly.

Number 1 Court is not only the most famous courtroom in the world; it also looks the part. It is woody and leathery and intimidating. Its oak-panelled walls have echoed to the voices of the finest advocates of the century. Dr Crippen stood in this very dock and heard the black-capped judge pronounce his death sentence from that very bench. Now the place was swarming with men in jeans and women piling their Marks & Spencer's macs among bundles of documents on the ushers' table. The paraphernalia of a trial in progress – cardboard boxes, foolscap pads and bulging binders – were scattered about the court. We sat or leant where we could and Adi set the video going on a TV set up by the judge's chair.

The video was a well-put-together account of what jurors are supposed to do and not do. Doubtless it is intended to be reassuring as well as informative, just as those emergency-procedure videos which have replaced the human cabin crew on aeroplanes are meant to be. But whereas most airline passengers are blasé about escape chutes and lifejacket toggles, all this stuff about juries was alarmingly new. We listened intently. We were told about taking the oath and about our responsibilities in court and jury room. We were instructed how to collect our expenses and put in for loss of earnings.

Some of it was distinctly daunting. Do not talk to a soul about what you are doing, other than your fellow-jurors on the case (even that is discouraged on American juries). Be careful about whom you speak to in local bars and cafés near the court. 'It is a Contempt of Court, which may be punishable by imprisonment, to obtain, disclose, or solicit any opinions expressed, arguments advanced or votes cast by jurors in the course of their deliberations ... It is also important that you tell the Court Usher immediately should anyone outside your jury approach you about the case or try to influence you about it.' We filed out of Court 1 feeling even more nervous than before, keeping a sharp look-out for furtive jury-nobblers.

The scene in the jury restaurant had grown calmer. The serving jurors had gone. The newcomers settled down for a morning of reading newspapers and magazines or simply staring into space. I counted twenty-two broad-sheet newspapers, the *Guardian* and *Independent* narrowly outnumbering *The Times* and the *Telegraph*. Not an *FT* in sight. Copies of the *Sun* were lying about everywhere. Otherwise honours were evenly divided between the *Mail*, *Mirror* and the *Express*. I could see only four people with books. Staring into space was easily the most popular occupation.

My fellow jurors seemed to be mostly young, mostly white, with a scattering of grey heads and black or brown faces. The men by and large were dressed as though they were off to Ibiza or the betting shop. There was scarcely a tie to be seen. Many wore trainers. Such is the modern male's blokeish terror of appearing respectable. The women were altogether smarter and less ill-at-ease.

Court dress is a subject people lecture you on the minute you tell them you are going to be doing jury service. These knowing types all tell you exactly the same thing, although you would think from their manner they were imparting some dark masonic secret. What they tell you is that if you want to get off, which of course they assume you do, you must go into court wearing a suit and tie and carrying the *Times* or *Telegraph*. This will infallibly signal that you are a well-educated, conservative, law-and-order sort of chap to the defence counsel, who will promptly exercise one of his three peremptory challenges and boot you out of the jury box.

The trouble with this engaging piece of folk wisdom is that it is wrong: in this country the defence has not had the right to exercise a peremptory challenge for more than a decade – although in theory but seldom in practice the prosecution can still 'stand by' someone it considers an unsuitable juror. Twenty-one years ago, up to seven jurors per defendant could be challenged 'without cause'. John Mortimer remembers a case where he and his fellow defence counsel had forty-nine potential challenges between them (he was persuaded *not* to challenge a tie-wearing *Telegraph*-reader, because the man had been spotted winking in a friendly manner at the defendants – only to discover too late that the man had a facial tic). In 1977 the maximum number of challenges dropped to three. Since 1988 it is none at all. The only way for the defence to reject a juror is 'for cause', i.e. by showing there is valid reason such as that a juror is the prosecuting counsel's cousin. Not even a Savile Row pinstripe and a Guards tie would qualify under that heading.

All the same, there were were four men wearing suits in the jury restaurant, looking smug. And, yes, two of them were scanning *The Times*; a third was doing the *Telegraph* crossword. What was the fourth planning to carry into court under his arm, I wondered – a copy of Margaret Thatcher's memoirs? Sure enough, within a couple of days of realising the ruse was redundant, the suits had disappeared.

Every half an hour or so Adi or another bailiff would read out a list of names, to which those called had to respond in school rollcall fashion. Some names sounded Asian or East European, over which the bailiffs occasionally stumbled, but most were recognisably British. These people were then assigned a court and led away, chattering uneasily, not so much like sheep to the slaughter, if you came to think of it, as slaughterers to the sheep.

Lunchtime came and went and my name had still not been called. I found a seat by the windows which, a notice warned, would trigger alarms if you tried to open them. Perhaps some desperate juror for whom the suit-and-*Times* trick hadn't worked had once escaped across the rooftops. I was deep into the latest Patrick O'Brian novel and had no desire to escape. At Southwark Crown Court ten years earlier I had got through two books between cases besides *Oscar and Lucinda*. One of them was *Bleak House*. Dickens's lampooning of the convolutions of the courts made an excellent homeopathic antidote to points-of-law fatigue. This is an affliction to which jurors rapidly succumb, when they are repeatedly sent out of court so that arcane legal matters can be discussed behind their backs – *pas devant les jurés*.

The introductory video makes it quite plain that there will

be lots of hanging about. 'You may find it helps to pass the time if you bring something with you to do,' it warns, and then kindly offers some suggestions, 'for example, a book to read, crosswords or knitting.' It was extraordinary how few jurors seemed inclined to take this advice. You could buy a pack of cards in the restaurant. There was also a shoe-box containing half-a-dozen books for jurors to borrow, all of which apart from a well-thumbed Ngaio Marsh were of the 'a turbulent epic of love and guilt' variety. But why no one has been enterprising enough to open the Old Bailey Bookshop on the premises is a puzzle. Perhaps the horrid truth is that there's no call for it. I didn't see anyone knitting either.

The Tannoy ding-donged. Adi read out a very long list of names, including my own. When he finished, he told us to go down to Court 9. But there was something odd going on. Most of the groups called down to other courts during the day had numbered fifteen or sixteen people. Yet there seemed to be at least sixty of us cramming into the lifts and clattering down the stairs to the third floor.

I am not clear how we all managed to fit into Court 9, but we did. It was far smaller and less impressive than Number 1 Court, and it was three-quarters full already. As we poured in, what seemed like dozens of bewigged heads turned towards us from the well of the court. The judge stared gravely down. We squeezed in anywhere we could. It was only then that I noticed the dock. It too was packed. There seemed to be at least a dozen men up there. It looked like Nuremberg without the headphones.

Something was definitely up. Was it a fraud trial, as some of the jurors were whispering, one of those cases that would last half a year and end in an acquittal brought on by evidential overload? This was a fate I dreaded. The only clue I could gather was a label on a box file where I spotted two names: Mereu, Jean-Marc and Moussaoui, Djemel. It would be an odd sort of fraud trial which included a Frenchman and someone who appeared to be an Arab.

What followed was interesting and entertaining but still provided no clue as to what was afoot. First the judge explained that the trial set to take place in this courtroom would be an unusually long one. Most only take a few days. This one was likely to last at least until 20 January 1997, with a break for Christmas. The reason for the panel being so large was that many of us might have a good reason for avoiding a long trial, and that would whittle the numbers down. Also, he said, anyone who had family or work connections with the police should disclose them and would be stood down. What he planned to do now, he went on, leaving us no time to digest this tantalising information, was to find a total of twenty-four people available to serve, of whom twelve would eventually be sworn.

The clerk of the court had a fat wodge of cards in front of her. At random she picked one and read out the name on it. The person called had to state in a voice loud enough to be heard whether he or she could be a member of this jury. Those who answered yes had nothing more to worry about at this point. But if you could not, you had to approach the bench and tell the court why. Again I was put in mind of some arcane rite of passage from one's schooldays. The judge seemed to be the kindliest of men, but it was plain that some of those who wanted to put forward an excuse found doing so in front of a room full of strangers awkward. One trembling middle-aged woman murmured something about her child-minder; another *was* a child-minder. Someone was related to a policeman. There was an extraordinary hat-trick of postmen. The judge chuckled appreciatively: even the judiciary, celebrated for its ignorance of the modern world, knows about the Christmas postal rush. They were let off. So was a woman with a disabled mother. Then, to mounting hilarity, came more postmen, bringing the total so far to six – a tenth of the panel.

And of course there were those who had booked their winter holidays. Should one have been surprised that it was invariably the types who had been reading the broadsheets upstairs who were off to the snow and sun? Of course not. But wasn't it rather galling that, of all the reasons offered for being unable to serve as jurors, this was the one that got the most automatic acceptance from the judge? A quick, understanding nod and off they went back upstairs, to be picked for a nice short trial which would leave them plenty of time to pack for St Moritz or Morocco. It looked like a fix and in some ways it is a fix. The better off you are, the more likely it is that you will have some pressing reason for skipping jury service, be it a chalet in Chamonix or a business trip to Bolivia. And who could be more sympathetic to such pleas than a well-paid lawyer, that cynosure of the professional middle classes?

Sure enough, once we were a few days into our jury service proper, the twenty-two quality newspaper readers I had counted among our first-day intake had been whittled down to half-a-dozen. It is an old story and a disreputable one. How ironic it is that the middle classes, so apt to boast about avoiding jury service, are invariably its chief detractors.

My name was called. For the sake of form I attempted a half-hearted excuse about being a self-employed writer. The judge did not buy it, though he added, 'Don't worry. It may never happen.' I was relieved, really. I could have come forward with a full-hearted excuse, the one any journalist can use with near-certain results, which is to say that one's work has brought one into close contact with the police. But I felt like leaving the decision to fate. By now there was an A team of a dozen potential jurors. I was on the B team. Now, said the judge, we twenty-four were to go home, consult our families about the feasibility of serving in a long trial, and return the following Monday, when the actual jury would be empanelled. I was suddenly rather keen to be on it.

SWEARING IN

A week had passed. We were back in Court 9. Today the clerk had only twenty-four cards on her desk. 'Members of the jury in waiting,' said the usher, 'will you answer to your name and step into the box as your name is called?' Gradually the jury box filled up. Several members of the A team were allowed to drop out now that they had had time to think about the implications. One said his wife had just told him she was having a baby. The reservists took their places in the box. We reached Juror No. 10. I cannot remember what Juror No. 10's problem was, but it convinced the judge. I heard my name read out and walked self-consciously across the court to take her place: second row, last but two on the left. No. 11 and No. 12 said they could serve. The jury was complete and ready to be sworn.

It is not obligatory to swear. Since the Oaths Act of 1888 agnostics and atheists have been allowed to affirm. Muslims may swear by Allah, Hindus by Gita and Sikhs by Guru Nanak. In our case, we all took our oaths one by one in the traditional manner, standing up and holding the Bible in the right hand: 'I swear by Almighty God that I will faithfully try the defendants and give a true verdict according to the evidence.'

No one stumbled. At least we were all literate. If we sounded nervous it would not have been surprising. The only other occasions on which such solemn undertakings are pronounced in public are weddings and christenings. We spend most of our lives blithely committing good and bad deeds careless of the eye of Heaven upon us. Yet here we were positively calling God's attention to ourselves and doing so in the presence of scores of stern-faced witnesses, many of them togged up like members of the Spanish Inquisition.

From this moment on, no member of the jury would be required or allowed to speak in court again. We would be a silent tribunal, giving away nothing except what could be read on our faces. In Britain, jury vetting is not a customary procedure, although it is allowed for the prosecution in certain cases, such as those involving official secrets. Since 1973, the court no longer even has the right to know our occupations. So until the day when the foreman delivered his or her verdict, neither the prisoners nor their counsel nor the press nor even the judge himself, however wise in the ways of juries, would know what to make of us. But that was not going to stop them trying.

The scrutiny had already begun. If I turned left, towards the dock, I found at least one of the defendants staring at me intently. Down in the well of the court, my gaze would meet that of a barrister and our eyes would lock. From his eyrie to our right the judge also looked down at one or other of us from time to time, with the unblinking curiosity of an owl. Presumably they felt that our muteness, the blurry anonymity conferred on us by being a body known as a jury, gave them some sort of licence to weigh us up in this unembarrassed fashion. Should any of them try it on the London Underground they would get thumped. But here it was OK.

Actually, it was better than OK: it was flattering and rather thrilling. For the true reason for their hunger to know us better was this: it was we twelve who had ultimate power in this court. They could boss us about like schoolchildren, but unless the judge stopped the trial prematurely it was we who held the scales of justice in our inexperienced hands. The lawyers might know each other and would be able to play on each other's strengths and weaknesses. They would know which of them, in their own terms, was getting the better of it. But we dozen un-case-hardened strangers would have no such knowledge, any more than an American would know which team was ahead in a test match after a couple of days' play. We were as stony-faced as sphinxes – and how they longed to have the answers to the riddles we posed.

Naturally, we felt the same curiosity about each other. Who were we? How would we get on together? What teams did we support? What were our politics? For the time being, I could only form a very general impression. We seemed to be a fair representation of the crowd up in the jury restaurant, except for the fact that we were all white, which was unusual. We were six men and six women, ranging in age from early twenties to mid-sixties. The women were nicely turned out; the men were in casual clothes but for two of us in ties and jackets. Socio-economic classes? I guessed there were five who would qualify as ABC1s and seven pretty definite C2s. None of us was on the dole, none was a student and there were just two pensioners, which rather blew a hole in Auberon Waugh's assertion that 'any jury nowadays is largely filled by the unemployed'. Nor did we have anyone who could not read or write. The judge had particularly asked those members of the original panel with reading difficulties to excuse themselves. No one did.

But these were early days, when it was enough simply to exchange first names and share our apprehensions about what lay ahead. We were a bunch of disparate people thrown together in unusual circumstances. We were like a group of holiday-makers setting off on a coach tour of the Rhine. But in our case, we had even less in common. We had not even chosen the same holiday from the brochure. What is more, we were all travelling alone. It might turn out to be an uplifting adventure for all of us. But at this stage it felt more like a mystery tour for mismatched singles.

THE CROWN'S CASE

Joanna Korner QC opened for the Crown. She outlined the case for the prosecution crisply. In the late afternoon of Sunday 24 March 1996 George Fraghistas drove his car into the NCP car-park at Lanark Road, Maida Vale, using a plastic card to open the garage doors. As he got out of the car he heard running feet and looked up to see a masked man coming towards him. There were three men altogether, he thought. Mr Fraghistas was hurled to the ground and bundled into the boot of a car at pistol-point, kicking and shouting for help. Someone got into the boot beside him. The man with the gun spoke in English with a Greek accent. Neither of the others uttered a word.

After a short journey, Mr Fraghistas was hauled out of the boot, a blanket was thrown over his head and he was thrust into the utility cupboard at 5 Hogan Mews. He was blindfolded, handcuffed, his ankles were bound, wax plugs were stuffed in his ears and taped into place. The next day he was forced to begin the ransom calls. Scotland Yard was alerted. Nine days after he was seized the police arrested two of the kidnappers in Golders Green in the middle of a ransom call to the Fraghistas household. Two hours later they found the kidnap victim, released him and his four captors were charged.

That, baldly, was what the Crown would now try to prove had happened.

It was hard to take in, chiefly because of its strangeness. Kidnapping for ransom is one of the most serious crimes on the English statute book, second only to murder. In this country, thank heavens, it is also one of the rarest, although there has been a little-publicised increase in recent years, mainly among immigrant communities. Of the nearly fifteen hundred crimes logged as kidnaps in England and Wales in

1996, most concerned gangland feuds, siege situations or domestic squabbles, and lasted no more than a few hours.

In the public imagination kidnapping for ransom is mostly the preserve of pitiless Sicilians and Colombians, the world leaders in the field. Terrorist kidnaps we are more familiar with: over the past thirty years British hostages have been held in the Middle East, Far East, South America and even Canada, though over here the IRA has generally eschewed this tactic.

Sure enough, the alleged kidnappers in our case were all foreigners, as was the kidnapped man. But still, it all sounded quite outlandish. Did such a nasty, un-British crime really happen among the law-abiding mansion-blocks of Maida Vale?

In front of each juror was a plastic water-cup, a yellow highlighter, an array of pencils and a cheap school exercise book. About a third of us began taking notes immediately. As a general rule, those first-day scribblers kept at it throughout the trial, filling a notebook every four weeks or so. Whether it was because they had greater confidence in their memories or were simply lazy, the rest scarcely ever wrote down a thing. One of the detectives on the case told me afterwards that this worried him greatly, since he knew how complicated things would become. As a journalist with an atrocious memory I realised that without a record of what we were hearing I would have nothing but confused impressions to go on even after a week, never mind the months we had been told to expect. Some of our notes did indeed turn out to be crucially important when the time came: the difficulty was in trying to convince some of the others that they were accurate. I suppose those who do not much use the written word in their daily lives are also mistrustful of it. Had we had a video they might have been less dubious.

Joanna Korner was the first barrister most of us had ever seen in action other than on the TV screen. My own courtroom experience was limited to a couple of libel trials and my previous stint as a juror in Southwark. Only one of my new colleagues had also done jury service before.

Miss Korner made a striking impression. She was exceptionally tall and elegant, with an attractive, angular face and short grey hair which blended becomingly into her wig. If she might not, at 46, be everyone's idea of Portia, she would certainly be right for one of those strong-willed women in the Roman plays. Her manner was head-girlish: drawlingly self-assured for the most part, but prone now and then to break into a self-deprecating, Joyce Grenfellish guffaw. I had her down for Roedean and Girton. I was wrong on both counts. That night when I got home I looked in *Who's Who* and learnt that she did not go to university; that in her time off she collected books and porcelain, went to the cinema and played tennis.

Slightly to my surprise the other jurors rather warmed to Joanna Korner as the trial got into its stride. They thought her clever and intelligible (as did the policemen in charge of the case, who had recommended her to the Crown Prosecution Service). I had imagined they would have been put off by her accent, such is the general disdain for talking posh in 1990s Britain. But if so, they would have had to show the same scorn for every other lawyer who opened his mouth in Court 9, including Judge Simon Goldstein who, despite being the son of an East End market trader, alumnus of East Ham Grammar and a supporter of West Ham football club, spoke with the refinement of a Trollopian bishop. Maybe, I concluded, people actually expect a court of law to be a bastion of poshness and so are undismayed by it. Perhaps they even find it reassuring.

It was time for the prosecution to produce its first witness and the jury to get their first look at George Fraghistas, the alleged kidnap victim. He cut an unremarkable figure, standing uncertainly in the witness box. He looked like the sort of businessman you find in Club Class on any scheduled flight to southern Europe: dark suit, dazzling white shirt, striped tie; middle-aged, middling height, middling build, a touch on the flabby side. His cheeks had a muddy Mediterranean pallor. He wore large wire-framed spectacles which he swapped for another pair to read the oath. There was nothing about him to indicate the trauma which the Crown said he had undergone eight months earlier.

If he seemed bewildered and apprehensive, it was a look the jury would come to recognise on the face of every new witness other than court-calloused characters such as the police and forensic experts. For some reason as I watched George standing there, blinking at the ranks of faces around him, I thought of the early Christians, thrust into the glare of the Roman arena, wildly uncertain of their fate.

The witness cuts a very lonely figure in a courtroom. He or she has not been allowed to follow the trial, knows none of the leading players except possibly the defendant, and is usually unfamiliar with court procedure. Barristers are not allowed to rehearse with them, as they are in the United States. These days there is a witness support set-up at the Old Bailey should help be needed. But nothing can alter the fact that while the ordeal lasts, it is the witness who is the centre of attention in this drama and on whom umpteen pairs of eyes are riveted.

To begin with, it was relatively easy for George Fraghistas. Name, address, age, occupation, status (bachelor), family (widowed mother, older brother, two sisters: well-off Athenians with a successful business, mainly in shipping). This was friendly fire. All Mr Fraghistas had to do was give his account, gently prompted by Miss Korner. Bit by bit, he shaded in the outline she had already sketched for us.

His story was both shocking and mundane. The first thought that flashed through his mind on seeing a hooded man running towards him in the car-park was that it was a friend of his, a man notorious for gruesome practical jokes. (Some friend, we thought.) When his assailants had wrestled him to the concrete floor and a gun was levelled at him, all he could think about, he said, was how gigantically tall the man with the gun looked (three of the four defendants were notably short). They tried to force a leather mask over his head but he begged them not to, saying he was terrified of suffocating: surprisingly, they desisted. He struggled so hard to avoid being put in the boot of the kidnappers' car that one of them jumped in beside him, forcing him to the floor, allegedly the burly French wrestler. The two men, victim and attacker, lay pressed together in the darkness like lovers for the journey to Hogan Mews.

Once installed in the cupboard, Fraghistas's sense of disorientation was compounded. He could not see where he was because he had been blindfolded. Someone spoke to him in a strange squeaky voice, like a child who has sucked the helium from a party balloon. His ears were plugged, his wrists hurt from the handcuffs and he was losing the circulation in his ankles, which had been tightly bound with adhesive tape. His wristwatch and glasses had been taken from him. Only the dim sounds of traffic, he said, gave him any idea what time of day it was. Gradually the regime was relaxed a little, along with his bonds. He was told to call his chief captor 'Petros'. He was fed quite well on chicken, prosciutto, even steak and ice-cream. He was brought cigarettes, fruit and tranquilliser pills. At first he was given a bucket to pee in; then an empty plastic mineral water bottle. Once a day he was led blindfolded to the lavatory.

Miss Korner spent long hours taking the court through the transcripts of the ransom calls. These were made by George, she said, under duress. The initial demands were dictated by 'Petros' and pre-recorded, then played down the line to the family, who had gathered at Mrs Fraghistas's flat. When they responded, it was George who had to talk to them. He said that one of the kidnappers was always standing behind his blindfolded head threatening to break his neck if he spoke out of turn. The conversations were being taped both by the kidnappers at Hogan Mews and by the police, who had speedily set up camp in Mrs Fraghistas's small living room.

These transcribed calls, page after page of them, had an unreal, almost bland quality when read out in studiedly neutral tones by Joanna Korner. Yet one could sense the tension with which each phrase was loaded, a desperate anxiety concealed behind even the most banal-seeming exchanges between George and his sister Marily, or George and Nicos, his fiery older brother. It was Nicos who became the chief negotiator.

The odd thing was that, as the days went by and the man in the witness box told the tale of his terror, it gradually began to sound quite matter of fact. Perhaps we were becoming case-hardened. It was partly the effect of the antiseptic courtroom. Had George Fraghistas been spotlit on a stage with the house-lights dimmed, his narrative would have sustained its dramatic drive. But a boxy modern courtroom with strip lighting overhead is no aid to the imagination. It is, however, a compelling setting when the drama is in the present tense and takes place before one's very eyes.

This was what occurred one day early on in the trial when Miss Korner asked the usher for one of the exhibits. He took it over to the witness box and held it up. It was a hood, made of heavy black leather. It was designed to cover the entire head, down to the neck, with a horizontal zip across the mouth. It was an almost comically gruesome thing, straight out of the sado-masochist's mail-order catalogue. Did Mr Fraghistas recognise it? Was this the mask they had tried to force over his head in the garage?

Mr Fraghistas stammered, blenched, bowed his head and

hid his face in his hands. He began to sob. The whole court tensed, then looked away, embarrassed. It was one of those moments, for sure, that would stick in the jury's mind. This was the kind of first-hand evidence we really could judge for ourselves. George breaks down in the box: a man under unbearable stress, suddenly reminded by this horrible object of those first frightening seconds in the car-park. His emotional collapse had allowed us a glimpse of the unvarnished truth.

Or had it?

The trial was still in its infancy, yet already second thoughts were becoming second nature. Antennae we didn't even know we possessed were erect and twitching. One found oneself asking questions which in other circumstances would have seemed absurdly suspicious. Was it possible, just possible, that George was play-acting? Could it be that he had planned something like this to win the jury's sympathy?

We were to see and handle a great many other exhibits during the succeeding months – more than a hundred of them. There was a scuffed leather jacket, a pair of handcuffs, a voice distorter, a set of hypodermic syringes still in their wrappers. The firearms expert demonstrated a stungun, made in Korea. It was called a Thundershot. He held it up and a crackling blue arc flared between its crab-like claws, a charge capable of paralysing Arnold Schwarzenegger. The other gun, a heavy black automatic, looked and felt like the real thing although it fired supposedly non-lethal ammunition. We passed it silently from one to another along the two rows of the jury box.

Each of these things was charged with its own capacity to shock, like the stungun itself. We were touching the texture of violence, feeling its hard edges, holding its dead weight in our hands. Yet none of these exhibits quite matched the sick-making menace of that mask. A while later, when the court had risen for lunch, some of us saw George huddled in a corner outside, with his face pressed to the wall, weeping.

THE JURORS

We had only been together as a sitting jury for a few days, but already we were showing signs of developing a group sense of responsibility. This became apparent when those of us who had seen George crying told some of the others about it. Poor George, they said. And then a couple of jurors pointed out earnestly that it would surely be wrong for us to let ourselves be influenced by something that had happened *outside* the courtroom. Shouldn't we wipe the scene from our minds? And the rest of us nodded gravely.

This was rather remarkable. We had had no guidance whatsoever about such matters. What was happening was that the jury was evolving its own code of behaviour, according to what it dimly understood to be proper and fair. The glue of shared experience was binding us into a group, as any amateur psychologist would have predicted. By now we had progressed from first names to surnames, ages, jobs. In the unhurried British fashion, we learned a little more about each other every day, joining up the dots as we went along.

Bob was the extrovert. That was clear before one had even met him. Right from the start I had seen this grinning, broad-shouldered young man swaggering about the jury restaurant, chatting to all and sundry. He seemed thoroughly at ease. He had an Irish surname but was born and brought up in Woolwich and went to the local Catholic schools. He might have been a bus conductor or a soldier. Actually he was a postman. Yeah. He could have got off, like the other posties, seeing Christmas was coming up. But he wanted to be on a jury, right, especially a good long one. He reckoned the court would compensate for his lost overtime. He was 25, worked out in the gym and played league football for a south London team ('semi-professionally' he insisted: £25 a match plus small bonuses). He was a cheery, cocky sort of bloke who let everyone know that he'd be volunteering to be jury foreman when the time came. He quite fancied the idea of standing up in court and delivering the verdict. He had eight GCSEs and knew a lot about cars, something which we would find useful later on. The detectives assigned to the case, who sat across court from us every day, sussed Bob as a weight-trainer straight away, just by the way he moved. They nicknamed him The Body-Builder and thought they saw him looking with special absorption at one of the defendants, Mereu the wrestler. From day one, Bob made a beeline for Kate.

Kate was the youngest of us. She was 21 years old. She was plump, pretty, sharp-tongued and wonderfully sour about men, women, the newspapers, the jury system and almost anything else that came up in our communal conversation until the day we were locked up to deliberate. Then she became quite steely and tough-minded. She had ten GCSEs and two BTec diplomas. She had a job (her first) providing what she called helpdesk support on the computer system of a big firm of City solicitors. She was a swimmer. Her boyfriend was a professional golfer working his way up the ladder. She would meet him off the plane after an overseas tournament, half-pleased, half-cross to be caught in the press camera lenses. Kate saw Bob coming a mile off. She kept him at bay with put-downs of a scorn that would have made lesser men shrivel. They bounced off Bob like airgun pellets off a rhino.

Sophie was the next youngest. She was small and sweet-natured and the only one of the women jurors who smoked. This consigned her to the ashtray-littered, male-dominated zone of the jury restaurant reserved for smokers, where she puffed away unconcernedly. It turned out that she too was a Post Office worker who could have got off if she had wanted to, but didn't. She was a sorter, but was surely headed for promotion. She was bright, and turned out to have an unerring ear for the tongue-twisting Greek names which jostled in the cast list. She was the only one of us to know which Petros was which and never to confuse Whatyoumacallitakis with Whatsernameopoulos. Perhaps this was her GPO training.

As well as a pair of postal workers we had a couple of cleaners. Keith's job was out at Heathrow. Sweeping up the debris of the busiest airport in the world might sound a touch dreary. But as far as Keith was concerned there could be no more fulfilling occupation on earth, since Keith's great passion in life was plane-spotting. Billy Bunter put in charge of the tuck shop could not have been more contented. A slow-moving, Smike-ish figure whose blundering at cards regularly provoked good-natured jeers from the other players, he seemed to derive an inner insouciance from the contents of his carrier bag, which included a pair of binoculars. When we were shooed from court for points of law, he would huddle over his clip-board of plane numbers like a Talmudic scholar. My impression was that he formed his opinions about what was going on in court early in the proceedings, then stuck to them doggedly.

Eddie was an office cleaner. He was a pleasant, bespectacled, shy young man who would have looked more in place behind a bank counter in Burgos, changing your traveller's cheques into pesetas, than in the Central Criminal Court. His full name was Eduardo. He was born in London of Spanish parents twenty-three years ago. Since I speak some Spanish, we would exchange a 'Buenos dias' every morning at the hand-dryer in the Gents'. But he seemed much happier being a thorough-going north London lad. He had even anglicised the pronunciation of his surname, in a fashion that must have been painful to his parents' ears. Eddie was a keen badminton-player. Somewhere along the line he had picked up some knowledge of electronics and telecommunications. In a trial where mobile telephones played a key role, this turned out to be an unexpected benefit.

Ah, the glories of random jury selection. Here was a case concerning four men of what you might loosely call Mediterranean background. And, as luck would have it, here was a London jury which included not only Eduardo but also Anna. Anna was an East Ender through and through, and noisily proud of it. But she was also as Italian as provolone. We had an excitable argument over the best kind of soup to make from Christmas turkey bones.

Once upon a time under English law, foreign defendants were allowed to ask for a jury *de medietate linguae*, half-composed of fellow countrymen, or at any rate non-Englishmen. That rather fair-minded practice fell into disuse in the middle of the last century. Our jury seemed to have almost resuscitated it. Two of our number had Latin blood in their veins. A third (myself) had grown up in a Latin country, Argentina, and even spoke a smidgin of tourist Greek.

Anna was 49, a working wife and mother. She was on the check-out at an inner-city Sainsbury's, a happy combination of London hard-headedness and Italian sentimentality. One minute she would be loosing off some cockney obscenity about the tiresomeness of a male juror, the next waving her hands in anguish over poor Mrs Fraghistas. Anna was unwavering on one theme: the strength of the *family* in the Mediterranean world. A son would never do that to his mamma, she would say to me firmly. A sister will always stand by her brother. And so on. These were valuable insights.

Pat was the only one of us who was not born in the UK. She was a fair-haired, apple-cheeked New Zealander, who had lived in London for years. She had come over to England on the obligatory European tour as a young Kiwi and had simply stayed put, though she still had the slightly distrait air of an antipodean who had only temporarily alighted in the motherland. Sure enough, she and her partner and their baby daughter were in the throes of uprooting to go and settle back in Auckland. Every day Pat arrived with a mobile phone and a satchel full of documents. She was a one-woman emigration department. One week she would be negotiating the sale of her home, the next organising the shipping of its contents. The rest of us had ringside seats. Pat sought Bob's advice on what sort of car to take out with them, prices back home being so exorbitant. The ladies were consulted about curtain materials. As the trial rolled on and one provisional deadline succeeded another, Pat's move became a sort of parallel drama. Would we finish in time, or would the jury have to shrink to eleven because one of the jurors had emigrated? In actual fact, the dilemma would never have arisen. Though I suspect Pat was the kind of person who dislikes being judgemental, she was very conscientious about her juror's role and would have seen it through however long the trial took.

Anna spent a lot of her lunch-breaks with Daphne. Daph was a handsome grey-haired woman in her late sixties. A retired secretary at the Factory Inspectorate, she never failed to be on time for court despite the fact that her journey to court was one of the longest. I sometimes followed her up the hill to the Old Bailey from Blackfriars tube station and she usually outpaced me. Daph was a Scrabble demon. We only had time for one full game, despite all the hundreds of hours we spent in each other's company. But she came armed with her Travel Scrabble and a diary of previous scores. I realised I was up against a player who not only knew all those beastly two-letter words beginning with 'x' but was also bang up-to-date about the newly allowed non-U word 'qi' (an Oriental life force, supposedly). Dangerous stuff. So when Daph described her chance encounter with a pair of police handcuffs and how they worked, we all listened. It was highly relevant.

The most outspoken member of our jury was Stuart. He was a self-employed builder in his early fifties, a Glaswegian with a passion for Rangers and an opinion on everything, mostly of a no-nonsense reactionary variety. He was tough, canny, down-to-earth and good company. He wasted no time at all in finding out exactly what the self-employed among us should be claiming for lost earnings. Naturally he was the one who started the card school and who proposed that we should set up a lottery syndicate. He smoked roll-ups, preferred beer to whisky, read the *Express*, outraged the women with his chauvinistic banter and never wore anything but trainers during the whole of the trial. He seemed to me to be an excellent juror, quick to grasp the essentials. His other talents included a cab-driver's knowledge of central London streets and a fund of information about previous criminal trials, especially those that had taken place at the Bailey.

The oldest juryman was Magnus, a 68-year-old former schools inspector with the Inner London Education Authority who had retired in 1988. He had a BSc, a PhD and was also a qualified educational psychologist. A beaming, bespectacled, invariably blazered figure, he had got his doctor to prescribe him speed to keep him awake during the trial. He was one of those old-fashioned Englishmen who have real, time-consuming *hobbies*, and are perplexed that the modern generation gets by without them. Magnus was a Rotarian; a movie buff who kept records of all the films he saw; he collected old postcards, stamps and cigarette cards and did so sufficiently seriously to make quite a bit of money out of it. While the rest of us kicked our heels waiting to go into court, he would pore over catalogues. Several times during the trial he trotted off during the lunch-break to attend an auction.

His other obsession was telling jokes. Four or five times a day he would begin: 'Have I told you the one about . . .?' As the weeks went by, the chorus of mock-protest that rose every time he said this grew louder. Magnus would plough on undaunted, shouldering aside our objections like an icebreaker under full steam. Everyone and anyone was a potential audience, until the time came when bailiffs, ushers and jurors on other cases would flinch at his approach as though he were the Ancient Mariner. Yet not once do I recall his repeating a crack. Nor did we ever see him looking one up in the tiny notebook he always carried in his pocket and which we believed must be crammed with risqué ribaldry from a lifetime's Rotary Club after-dinner speeches. In any case, the amiable wisecracker was also pretty wise. To have a qualified psychologist on the team was a bonus: every jury should have one.

The conventional wisdom among lawyers is that older jurors are more inclined to be conservative and less inclined to acquit. My observation is that this is an unjustified prejudice (Magnus was a liberal-minded *Independent*-reader). More to the point, since experience of life is the only resource a juror brings to the undertaking, the longer that life has been, the better.

In the witness box, we operated in pairs. This was because the documentation in the case was so massive and the binders which contained it so cumbersome that had we each had a set the court would have been hidden from us behind ramparts of files. My team-mate was a petite, sharp-faced, auburn-haired young woman called Terrie. She looked about 30, though later confessed that she was 41. She had worked for a tour-operator in Spain for some time, had lived out there and loved it (another Latinate element in our jury). Now she had a job at a hotel in Essex which she loved rather less and was thinking of leaving. The trial, she confided, would be a useful time for reflection. It might even be a turning point. She took notes assiduously and managed our set of documents with busy efficiency. When we all gave Christmas cards to each other I wrote in hers: 'To my bundle-partner', which she did not quite know how to take.

As for myself, 51, I struck the others as rather stand-offish, one of them told me later. I read books. I dressed stuffily. I knew shamefully little about football or cards. And I preferred getting out of the place and exploring the local City eateries to lunching in the jury restaurant. But I was not the only fan of *Larry Sanders* and *The Simpsons* in the group and I had at least watched *Friends* and *The X Files* a few times. As a former newspaper editor I could answer the odd question about the forthcoming general election. And as a married father-of-four I was able to explain to Kate, who demanded the information in a loud and unembarrassed voice one morning while she was reading a magazine article, how an IUD worked, though I suspect she was having me on.

Although comradeships were established quite quickly, I think we all instinctively understood that it was best not to form into camps: one day we would be locked up together to reach a verdict and would not want to be taking sides for the wrong reasons. There were no outbreaks of cliqueishness. If we did gang up from time to time against someone's particularly maddening behaviour, we managed to keep it good-humoured.

Magnus the educational psychologist could probably explain this as a manifestation of group protective behaviour. Solidarity was our best defence against the bossiness of the court and the risk of making fools of ourselves. But I am sure those national characteristics of tolerance and decency which the British are supposed to have discarded soon after the Second World War had something to do with it too. My parents' generation never tired of saying the war brought out the best in people. Maybe jury service does the same in a lesser way, the sobering ambience of the court turning even men prone to behaving badly into jurors behaving, well . . . well.

USHERS

It is the ushers who keep the wheels of justice turning. They have various functions in court, such as administering the oaths and handing around exhibits, but their main job as far as we were concerned was acting as shepherd-cum-sheepdog to their flocks. One minute they would be jollying the jurors along, making them feel wanted, explaining what barristers' wigs are made of; the next they'd be nipping at their heels and rounding up the stragglers to herd them into court on time. Woe betide the usher who lost one of his sheep. And woe betide the lost sheep.

Many ushers seem to tell the same story to new jurors, claiming that they were there when it happened. The story is that one day a London court was held up for a quarter of an hour because a woman juror was late back from lunch. When the jury was safely penned in its box again, the judge, a beak of the old school, asked the woman juror to stand up. 'Will you please tell the court why you were late?' he said mildly.

The woman explained that she was sorry: she had been doing some shopping in the sales and had misjudged the time it would take to get back. 'Oh yes?' responded the judge in a good-natured way. 'And what did you buy?'

'I bought a coat,' she answered.

'What did it cost, may I ask?' said the genial judge.

'A hundred and twenty pounds.'

'Clerk,' snapped the judge, all trace of amiability vanishing, 'fine that woman a hundred and twenty pounds for lateness!'

One of the ushers gave us this account during our first week. Later I learnt from a juror on another trial that they had been told the same tale by their usher. Later still, I read a feature in the *Sunday Telegraph* by a journalist colleague, Carole Dawson, who had just done jury service, in which she recounted the same sequence of events – only the coat had cost £150. Well, perhaps judges do this sort of thing at intervals, just to keep jurors on their toes. But since I first heard the story back in 1976, identical in every detail except that the coat had then cost £75, I suspect it is really one of those urban myths, which ushers find handy for scaring their charges.

We had a number of different ushers looking after us during our four months. Apart from one with a sour face and a mobile-phone phobia, they could all have done a good job as Butlin's redcoats. One of them was a come-hitherishly made-up young woman with a winning smile. Even in her subfusc robes she looked less like an usher than an usherette. But mostly we were in the hands of Roy, a moustachioed RSM type with the belly of an ex-butcher – which he had indeed been for thirty-two years. Roy was a card. His unvarying catchphrase to chivvy us into court was 'Let's rock and roll'. He had a knack of cupping his roll-up in his fist that suggested a lifetime of surreptitious smokos. Sophie confided in me after the trial that she thought we would never have been such a good team had it not been for Roy's patient friendliness. A motion to enroll him in our lottery syndicate was carried *nem. con.*

Every morning Roy would round us up, joshing if we were all present and correct but as stern as he was capable of being with latecomers. My bundle-partner, Terrie, was the chief object of these admonitions. Floods, fires and bomb-scares took it in turn to disrupt Terrie's journey into the City. More than once she was summoned before the clerk of the court for a dressing down. Even the judge was driven to deliver an oblique wigging. But nothing could re-set Terrie's inner clock, which automatically seemed to add half an hour to any given deadline. Poor Terrie was furious when she discovered that Stuart was running a book on her exact time of arrival. How she discovered was that one morning Stuart gave her a smacking kiss and announced, 'A nicker, a nicker. Ye've won me a quid, lassie!'

In truth, judges are in no position to get high-falutin over jury time-keeping. Court hours hardly convey a sense of urgency in the first place: 10 a.m. to 4 p.m. with fifty minutes for lunch would not strike a fair-minded person as onerous. Add to that a coffee-break in the morning, a tea-break in the afternoon and, as I say, you would not form the impression that time was of the essence in an English trial.

What really brought this home, though, were the almost daily intermissions during which the court would discuss sundry 'points of law' in the absence of the jury. Sometimes we would be kept hanging around for whole mornings. Eventually we would be brought back into court – only to be told we could break for lunch. Warned on pain of unnamed retributions to be back at five to two, we might spend a further hour in idle suspense, wondering what on earth was going on.

One morning my tube station in north London was closed because of a fire. I ran home and my wife gamely agreed to drive me in to the City. Half an hour later we were still only at King's Cross. The traffic was abominable. I got out and walked the final two miles at top speed, arriving at the Old Bailey panting and perspiring. No one seemed impressed by this show of dedication to public duty, which was not surprising since an hour later we still hadn't gone into court.

Occasionally His Honour Judge Simon Goldstein would give us a rough idea what the hold-up was all about, but usually not. This was profoundly irritating, especially as the public gallery was not evacuated during these legalistic conferences and the press could look on (though not report) to their hearts' content. It made us feel like children forced to leave the room while the grown-ups discussed something supremely interesting behind our backs. When I learned after the trial about some of the hair-raising stuff that had indeed been discussed in our absence, it merely confirmed a suspicion that a British trial is not always the quickest or surest way to arrive at the truth, even if it is the fairest. On reflection, I thought crossly, it is not blindfolded Justice with a set of scales in her hand that should symbolise the impartiality of the law: it is a blindfolded juror holding a styrofoam coffee cup.

DEFENCE TACTICS

On 4 December Joanna Korner sat down and Michael Gale QC stood up. Roy the usher had explained the order of play for each of the Crown's witnesses: first the prosecution's evidence-in-chief, then the cross-examination, one after the other, by each of the defence counsel representing the four accused, and finally the prosecution's re-examination.

Presumably someone had also described all this to George Fraghistas. As a citizen of Greece, he would be even less familiar with our courtroom ways than the average Briton, who at least has a nodding acquaintance of them via television. But as Mr Gale began his distinctly hostile line of questioning, the look on George's face grew more and more indignant. The whole purpose of the adversarial system is to test the Crown's evidence before a jury. This sounds reasonable enough in the abstract. In practice it often means putting witnesses on the rack and treating them as though it were they who were in the dock. George was obviously ill-prepared for this change of gear. Yesterday he was a victim. Today he was suddenly being treated as a villain.

The defendants' case was bold and unexpected. They did not deny that they had been caught by the police *in flagrante delicto*. They could hardly do that, since the events of 2 April 1996 were indisputable. Their argument was that it was no *delictum*. It was merely a ploy, planned by George and executed by themselves on his orders, to extort money from his own family. What is more, he had assured his associates that it was money to which he was entitled anyway. So the kidnap was no kidnap, the victim was not a victim, and even the ransom was not really what you could call a ransom, more like an advance on his eventual inheritance. The man in the witness box, Mr Gale wanted us to believe, was the ringleader of the plot, driven to this heartless means of helping himself to the family coffers by the shakiness of his shipping business and the size of his gambling debts.

As Mr Gale progressed with his attempted demolition of the witness's character, dwelling insinuatingly on his financial secretiveness, George's face took on a grimace of sulky outrage. 'Are you from the Inland Revenue?' he burst out at one point. Hitherto he had been a patient, amiable witness, deserving of every sympathy. But Mr Gale had led us upstairs and shown us a Dorian Gray portrait in the attic. It was not such a pleasant sight. What is more, some of its features *could* be made to fit the now angry-looking man in the witness box.

I found this unsettling. Until now the prosecution account had seemed as watertight as a diving bell. These trickles of doubt were my first intimation that it might not, after all, be an open-and-shut case. Naturally, we were not such fools as to have believed it ever would be. Jurors pick up jury folklore very quickly in the coffee queue and it is conventional wisdom that trials always turn out to be less straightforward by the end than they seem at the beginning. The good juryman's motto is: 'I'm keeping an open mind.' I must have heard my colleagues use it five times a day. It was a pious expression of our conscientiousness, I suppose. It was also a useful mantra to ward off the gusts of confusion that now began to eddy round us.

What really shook me about George was his gambling. He did not merely frequent casinos such as the Ritz and Crockford's. By night he practically lived there. Sometimes he would jet over to Palm Beach just for the gaming. He played with a dedication and on a scale that were truly astonishing. Pop-eyed, we heard that he regularly put down a quarter of a million pounds in a single evening. Sometimes he lost six-figure sums. Sometimes he won. George denied none of this, though he was clearly embarrassed. He said it was something he hid from his family. He was not proud of it, though he admitted that on one occasion he had had a win of a million pounds. 'That,' he said with a sheepish grin, 'was a highlight.' So it must have been, even for a man who seemed to regard anything under a hundred grand's worth of chips as pretty small potatoes. It was not just myself who goggled at this peep into the nocturnal world of London's high-rollers. The barristers were just as open-mouthed, exchanging incredulous glances.

Here was yet another element of unfamiliarity to be grappled with by the jury. Already we had a multi-national cast-list, swollen by a retinue of interpreters. The defendants were accused of an unusual crime. In response they were putting forward an explanation which was positively Byzantine. The setting had been strange enough when it concerned only the arcane business of international shipping. Now the lights had dimmed and we were being invited to peer over expensively tailored shoulders at baize tables piled with enough chips to buy or lose an oil tanker in a single night.

Trial by Jury

Theoretically, the twelve members of a jury share a wide enough variety of knowledge and experience to have a collective grasp of what is going on in court. In practice, as we were discovering, a jury can easily find itself embarked on a journey without maps in completely alien terrain.

What was one to make of a man who gambled as heavily as George? Did it mean he was as unreliable as an alcoholic, or as devious as a drug addict? We did not know. Stuart the Rangers supporter had a weekly accumulator bet on the football results: he had once come within a whisker of a whopping win. Ex-schools inspector Magnus told us he used to bet on general elections, though after barely recovering his stake money in '92 he had no plans for '97. But apart from these two we were all non-punters (if you excluded our lottery syndicate) and had no means of forming a useful view. Copies of George's current account produced by the defence showed his bank balance going up and down crazily, without ever plunging seriously into the red. Over a period, he seemed to come out even.

If the defence team calculated that the jury would be revolted by evidence of such profligacy, or repelled simply by the careless wealth of George Fraghistas, they were probably going to be in for a disappointment. Had he been a home-born toff in the Lord Lucan mould, the reaction might have been more hostile. But George was Greek and therefore a non-combatant in the class war. Besides, his rather modest, unflamboyant manner was disarming. He was neither a jet-setter nor a spiv. He did not drink, he told us. He could not even be accused of starving his wife of his company to feed his habit, since he was a bachelor. All the same, if Mr Gale's probing did not produce a blanket condemnation, it did strike home with one very telling revelation. This concerned George's bouncing cheques.

Mr Gale explained that top casinos are accustomed to give

favoured patrons credit by letting them fill in house cheques for an agreed amount. The casino then presents these cheques at the client's bank and, after the usual period for clearance, the sum is transferred to the casino's account. George used this facility frequently. However, in a couple of instances a while before his kidnap, cheques for sizeable amounts had been returned, with a request for representation. In other words they had bounced. Despite courteous reminders from his creditors, George had done nothing about them. By the time of his kidnap, one casino had resorted to making sharpish telephone calls to goad him into action.

This was evidence, Mr Gale quite reasonably suggested, that Mr Fraghistas was in financial trouble and that the duns were after him. So here was a motive for devising the scheme to terrorise his family into parting with a multi-million dollar 'ransom'. What is more, it was suggested, a man who knowingly bounced cheques for large amounts of money was by definition dishonest and could not be trusted to tell the truth, even under oath.

George struggled to refute this last point but he was not convincing. He claimed that signing cheques which he knew would not be covered by the bank was his way of rationing his gaming, since any casino holding his dishonoured cheques in the till would not let him play. In any case, bouncing cheques on casinos was not really dishonest, since they were used to it: for example, he said, even establishments where he owed money still invited him to lunch as an honoured guest and friend of the house.

These explanations sounded disingenuous at best and at worst plain babyish. Mr Gale's harping on the theme of tax avoidance had, unsurprisingly, done George Fraghistas not a jot of damage. But the matter of the worthless cheques seemed to me to have dented him near the waterline. Had it not been for what one might call a presentational problem, the impact would have been even greater.

The problem was Michael Gale QC himself. I have no doubt that Mr Gale is a very able barrister. His oratory was remarkable. For one thing, when it wasn't targeted witheringly at George Fraghistas, it seemed to be addressed over the heads of us rude mechanicals in the jury box to some invisible audience of impressionable law students. For another, it demonstrated those perhaps rather neglected, old-fashioned rhetorical skills, the sustained sneer and the condescending put-down. 'Come, come, Mr Fraghistas,' he would say in a snappish tone that Jeremy Paxman might have envied. He had an extraordinary mannerism of asking George a question, then abruptly turning his head away to smirk at the jury. 'D'you follow me?' he would say, looking down his nose at us but addressing him.

A section of the jury soon began logging every 'D'you follow me?'. One of the interpreters sitting in the dock realised what was going on and grinned appreciatively. The witness was less amused by his inquisitor. 'You're out of your mind. You're crazy,' George exploded at Mr Gale after a particularly inflaming proposition of the 'I put it to you, Mr Fraghistas' variety.

A jury's job is to reach a verdict based solely on the evidence. But it would have to be composed of archangels not to be swayed by ordinary human likes and dislikes. It seemed surprising to me that Mr Gale could not detect the effect his approach was having. After one of his more pointed accusations, George gave a snort of derisive laughter. Instantly Mr Gale fixed him with a headmasterly glare. 'Did you laugh?' he barked. George's soft face crumpled like a small boy's. 'No, sir,' he squeaked, though we all knew he had and we all knew why he'd said he hadn't. Some childhood lessons are never forgotten.

I had the impression that even the judge found Korkolis's counsel trying, though Mr Gale was a recorder, a part-time fellow-judge (and a much admired one, according to Roy the usher). Once My Lord rapped him for clumsy use of language; another time he gave him exasperated guidance over the course of his cross-examination; and he ordered one particularly insensitive sally to be struck from the record altogether.

Not yet two weeks into the trial and our opinions had been set oscillating like a bank of echo-sounders. Mr Gale was scoring some palpable hits. He had raised niggles about George's financial probity that would not go away. Yet he was doing so in a manner liable to provoke as much sympathy for the prosecution's principal witness as doubt about his testimony.

POLICE VIDEO

We discussed all this fairly freely among ourselves whenever we could do so without being overheard. We had not yet been given our own jury room in which to forgather and pass the time during breaks for points of law. To begin with we didn't even have anywhere to sit, but had to stand about in a gaggle outside the lifts, sometimes for what felt like hours. The seats outside the courtrooms were reserved for witnesses and lawyers, with whom we were supposed to have no contact whatsoever. This was understandable. Roy the usher told us alarming tales about witnesses – even defendants on bail – brushing up against jurors and whispering the antithesis of sweet nothings in their ears.

In fact the Old Bailey is so pressed for space that jurors frequently find themselves caught up in a highly improper mêlée of lawyers, police, witnesses and journalists. Besides, there was only one set of loos for either sex on each floor, so inevitably there were times when I would find myself in the next stall to a barrister or witness. We would stare fixedly ahead at the tiles in awkward silence, though by now we all knew each other as well as people can who have never exchanged a word but see each other every day.

The safest place for the jury to swap views was in the lift, which bore a prominent notice saying: 'Do not discuss cases while travelling in this lift'. When there were just the twelve of us inside there would be a spontaneous outbreak of contempt-of-court ribaldry. As the trial wore on, we began to be treated more like grown-ups: we were allowed to use the seating outside the courts, so long as we could be trusted to keep to ourselves. Later still we were awarded the privilege of our own jury room. This had the advantage of being private and of possessing its own lavatories – one for boys, one for girls – but the disadvantage of forcing us to spend a lot of time hugger-mugger round the table. The chatter was distracting if one was trying to read a book or fill in New Zealand immigration forms. On one thumb-twiddling morning the subjects under discussion were as follows:

The colour of cigarette filter tips.
Religious divisions in Glasgow, with special reference to football.
Does the Pope keep a mistress?
What did everyone think of leather sofas?
Boxer shorts for men: the pros and cons.

Inevitably, there was also a joke from Magnus. Question: 'What are a monk's vices?' Answer: 'Nun.' Bob observed that Kate was putting on some make-up. 'Hey,' he called to her in a spurt of wit: 'Old paint-your-wagon!' Whereupon twelve Lee Marvins of either sex burst into a spontaneous chorus of 'I was born under a wanderin' star' which must have startled Judge Goldstein in his room next door.

One morning in December we trooped down to a tiny courtroom just off the Grand Hall which is a sort of electronics studio for the playing of taped and filmed evidence.

We were to see a video shot by a cameraman from the Met minutes after the police stormed Hogan Mews. We were a very rum audience: lawyers, witnesses, jurors, defendants, interpreters and prison officers, all pressed together on rows of chairs in a space smaller than a Soho preview theatre. (I learnt after the trial that George was able to look over Sophie's shoulder and read her notes. He made out the word 'chips' and glumly realised that she had homed in on the gambling.) The judge and the clerk of the court sat facing us, just feet away, watching on their own monitor.

The video was silent and rather eerie. This was our first sight of Hogan Mews except in photographs. The camera wobbled slowly from room to room, lingering meaningfully on a pair of handcuffs and a mask, inexplicably on a detergent bottle, messy heaps of clothes and an unflushed lavatory bowl. At one point George was standing in the doorway of the cupboard, pale, stubble-chinned and wearing a dressing gown. The silence was broken when we heard him say something about his mother, addressed to one of his invisible rescuers. Had someone telephoned her, he asked indistinctly. Like the moment when he was shown the leather mask in the witness box, this was a rare bit of direct, living evidence which the jury could judge with its own eyes and ears, even if it was only on video.

The film was played through twice. Comparing notes afterwards, four things appeared to have stuck in the jury's minds: the kidnap paraphernalia such as the handcuffs and the mask; the copy of a gay magazine lying on a table in the living room; a close-up of a Polaroid photograph torn into shreds; and the brief glimpse of George himself. It was at this point that we began to play detective. All juries do it to some extent, I suspect. (It was one of the accusations levelled by the defence against the Louise Woodward jury.) The temptation to second-guess the police is just too great. In our case we were to have so much time to reflect and so much contradictory evidence to go on that the Sherlock Holmes in each of us would have a field day.

It was the magazine that got us going. Which of the defendants was – or were – gay? Could bachelor George be gay himself? This was a theme we never quite let go of throughout the whole trial, though our curiosity was not finally satisfied until after the verdict.

The Polaroid: why had it been torn up into confetti-sized morsels? Should we ask if we could piece it together if the police had not already done so? (Daphne the Scrabble-player was keen to volunteer for this task.)

And George: was his demeanour as shown in the video really that of a newly released kidnap victim? Shouldn't he have been crying or breaking down or something, rather than smiling and composedly asking if someone had telephoned his mother? There was much uninformed speculation on this score. (Months later I learnt that George himself was struck by his own appearance: 'I was quite scared when I saw the video. Looking myself at the video it doesn't show like I was locked in the cupboard. I am quite normal.')

Back in Court 9 Mr Gale was still on the attack. George had by now taken to responding with a repertoire of shoulder-shrugging, eye-rolling and mute appeals to the judge. Once he broke out with an angry 'Are you out of your mind?' which earned him a rapping from the bench. At one point in the taped telephone conversations between George and his brother, Nicos appeared to lose his temper. Mr Gale implied that this was because Nicos had begun to suspect that George was not the victim of a real kidnap. George reacted to this suggestion fiercely, casting aside decorum. His brother was not getting at him: he was getting at the kidnappers *through* him. 'Nicos was trying to break Petros's balls,' cried George. 'But in the process he was also breaking *my* balls.'

We were now into the third week of the trial, an important

watershed for self-employed jurors. This was the point at which Stuart and I could raise our loss-of-earnings claims from the £40 or so a day payable during the first fortnight to a munificent £89.60. It was confirmation that we were now senior wranglers, long-serving jurors, and very welcome too, considering the potential earnings both he and I had been losing until now. Later the sum would go up again, to just over £96 a day. 'Not bad, eh, Trev?' said Stuart. He rubbed his hands with the satisfaction of an escapee from the cash-flow crisis which is the lot of the self-employed in modern Britain. Not bad at all.

I would like to have used some of the extra lolly to buy George a drink. Not because I was a hundred per cent convinced he was telling the truth or out of sympathy for what he was undergoing in the witness box, where the next defence barrister had now taken over the pummelling, but simply because he cut such a lonely figure. Witnesses may talk to no one about the case while they are in the box – unlike the defendants, who were having constant tête-à-têtes with their solicitors. Not only did George have to keep clear of the lawyers; he could not even unburden himself to his nearest and dearest, who would themselves be giving evidence.

George was the only one of us, save possibly the judge, who had no one to chat to in the coffee-breaks or share a fag with, no one to take to lunch or go home to in the evenings. He was in purdah. When one of the defence barristers concluded his cross-examination by saying nastily, 'You are a cheat with a T and cheap with a P,' George had to suffer in solitary silence. One day he announced brokenly, 'I feel that every time I get out of this court I have just given birth.' Then he added with a tight smile, 'To twins!'

Eventually it was all over. The judge released him, thanked him, and let him know that he could now rejoin the human race. George had been in the witness box for eleven days.

He climbed down, looking sad and tired. It would be many weeks before we were to see him again.

We wondered who the next witness would be. There were many, many more to come, the usher had warned us. How on earth would we know which of them to believe? In everyday life it is normal and polite to take what people say at face value. Here in court it was our job to be aware that every witness was a potential perjurer. From what they told us, we twelve had to decide on the facts of the case. But of course if the facts were straightforward, this trial would not even be taking place.

DO JURIES WORK?

There is an immense amount of research into the efficacy of juries as finders-out of the truth. None of it is conclusive. How could it be? There is no way of measuring the correctness or otherwise of a verdict with a hundred per cent accuracy. There have been painstaking projects to assess how far judges agree with their juries' decisions, likewise barristers and the police. One might suppose that where judge and jury were in accord one could describe a verdict as correct. But what if there were a successful appeal based on fresh evidence, say, or proof of misconduct by the police? Notorious miscarriages of justice occur with depressing regularity. Such verdicts would by definition have been incorrect. But who could blame the jury?

Tests have been made with mock juries, sometimes sitting in parallel with real ones. The results have been intriguing, but of course such experiments can only approximate the tension and the tedium of the real thing. There are whole libraries of material based on post-trial interviews with jurors in the United States, where such research is allowed. In this country even the most anonymous probing into how jurors reach their verdicts is strictly forbidden. Any doubt on this score was firmly scotched under Section 8 of the Contempt of Court Act 1981, after a juror wrote the inside story of the Jeremy Thorpe trial in the *New Statesman*. Since then, although jurors do not swear an oath to stay silent, they are liable to prosecution if they do not. So is anyone who tries to persuade them to reveal the secrets of the retiring room. A Royal Commission recommendation in 1993 that this restriction should be lifted for the purposes of academic study was not acted upon. And even in the US, where almost anything goes and interviews with jurymen on the very steps of the courthouse are commonplace, the taping or filming of deliberations in the jury room itself is not permitted.

I think the complete lifting of this ban would be a bad idea, though it goes against the journalistic grain not to want to know more. Verdicts must not only be unassailable: they have to be seen to be so, other than through the appeals mechanism (even then, it is not the quality of the verdict that is under review but the fairness and correctness of the trial that led to it). Likewise jurors should not have to worry about being mocked or menaced by having their conduct in the jury room exposed in the newspapers.

My own guess is that even the most thorough investigations would fail to answer any of the great questions about juries beyond reasonable doubt. All the same, not to allow properly monitored, anonymity-preserving, carefully targeted academic research seems unnecessarily defensive. Belief in the jury system is an act of communal faith and political will. But if mystique is all it has going for it, we should be worried.

The history of the English jury is blotted with hair-raising stories of jurors playing pitch and toss or 'hustling half-pennies in a hat' to reach a verdict. There has been a recent case where some members of a jury consulted an ouija board. Every lawyer can tell you anecdotes about deaf, drunk or disqualified people sitting on juries. Nevertheless, it is broadly correct that in England and Wales most judges and most lawyers – even most of the police – accept that juries are reasonably reliable assessors of the facts.

An even greater majority would agree that whatever their reservations on that score, the system confers a unique legitimacy on the judicial process. As a distinguished prosecuting counsel put it to me, 'The strongest argument for the retention of the jury is that it is the only involvement the public has in the criminal justice system. Confidence in our system may not be high: it would be reduced even further if it were left to lawyers and judges alone.' The jury-less Diplock courts that have been imposed on Northern Ireland since 1973 for fear of prejudice and intimidation have worked extraordinarily well, I am told. But they are a symptom of a deeply troubled society and are tolerated by the community only so long as there is no alternative.

About a quarter of contested Crown Court trials in England and Wales end in acquittals. That may seem rather a high proportion, given that the Crown Prosecution Service is supposed to proceed only with cases that have a good chance of a conviction. But for the record, a senior British judge, Lord Salmon, said in 1974, 'I do not believe that . . . there is more than about two per cent of the men brought to trial who are wrongly acquitted.' Other judges put the figure higher – but no one can say with any certainty what the proportion really is.

Most American judges claim to be broadly in favour of juries and confident that verdicts are overwhelmingly correct. Although there is a large element of motherhood and apple pie in all this, academic studies here, too, have tended to support the view that perverse jury verdicts are rare. *Jury Trials* (OUP, 1979), an analysis by John Baldwin and Michael McConville of hundreds of cases tried in Birmingham and London in the mid-1970s, did come up with some disturbing statistics – for example, they identified forty-one out of a hundred and fourteen acquittals in Birmingham as questionable, and there was a significant though much smaller proportion of dubious convictions. (The ratio of questionable verdicts was lower in London.) None of their research led them to any clear explanation for this anomaly, other than that 'trial by jury is a relatively crude instrument'. But Baldwin and McConville do declare emphatically that 'there was no evidence . . . to suggest any relationship between the composition of the jury and the verdict returned'.

That information might have been a comfort to George Fraghistas had he known it. Our twelve faces staring at him across the court must have unnerved him. I am sure that at times we looked stupid or confused, at others merely expressionless. He would have seen one or two of us nod off. At any rate, very little about our appearance can have inspired him with confidence.

GEORGE'S MOTHER

Rhea Fraghistas took her son's place in the witness box on Friday 13 December. She was a slim, well-groomed, quietly dressed woman who I guessed was in her late sixties. She had obviously been even prettier when she was young. She had bluey-grey hair and a calm face – not at all the grim-visaged shipping tycooness I had been half-expecting. This was going to be a problem for the defending counsel: if they bully this nice-looking elderly lady, I said to myself, the jury will say boo.

We settled back with the anticipation of a theatre audience, hoping to learn more about George by observing his mother. Joanna Korner took her through a set of questions which quickly challenged the defence's insinuations that there was friction among the Fraghistas clan. 'We are a very united family,' said Mrs Fraghistas firmly. 'In Greece, most families are very close. That is the rule rather than the exception.' She left hanging in the air the unspoken suggestion that perhaps this was not the case in Britain.

'If George wanted some money, what happened?' asked Miss Korner.

'I would give it to him. The same with all my children. And sometimes George would send *me* money.' Bang went any idea – for the moment at any rate – that George would normally have a problem extracting funds from his mama. Yes, she knew George gambled. No, she did not approve. No, she had never given him money to pay off his casino debts. And if he had asked for help of that kind? 'I would probably have given it to him. He is my son. But I would have made conditions.'

'Such as stopping?'

'Of course, stopping.'

Mr Gale used his cross-examination to search for a breach in this solid maternal wall. 'In England, if one company lent money to another, it would have to show up in the books,' he said.

'But this was Greece, not England. As I said, we are a family,' replied the witness patiently.

Once again, one was aware of the cultural dissonance resonating around Court 9. Mr Gale found it impossible to picture a business, even a family business, which allowed its directors to shovel large sums of money from one member to another as the need arose without accounting for every penny. Mrs Fraghistas seemed to find it equally puzzling that these English lawyers couldn't imagine such an amiable and relaxed state of affairs. It was put to her that perhaps George would have been scared to come to her for money to cover gambling debts, had he known she would try to put an end to his bad habits. No, she didn't think so.

'But, Mrs Fraghistas, you agree that you told the police he was a naughty boy . . .'

She said she was referring to when he was a boy – a naughty *little* boy.

The judge intervened: 'Mr Gale, Mr Fraghistas is 43.'

Mrs Fraghistas told Mr Gale she thought it very unlikely that George would go back to his old ways at the tables after his recent experience.

She left the courtroom looking desolate. Mr Gale's closing shot of the day had been to inform her that George *had* been back to the Clermont to gamble, *since* the kidnap. Did she know that, asked the sneak of the Bailey triumphantly? No she did not, she had said, crestfallen.

I doubt if I was alone in liking Rhea Fraghistas. I heard a woman juror say, 'I wish she was *my* mother.' The transcripts of telephone conversations between George in the cupboard and Nicos at his mother's flat showed that Rhea was ill with anxiety during the kidnap. Could George really have put her through this deliberately, as the defence alleged? She said with complete conviction, 'My children always try not to worry me.' She could be quite funny. Asked to describe the family business she began, 'If you will now listen to some shipping information . . .' Challenged to admit that her late husband had played poker with a certain Greek minister she said with a shrug of her shoulders, 'My husband played poker with half of Athens.'

Her English was fluent. She very seldom turned for help to the interpreter seated beside her in the witness box. She stood her ground in a way that must have pleased Joanna Korner and her junior, Jeremy Benson.

'Does George have an account in Geneva?'

'Ask George,' replied his mother.

'But I thought you were a very united family?'

'Yes, but we are not in each other's pockets.'

The barrage did not slacken. Did she ever think that the

kidnap was a fake? Never. Did she believe that George was really in debt? No. Why not? Because if he'd really been in debt he would have come to her for money. 'As I have said, we are a *family*.'

The judge leaned towards her kindly when she had finished. 'You are now free to talk to your son. You can have dinner with George and talk to him about anything you like, including this case.' His thoughtfulness did not go unnoticed. She had been an impressive witness. She had done all that a mother could for her son.

Exactly, a sceptical juror might have reflected. Even if George *had* been trying to terrify her into parting with millions of dollars, and even if she *had* suspected him all along, she was just the sort of mother who would have stood by him, wasn't she? She would have wanted to protect the family name, wouldn't she?

SCENES OF THE CRIME

Before Mrs Fraghistas took the stand the jury had done something which made us feel rather bold. We had asked to visit the scenes of the crime – the kidnap HQ at Hogan Mews and the Lanark Road car-park where George had been seized. This would be arranged, said the judge, making it sound as though jury tours of kidnap hideouts were all part of the Old Bailey service.

The jurors were very excited about the jaunt. Here was a chance to put the courtroom narrative with which we were now so familiar into a three-dimensional context. Bob the postman saw this trip as raising the whole status of our task. A jury being escorted to the *mise en scène* was serious stuff. He was now quite confident that our deliberations at the end of the trial would take days rather than hours. We would therefore have to be sequestered in a hotel for several nights. He grinned significantly at Kate as he explained this. Juries were always sent to top-grade hotels, he said. He hoped ours would have a gym, so he could keep up his training. Several jurors began discussing what they should pack on the morning we began our deliberations – just in case we were cut off from the world without a toothbrush and a nightie.

All this seemed a bit premature. Several of us were appalled at the idea of extending our enforced intimacy in an almost certainly gymless hostelry, probably somewhere out on the M25. But the idea took hold and remained a potent lure for the rest of the trial.

The expedition to Hogan Mews and Lanark Road took place on a Monday morning. When we trooped into court there was no one there except the judge and the clerk, both dressed in mufti. We were warned not to talk to a soul except the usher from now on. One almost expected to be told to walk in a crocodile, holding hands.

The jury was led out of the back of the Old Bailey into a yard where a full-sized tourist coach awaited. We spread ourselves around the interior in a suppressed holiday mood, feeling foolishly outnumbered by empty seats. We left a large space between ourselves and the judge. He sat near the front in a natty overcoat looking rather small away from his dais and bereft of his paraphernalia.

Forty minutes later it was plain we were lost. Although both Lanark Road and Hogan Mews are clearly marked in the London street maps, we were way off target. I could hear the judge giving the driver some unconvincing instructions. Considering that His Honour Judge Goldstein was near enough a local man, as I had discovered from *Who's Who*, living quite close to our destinations, this was slightly disconcerting. Was someone incapable of finding his way around his own neighbourhood the best man to go into the legal jungle with?

I murmured as loudly as I dared from the back of the bus that we ought to be going the other way. Stuart, the one-man *A-Z*, joined in. The judge, the clerk and even the driver pretended not to hear. The usher, looking a bit flummoxed, checked whether we jurors really knew the way. There then ensued an A.A. Milne-ish parody of English judicial procedure in which I told the usher, the usher told the clerk, the clerk told the judge and the judge told the driver which way to turn. The driver, understandably sceptical of all this palaver, eventually stopped the coach and went to ask directions. By then Hogan Mews was just around the corner.

We turned down a quiet street from the Regent's Canal in Little Venice, where the narrow boats are moored. The entrance to Hogan Mews is just off Porteous Road, opposite a characterless eight-storey estate called John Aird Court. It was rather a glum little mews, no more than fifty yards long, consisting of identical small town houses. I saw Neighbourhood Watch stickers in two windows, but only one burglar alarm.

There was a gaggle of overcoated lawyers waiting for us outside Number 5. Michael Gale was wearing a bowler hat, which the jury thought hilarious. He looked like a character from one of the late Jak's cartoons in the *Evening Standard*. Where else has one seen a bowler hat *in situ* in the last twenty years except in the vicinity of the racetrack? Miss Korner must also have been uneasy at going about wigless. She was splendidly decked in a brown velvet Mabel Lucie Attwell creation.

We surged into the house, retracing the steps of Detective Sergeant Hawkins and his men seven months earlier. Immediately to the left was the downstairs lavatory into which Mereu had been shoved. It had a tiny window, which none of us noticed, but whose size would eventually become an issue of some significance. Ahead was the kitchen, now a good deal tidier than in the police video. The door to the cupboard-cum-utility room off the kitchen was open: it looked even smaller and more cell-like than I had expected. Only one of us could get in there at a time to inspect it.

This was the airless hole where George had expected to meet his death. He said he had begged 'Petros' if 'he could kindly use a gun while I sleep instead of a lethal injection. And he agreed, which put me at rest a little bit'. Towards the end of his ordeal 'Petros' terrified him by saying that the guards had grown to like him and wouldn't be prepared to kill him – so Mereu and Moussaoui were to be replaced.

A tall black man was lounging in the sitting room upstairs, presumably the present tenant or maybe the landlord. He was trying to look indifferent to this weird invasion of besuited swells and jean-clad jurymen. We poked about like house-hunters, our numbers emphasising the smallness of the place as we squeezed past each other on the stairs, scrummed into the bathroom and peered over each other's shoulders into box-like bedrooms. 'It's really naff,' whispered Kate. 'I couldn't bring up my family in a place like this,' Anna said scornfully. The jury seemed rather chuffed that the mews-dwelling classes lived in such cramped soullessness.

There was nobody guiding the jury around. We remembered that George had said he had only once been upstairs. Blindfolded, he had been half-pushed, half-carried up to the bathroom one day, convinced that they were going to kill him there. He had been in a state of terminal terror as they led him to the side of the bath. But they only wanted him to have a proper wash. He had left his fingerprints on a hair dryer.

It was on our own initiative that we looked into the garage, discovering that there was a door leading straight from there into the house. So George could have been unloaded from the boot and taken inside – or strolled in unaided – without any of the neighbours observing what was afoot. That had not previously been clear to me.

We got back into the bus to drive to Lanark Road, reversing the order in which events had occurred on 24 March. It did not take long.

The NCP car-park in Lanark Road would win a location manager's approval as the setting for a kidnap. It is an ill-lit, low-ceilinged place with oil-stained floors and shadows in the corners. One would feel a prickle of unease parking there at night, among the squat pillars and the tick of cooling car engines. We could see BMWs, Mercedes, Rovers and a Porsche. There was a long, low Ferrari lovingly wrapped in a bright red dust-sheet. Our two parties – judge, barristers and clerk in one group, jurors and usher in the other – milled around talking in low voices, like visitors to a grotto.

We had seen the police photos. Now, feeling rather self-conscious, we were able to stand by the bay marked out in faded white paint where George thought he had parked. I tried to imagine him hearing the sound of running footsteps behind him: whirling round, the sight of a hooded man wearing an anorak and motor-cycling gloves approaching through the gloom. Could it be a joke? That had been his first thought, he had told the court. Knocked against a car with a hand over his mouth, then forced face down on to the gritty concrete floor, he was aware of two other men struggling to pinion him. It was no joke.

Even when he raised his head, he could see only one of the three. The man loomed over him 'like a giant', holding a gun. Several hands tried to force a leather hood over his head: claustrophobia and panic. He fought and kicked to stop himself being crammed into the boot of a car. The boot lid was slammed on his ankles again and again to make him pull them in. He screamed. A man jumped in beside him. The lid closed. Claustrophobia and panic again. The car started up and swerved out into the street. No one had heard his shouts for help.

We timed the opening and closing of the garage doors

and examined the other exits. We paced out the alleged length of the alleged gunman's alleged run towards George, keenly aware of the difficulty of judging distance in such unscientific circumstances. Bob wanted to re-stage the attack among ourselves. The message was conveyed to the judge. The answer came back: no. Decorum was preserved.

We were bussed back to the Old Bailey in a somewhat muted mood. I was unsure whether our outing had really enlarged our understanding or merely titillated our curiosity. In my own case, the visits had sown a couple of nagging doubts. Was it logical that a gang of professional kidnappers would choose a hideaway so close – less than a quarter of an hour's drive – from their victim's home, rather than some isolated place in the country? And wasn't it strange that none of the residents of Hogan Mews had seen or heard anything out of the ordinary, given the closeness of the houses and the smallness of the mews?

CHRISTMAS IS COMING

It was the night of Jeffrey Archer's shepherd's pie and champagne Christmas party. John Major was there. His government was tottering towards electoral defeat in a few months' time. Top Tories were disembowelling themselves with the self-absorption of suicidal samurai. Yet the PM himself was boyishly animated, surrounded by a knot of admiring women. The condemned man enjoys a final fling, I thought ghoulishly, still in juryman mode.

The language of politics is full of courtroom metaphors. After eighteen years of mixed fortunes, the Tories would be described as being in the dock, defending their record, putting their case to the public and submitting to the judgement of the electorate. Rasher columnists of the Woodrow Wyatt persuasion might fall back on that other journalistic standby, claiming the jury was still out. Actually, by December '96 the jury was positively hammering at the courtroom door.

The parallels between the democratic process and trial by jury are quite illuminating, after a couple of glasses of Lord Archer's Krüg. The great mass of uncommitted voters who swing elections reach their verdict in much the same way as a jury: by assessing the evidence, listening to the advocacy and judging the honesty of the witnesses. Anyone querying the fitness of juries to try serious criminal cases is poking a sharp stick into the belly of democracy. 'Each jury is a little parliament,' Lord Devlin said. You cannot logically mistrust the one without condemning the other. You might even argue that a jury trial is a purer expression of popular will than a general election. Malice, bias, credulity and boredom influence both undertakings. But at least the juror, unlike the voter, is untainted by self-interest.

The following evening my wife and I were invited to another Christmas party, given by Jonathan Aitken's mother. His disastrous libel case against the *Guardian* was still some months away. Had I known then that he and his lawyers would argue successfully (on grounds of complexity, upheld on appeal) to have it heard before a judge alone, without a jury, I would have been very surprised. Aitken had been a journalist before he went into business and became an MP. Any newspaperman objects to the idea of libel juries setting damages. But when it comes to judging whether a person's reputation has been unfairly harmed, who fitter for the task than twelve members of the public? After all, it was a jury that had acquitted Aitken of charges under the Official Secrets Act earlier in his career. To avoid the jury in this case did not look good – and, as it turned out, did him none.

That morning the jurors had exchanged Christmas cards, some containing printed verses. The ceremony took place in the jury restaurant with all the punctiliousness of Japanese salesmen swapping business cards. 'Stuart, Terrie, Trev, Anna . . . these are for you.' The GPO two, Bob and Sophie, must have felt quite piqued as one hundred and thirty-two envelopes changed hands without their aid. Terrie was keen on arranging a Christmas party: should we book a table for twelve at the Café Rouge? Oh, no, said some: too posh. Too late, said others. Let's wait and see, suggested those with grim experience of office Christmas outings. A tipsy jury would lead to fines, for sure; maybe even a mis-trial.

The festive season was putting out green plastic shoots all over the Old Bailey. Holly leaves sprouted in unobtrusive corners. The jury restaurant started trailing its special Christmas lunch menu. One half expected Roy to turn up in false whiskers and a red bobble-hat. Merry greetings had been pinned up in the jury cloakroom, where there were sometimes as many as three people passing the time of day, slowly and inaccurately hanging up coats and handing out numbered discs. One snowy morning I came in wearing my one and only hat, a dark blue trilby. I handed it to the heroically lethargic West Indian in charge that day. When I collected it later, I discovered he had folded it up like a newspaper and stuffed it into my coat pocket, ruining it for ever. Perhaps this was why Mr Gale stuck to a bowler.

SELF-DEFENCE

By now Nicos Fraghistas had taken the stand. He was trimmer and more youthful than his younger brother George. He seemed to fizz with nervous energy. After the trial was over, at a funeral in Oxford, I got into conversation with a solicitor from one of the big City law firms. It emerged that he knew Nicos. How come? Oh, through water skiing, of course, he replied. Water skiing? He might as well have said bird-watching or amateur theatricals. He could see I was puzzled. 'Didn't you know Nicos Fraghistas is a champion water-skier in Greece? We ski together every summer.'

I could not fault Miss Korner for not eliciting this information about Nicos's aquatic prowess, even had she known about it. It was of no conceivable relevance to the trial. But in retrospect it helped to explain his debonair manner. There was a Jack Lemmonish jut to his chin as he gave his answers. He smiled a lot and peered eagerly around the courtroom. He had to be persuaded to sit himself on the little flap-down seat hinged to the back of the witness box.

Nicos was temperamentally incapable of giving yes or no for an answer. He would rattle on excitably for several minutes, only to conclude by saying with a radiant smile, 'My Lord, may I elaborate?'

My lawyer friend at the funeral told me that the faster a water-skier is capable of taking a slalom course, the shorter he has his tow-rope. So far as his evidence was concerned, Nicos seemed to prefer the long-rope approach. We sat back and allowed ourselves to be entertained.

On Wednesday 18 December we spent the morning lolling about in the jury room. It was a longer than usual point of law. Lunchtime approached. Something was afoot. Leanne, the usher with the lip-liner and big eyelashes, was standing in for Roy that day. She confirmed that there was a major development. We fell to speculating. My own guess was that one or both of the Frenchmen was going to change his plea. Up to this point the two elderly barristers representing them had said almost nothing in court, merely 'adopting' the cross-examinations by their learned friends Mr Gale and Mr Patrick Curran, representing Zografos.

It already seemed plain to me that, even if the defence story of a conspiracy involving George proved to be true, and that therefore there had been no actual kidnap or false imprisonment, the men in the dock could at least be held guilty of blackmailing the Fraghistas family. Might Mereu and Moussaoui not see some merit in cutting and running now, pleading guilty to one of the charges and avoiding any deeper quicksands that might lie ahead? Maybe all four of them would take that line? It seemed ominously plausible. I for one would be desperately disappointed if our trial came to a premature end that very day.

The trial did not come to an end that very day: quite the reverse. At two o'clock in the afternoon the jury was called into court. We were in a state of keen anticipation. The judge addressed us directly. Mr Korkolis, he told us, the principal defendant, had decided to dispense with his barrister, Mr Gale. From now on Mr Korkolis would represent himself.

There was a kind of weary fatalism in the judge's voice. Perhaps it was a fore-echo of what he feared was to come. Carefully he explained that everything possible had been done to alter Mr Korkolis's decision, but that the defendant had every right to stick to it. This would add difficulties to the jury's task and to everyone else's, he said. It would certainly extend the length of the trial. But there it was. Did he roll his eyes ceilingwards and sigh? I rather expect he did.

The jury was removed so that further legal niceties could be explained to Mr Korkolis. I felt a pang of sympathy for him. I tried to imagine what it would be like to conduct a highly complex case with no legal training and in a foreign language from the confines of a cell in one of Her Majesty's overcrowded prisons.

As we mooched about outside the courtroom discussing the likely fallout from this bombshell, Mr Gale sloped past, heading for the stairs. He had his bowler hat on and was carrying a briefcase. He looked thoroughly peeved. I felt a stab of sympathy for him too. To be publicly rejected in this fashion must be a pretty rare occurrence in a QC's CV. Was it possible, I wondered, that Korkolis's brief to him had simply been too outlandish for him to present convincingly?

Was that why this experienced barrister (rather a hero of Roy the usher's, I later learnt) had papered over the thinness of his case with sneers and innuendo? 'Tell you what,' said Bob, as we watched him make his exit, 'why don't we say, "Mr Gale, you've been sacked. *D'you follow me?*" ' Everyone laughed cruelly.

When we reassembled in court there was an empty space where Mr Gale had sat. His junior soon followed him out. Mr Korkolis was in his same seat in the dock, flanked as always by his own interpreter on one side and Zografos on the other. The difference was that now he was barricaded behind the boxes of documents he had inherited from his ex-counsel. In front of and below him was his solicitor, sticking gamely to his post: a thin-faced, anxious-looking young man. As Korkolis's only guide to the law and go-between with the court, I guessed his problems would henceforth be multiplied a hundredfold.

Korkolis himself was now an object of extra-close attention. He presented a small, wiry, putty-coloured figure. He was not altogether unappealing. He could have been the cousin of an old friend of mine, a bazouki-playing Queensway restaurateur called Stelios at whose gingham-covered tables I drank too much retsina in the 1970s. Stelios always offered his regular customers a glass of brandy on the house. 'This was my grandfather's brandy,' he'd say solemnly, though no one believed him. Korkolis looked as though he could turn on the same sort of twinkly Hellenic charm.

In contrast to the starched white neckbands and shiny shoes of the lawyers, he wore a baggy grey round-necked sweater with no shirt underneath, from which his head emerged like a tortoise's. His hair was cindery and his skin gleamed with an unhealthy prison pallor. Only his thick black eyebrows and perpetual half-grin animated his face.

After the ponderous condescensions of Mr Gale, Korkolis

was rather a tonic. He picked up where Mr Gale had left off, cross-examining Nicos as coolly as could be. His English was heavily accented and rapid. He seemed to have tuned in to the cadences of courtroom delivery with an uncanny ear. His questions were larded with the word 'alleged' and phrases like 'it has been suggested that'.

He waved his arms about a good deal. But then so did Nicos, whose outrage at being addressed by the supposed kidnapper and near-murderer of his brother was quickly apparent. Quite soon they were haranguing and interrupting each other as though they were in an Athens *kapheneon*. The court stenographer must have been going mad. Eventually the judge's patience wore out. No, I'm sorry, he said, this won't do. 'Mr Korkolis never listens to the answers. Mr Fraghistas never listens to the questions.'

It was a very odd situation. Here was the hostage's brother, who had been the chief negotiator with the kidnappers, being questioned by the very man he'd not been able to speak to during those desperate nine days: the shadowy figure who called himself 'Petros', who had allegedly threatened to kill George and had held his frantic mother to ransom for three million dollars. It was now 'Petros' who was putting the questions and demanding answers; it was Nicos, the cocksure figure who had hitherto been filled with righteous indignation, who had to answer them. All this was taking place within the polite conventions of an English courtroom. Had the confrontation been held outside the Old Bailey there would have been blood in the gutter for sure. One could sense Nicos's frustration. Where George had managed scarcely to look at the prisoners at all, Nicos could not avoid doing so, his interrogator being one of their number. Challenged by Korkolis to explain the curt tone he had adopted towards George during the ransom calls he burst out, 'I was telling *you*. I was talking to *you*.' It was his first chance to address his family's tormentor face to face.

'Do you have any underworld connections?' asked Korkolis unexpectedly. He referred to a telephone conversation Nicos had had from Mrs Fraghistas's flat with a Greek businessman acquaintance. The call had been routinely taped by the police which was how Korkolis knew about it: we had the transcript in front of us. The businessman had offered Nicos to send over 'top, top, top people' to do a little private investigation as to the missing George's whereabouts. What might it mean? What was 'top, top, top people' if not Mafia-speak for heavies? Mr Gale could not have done better. Korkolis was making us think.

He was also making us laugh. His gallant attempts at courtroom legalese occasionally took a grammatical tumble. 'Did your brother had a Bentley?' he asked fiercely at one point. At another, reverting to the alleged hostility between the two Fraghistas brothers, he said, 'You called your brother a wonker!' He asked one of the policemen who had searched Hogan Mews, 'Was there anything in the rubbishes incriminating?'

Judge Goldstein looked on with the controlled exasperation of a top boxing referee forced to oversee a low-grade wrestling match. He had already made it abundantly clear that he found Korkolis's prolixity trying. Now he wearily addressed the witness: 'Mr Fraghistas, you are as bad as he is.'

As the hours ticked by on the courtroom clock – the slowest clock in the world – and the jurors fussed around with their water carafes to keep themselves awake, what had seemed like a chaotically confusing approach by Korkolis gradually took on recognisable shape. He was determined to prove that not only was George in on the plot but that his family had become co-conspirators too. They had quickly twigged what was afoot, wanted to avoid a scandal and had somehow embroiled the police into helping them do so. Korkolis's tools were hypothesis and insinuation. He deployed them if not with skill then certainly with exhausting relentlessness. His questions invariably started with an 'if': 'If you were kidnapped . . .'; 'If you were a very experienced detective from Scotland Yard . . .'; 'If your own brother was held hostage . . .' He would then weave through a complex train of suppositions, concluding with an explosive 'Answer: yes or no!'

Korkolis's 'Yes or no!' replaced Mr Gale's 'D'you follow me?' as the jury's favourite catchphrase. Often it left the witness baffled, casting beseeching looks at the judge to intervene. With measured frequency he did so, his patience showing creeping signs of wear and tear. While preserving his courteous manner at all times, he now and then began to sound quite snappy. 'What we do not do in an English court, Mr Korkolis, is play games.' One morning he startled us all by his outspokenness. 'I am becoming quite cross,' he rumbled. Coming from Judge Goldstein this was the equivalent of a thunderbolt from Zeus.

But it had less impact on Korkolis than English insect-repellent on a Greek mosquito. He gabbled on undaunted, never using one word where a peroration would do, swinging entertainingly from racy idiomatic English ('George was in on the plot with us') to mangled grammar and sublime mispronunciations. 'Did you ever cross your mind . . . ?' he would ask the witness insinuatingly, and then go on to question him about 'weepons' and 'sweetcases'.

We did learn an engaging Greek phrase in the course of it all. This was *'anthropos das nichtas'* – a man of the night, a night owl. It would help to keep the principal characters in our minds over the forthcoming break, these gambling Greeks who ventured out at midnight and seldom roused themselves before midday.

Our Christmas party would not have appealed to an *anthropos das nichtas*. It was held at lunchtime in the pub across the road, which smelt of disinfectant. We had steak sandwiches and lager. Wishing each other 'Happy Christmas', 'Feliz Navidad' and 'Buon Natale' our gang of twelve dispersed into the early winter darkness.

HISTORY LESSON

The court would not be sitting again until 6 January. But I found it impossible to put the trial out of my mind. For one thing, it was clearly going to take up a great chunk of the new year, far greater than anyone had anticipated. Korkolis's line in self-defence was often more entertaining than Mr Gale's had been. But it was also immeasurably more long-winded and repetitive.

By now I was so absorbed I didn't mind. Korkolis himself was a riveting study. He was as bumptious as a cockerel. Yet he had moments of charm – and had become quite skilled at seizing an opportunity for sympathy. When the judge rapped him for not having prepared his material before coming into court, Korkolis responded with scarcely a hint of self-pity, 'My Lord, it is hard to prepare. You know the conditions.'

Korkolis was taking the leading defence role in a serious criminal trial with no more than his own sharp wits to aid him. In doing so, it seemed to me, he was calculatingly targeting the twelve members of the jury. He was shrewd enough to realise that, whatever the legal arguments or the weight of the evidence, it was not the judge or the barristers or the police he had to convince: it was us. He must have known he had won some points by sacking his counsel and stepping into the advocate's role himself. He had seen our lips curling. He was clever enough to understand that the British sense of fair play and love of the underdog could be recruited to his side. He would play the victim; he would try to align us with himself against the playboys of the West End world like George Fraghistas and his family.

He had also probably worked out by now, with a little help from prison friends, that even if English juries could not be wooed they could sometimes be baffled and bored into acquitting.

I thought about him with some sympathy over the holiday while I was stuffing the turkey and hoovering needles under the Christmas tree. I pictured him in his cell, stooped over law books written in a language which makes even native speakers stumble, summoning his solicitor for urgent conferences, rehearsing his lines.

I began doing a bit of homework myself, dipping into what books I could find about the jury system. They were few but illuminating. One of them, *Taking Liberties: The Criminal Jury in the 1990s* (Weidenfeld & Nicolson, 1990) by Sean Enright and James Morton, helped me to put the jury into an historical context. Geoffrey Robertson's admirable *Freedom, the Individual and the Law*, which I caught up with in its seventh edition (Penguin, 1993), provided a contemporary gloss. Then there was W. R. Cornish's *The Jury* (Allen Lane, 1968) . . . But stop. I had no plans to become an academic expert. I merely wanted a bit of background.

If Korkolis was gambling on an English jury's being stroppy, anti-establishment and resentful of the rich, it was not altogether a bad bet. Native stupidity might shorten the odds on an acquittal even further. Our jury system owes its fame – and notoriety – to outbreaks of wayward behaviour, even though the truth is that it has been a prop of authority far more consistently than it has been a check on it. Some would say that this is the great charm of the British jury. It may tog itself out like a mini rent-a-mob in blue jeans and Nike trainers. Its battle honours may include glorious instances of giving two fingers to the authorities of the day. But it remains on the whole a pretty conservative institution.

Trial by Jury

Trial by jury has existed in these islands for more than seven hundred years in one form or another. Naturally, it has evolved a great deal over that period. Back in the early part of the thirteenth century a jury might number anything between two and four dozen members. Picture the scene. They would all be men, generally of some rank and substance: a congregation of the sort of neighbourhood worthies who today would probably be JPs, Rotarians or members of the local Conservative Association.

In complete contrast to our present-day conventions, they would be chosen precisely because of their knowledge of the defendant, or at any rate his background, and their familiarity with the circumstances in which the alleged offence occurred. Nowadays, of course, total ignorance of all such matters is a juror's prime qualification, impartiality having become the jewel in justice's crown (and a great obstacle to truth-finding, the police might add, *sotto voce*).

But seven centuries ago there were worse things to fear even than a biased jury. Trial by ordeal effectively came to an end in 1215, at the instigation of the Vatican. But for centuries it had been the routine way of deciding guilt and innocence. Ordeal by battle, ordeal by fire and ordeal by water must have seemed almost as barbaric then as they do now, even if the innocent had greater faith in the Almighty to intervene on their behalf.

The ordeals came in ingenious variety. Pulling an object out of a vat of boiling water with one's hand or walking several paces holding a red-hot iron were two of them. The verdict depended on how swiftly the burnt hand healed. In the ordeal by water, the alleged felon was tied up and tossed into a pond. Perversely, floating on the surface was considered unnatural, and therefore proof of guilt. If you sank like a Mafia corpse you were acquitted – but risked drowning anyway. A less agonising ordeal required the eating of a bun or 'cursed morsel' in which a feather was secreted. If the result was a coughing fit, it was thumbs down. If you munched away contentedly and could get out the words, 'This bun or cursed morsel is delicious, as light as a feather', you were in the clear.

Even then, there were juries. They were employed to decide whether an accused person had a case to answer and, if so, to select which form of ordeal would be appropriate. After 1215, they began to act not only in this role as a 'petty jury' or 'jury of presentment' but to try the cases, too. By 1220 trial by jury was established as the normal procedure.

The experience could be tough for these early jurymen. Once a petty jury had accepted that the defendant had a case to answer, woe betide the jurors who then decided to acquit. They would usually be fined, on the assumption that it was a perverse verdict – an assumption that was to hold good for hundreds of years to come. No doubt there are judges who wish it still held good today.

In the 1360s it was decided that unanimous verdicts would be a good idea and that huge unwieldy juries were out of date. Enter the twelve good men and true who have been with us ever since, unchanged but for allowing women to join their number in 1919 and some subsequent adjustments to age and status. Why twelve? No one really knows. But there were twelve apostles and twelve tribes of Israel and twelve pennies to the shilling. Maybe, as Lord Devlin has suggested, the number chosen was simply the expression of 'an early English abhorrence of the decimal system'.

TRIALS AND TRIBULATIONS

If the composition of juries changed in the fourteenth century, conditions in those far-off days did not, nor would they for centuries to come. Because jurors tended to be local men, known to the defendant, the risk of jury-tampering was great. To counteract this, juries on serious cases, once sworn, were not allowed to separate until the end of the trial. For the same reason it was considered proper that juries should be deprived of food, water and heat during their deliberations. This was to prevent one side or the other from getting to the jury and corrupting its members with tasty titbits, strong drink, or out-and-out bribes. On a cold night even a log for the fire would presumably have been considered an inducement. If the effect of these privations was also to speed up the verdict, so much the better. 'The hungry judges soon the sentence sign,' wrote Alexander Pope in *The Rape of the Lock*. 'And wretches hang that jurymen may dine.'

The tale is told of how once, during a lengthy jury deliberation, the usher asked the judge if he could give one of the jurymen a glass of water. 'Well,' said Mr Justice Maule, 'it is not meat, and *I* should not call it drink; yes, you may.'

In his jolly book, *Great Legal Disasters* (Arthur Barker, 1983), former judge Sir Stephen Tumim recounts the story of the acquittal of the Seven Bishops in 1688. Their petition to James II to stay within the Church of England had led to their being charged with seditious libel. The jury was locked up for the night with nothing to eat or drink and without even a candle. When bowls of water were sent in for them to freshen up at four in the morning, they drank the lot.

Although this was what we would now recognise as a vetted jury, thought to be thoroughly pro-King, eleven of its members had decided by dawn in favour of not guilty. The exception was a man called Michael Arnold. He was the royal brewer. Poor Mr Arnold. 'Whatever I do I am sure to be half-ruined,' he reflected. 'If I say not guilty I shall brew no more for the King; and if I say guilty I shall brew no more for anybody else.' He hung out for guilty. The others, led by a landowner called Thomas Austin, wanted to change his mind, since there were no majority verdicts in those days. Mr Arnold said he was too hungry to argue. Whereupon Mr Austin made the following threat: 'If you come to that, look at me,' he said. 'I am the largest and strongest of the twelve; and before I find such a petition as this to be a libel, here I will stay until I am no bigger than a tobacco pipe.'

The brewer, even more appalled at the prospect of communal starvation than of losing his royal client, gave in. The bishops were freed. The jury chalked up one of its celebrated triumphs over the State. And not for the last time, the wisdom of treating jurors like prisoners was shown to be questionable as well as cruel. In this case it had been both ineffectual *and* self-defeating so far as the Crown was concerned. Yet well into the nineteenth century verdicts were still being overturned if it was discovered that victuals had been smuggled into the jury room. It was not until 1870 that deliberating jurors were allowed a fire in the grate and food in their bellies – and even then (as now) only so long as it was 'procured at their own expense'.

For much of its history there was another disagreeable reason for wishing to escape a jury summons. This was the State's tendency to believe that (a) anyone committed for trial was by definition guilty and (b) the jury's task was not to remain impartial or reach its own opinions but to follow the judge's instructions to the letter, especially when invited to return a guilty verdict. Failure to act accordingly could and did lead to fines, imprisonment or being 'accounted infamous'. Under the Tudors, the Court of Star Chamber was notoriously swift to punish juries which returned verdicts contrary to the weight of evidence, i.e. in defiance of the Crown.

Naturally, most juries toed the line. But some did not. And it is to these stubborn men that the jury system owes much of the sanctity and sentiment attached to it today. There was the case of John Lilburne, the Leveller, in 1653. He was already heading for the history books thanks to a heresy case against him in 1637. He had been pilloried for refusing to answer questions on oath. He appealed to the House of Lords which agreed that it was 'contrary to the laws of nature and the kingdom for any man to be his own accuser' – thereby helping to establish the right to silence.

Sixteen years later Lilburne faced a death sentence at the Old Bailey for flouting an exile order decreed by Parliament. He appealed to the jury to ignore the judge and to regard themselves as 'equal judges of law and fact'. The jury did just that, acquitted him, and consequently found themselves in very hot water. They were summoned to account for their actions before Cromwell's Council of State. Five of them adopted the explanation offered by their foreman, Thomas Greene, that he 'did discharge his conscience'. Surprisingly, the jurors were not punished, perhaps because Lilburne was a popular figure, perhaps because the regime did not wish to appear as high-handed as the lately deposed monarchy. The long-term significance of the case, however, was that those references to conscience and to a jury's being equal judges of fact and law struck a chord which has never since been silenced.

Seventeen years later, in 1670, came an even greater victory for the English jury in its slow march towards independence. Law students learn that it is one of the key events in establishing the jury's right to follow its own conscience, even to the extent of disregarding the letter of the law and the directions of the judge.

This is always said to be the case that ignited 'the lamp which shows that freedom lives'. It is known as Bushell's Case and there is a plaque in the Old Bailey whose beautiful curly script commemorates 'the courage and endurance' of those involved. It concerned two Quakers, William Mead and William Penn (as in Pennsylvania). In 1670 they were charged with conducting a seditious assembly. They had been preaching in Gracechurch Street, despite laws aimed at suppressing Nonconformism. The jury refused to convict. The judge angrily locked them up for two nights 'without meat, drink, fire and tobacco' – and, heaping indignity upon discomfort, no chamber pot either.

Undaunted, they stuck to their not guilty verdict. William Penn shouted his encouragement to the jurors: 'You are Englishmen. Mind your privilege. Give not away your right.' 'Nor will we ever do it,' cried their foreman, Edward Bushell.

The Recorder of London was outraged: 'I am sorry, gentlemen, you have followed your own judgements and opinions, rather than the good and wholesome advice which was given you. God keep my life out of your hands, but for this the court fines you 40 marks a man; and imprisonment till paid.'

The entire jury was banged up in Newgate, just around the corner. Four of them, led by Bushell, refused to pay and spent months in prison. They appealed against their incarceration by a writ of *habeas corpus*. The Lord Chief Justice, Sir Robert Vaughan, decided they should be released, asserting 'the right of juries to give their verdict by their conscience' or, in the words of the Old Bailey plaque, 'according to their convictions', irrespective of the judge's directions. In *Freedom, the Individual and the Law* Geoffrey Robertson says ringingly: 'Bushell's Case is the foundation of the constitutional independence of the jury: it can do justice, whatever the law may be.'

In other words, juries can take the law into their own hands. It is this right that underpins the belief that the jury system is our shield against official high-handedness. As the present Lord Chief Justice, Lord Bingham, has put it, the jury is 'one of the great safety valves that prevents the

State from behaving in an oppressive way'. In the eighteenth and nineteenth centuries, it was this right that helped juries save many petty criminals from the gallows. It was invoked to nullify unpopular laws in colonial America, where the jury is even more highly venerated today than it is in this country: there is a group in the US called the Fully Informed Jury Association one of whose principal goals is to ensure jurors know of this right to disregard the law and follow their consciences.

More recently, a 1985 Old Bailey jury refused to convict a senior civil servant of breaching Section 2 of the Official Secrets Act, which he plainly had, despite unambiguous directions from the judge. Clive Ponting had passed documents to a Labour MP showing that Margaret Thatcher's government had misled Parliament about the circumstances of the sinking of an Argentine warship, the *General Belgrano*, during the Falklands War. The acquittal was widely celebrated, says Geoffrey Robertson, for upholding the traditions of 'the gang of twelve'.

Six years later, a jury acquitted Michael Randle and Patrick Pottle of organising the escape from prison of the MI6 traitor George Blake in 1966 – even though they had written a book confessing all. Presumably the jury shared the authors' indignation at the length of Blake's forty-two-year sentence, and disapproved of the quarter-of-a-century delay in prosecuting.

(In September 1999 the jury in the trial of the Earl of Hardwicke and a friend, who had been entrapped by the *News of the World* into arranging a cocaine deal, reluctantly reached a guilty verdict, but made their feelings known in a note to the judge: 'Had we been allowed to take the extreme provocation into account we would undoubtedly have reached a different verdict.' The judge quite properly took on board the jury's concerns and freed the two men, giving them suspended sentences.)

I don't suppose Constantinos Korkolis was doing the same sort of background reading as I was. But if he had, there it was in black and white: the jury was all-powerful. According to an Oxford University Penal Research Unit study in 1974, some 14 per cent of acquittals can be described as 'sympathy verdicts' in which, as Geoffrey Robertson puts it, 'the jury strives to find a reasonable doubt because it believes, with good cause, that the defendant has been the victim of oppressive police behaviour or has in any event suffered enough'.

NEW YEAR, NEW WITNESSES

6 January 1997. The jurors were happy to be back in court. So was Mr Korkolis. He resumed his new role as chief defence interrogator with as much brio as if he'd been off for a bracing Christmas skiing holiday, though he looked pastier than ever.

Detective Chief Inspector Laurie Vanner was in the witness box. He was the man in charge of the Scotland Yard operation which had put Korkolis in the dock. He was evidently a policeman of great experience and authority, a persuasive witness for the prosecution. Then came the cross-examination. This was the first witness Korkolis would have to himself from start to finish and the first of a great many police witnesses we were to hear from. Not many accused men get the chance to twist the long arm of the law themselves, or would want it. Korkolis made the most of it.

Everyone in court, from the judge down, was much too polite to show any overt sign of disdain for the man in the dock, relentlessly going over the same ground again and again. But it was plain from the exasperated raising of eyebrows beneath wigs what was going through their minds. The police witnesses picked this up quickly. From time to time they would turn beseechingly to the judge and say, 'I am confused, My Lord.' The subtext was plain: 'Must I really bother to decipher this impertinent gobbledegook?'

But the truth was that, in his tiresome way, Korkolis was managing to show up some definite weaknesses in his opponents' armour. These were not so much in the prosecution case as in the way the police had conducted the operation. Several detectives contradicted each other in minor details. Strange gaps revealed themselves in the time-table of events that led up to the arrests. The detectives had relied on some wild assumptions. Risks had been taken that sounded worryingly unprofessional to laymen's ears. How did these errors square with Scotland Yard's world-famous reputation, Korkolis wanted to know? Were they mistakes – or signs of an extraordinary conspiracy between themselves and the Fraghistas family, as he maintained? At one point Korkolis needled DCI Vanner into remarking loftily, 'I cannot micromanage an operation from a red centre.' Exactly the sort of shifty-sounding jargon to make a juror freeze – and incidentally arouse some anxiety about what might have become of good old-fashioned policing at the Yard.

We had now been at it for twenty-four days. On 8 January the judge announced that the trial would be going on at least until St Valentine's Day. Out of curiosity, I asked the other jurors whether, were the verdict required that very day, we would be likely to agree. No, we would not, it seemed. Several voices were raised indignantly. It was improper even to think about it yet. We must keep open minds. It was too soon to judge. We would have to go back through all the evidence before we could even begin to reach a decision. It would be a hotel job, for sure.

My liking for the Fraghistas family blossomed into a full-blown crush with the arrival of George's sister Marily. She was very pretty in a modest, unselfconscious way, answering the prosecution's questions quietly but with great firmness. It was Jeremy Benson, Miss Korner's junior, who was conducting the evidence-in-chief on this occasion. Every once in a while she allowed herself a smile which swept the court like a sunbeam – though she took care it never shone on the men in the dock. I suspect quite a few of us were smitten, including some of the lawyers.

Is there an equivalent of the Stockholm Syndrome in a long-running court case? Hostages are known to form attachments to their captors, partly out of self-preservation but chiefly out of the need to keep a hold on their humanity. In Court 9 one could feel something growing between jurors, barristers, witnesses and judge which if not exactly a bond was certainly a sense of being all in this thing together. It extended to Detective Sergeant Hawkins and his sidekick Detective Constable Ian Slade, who were in court nearly every day. It even embraced the defendants, who suffered from the boredom and the hold-ups just as the jury did and were guarded with only slightly more severity. Every morning they nodded to us in a friendly way, which didn't go unappreciated.

At any rate, one could sense a determination on the jury's behalf that this trial should come out well in the eyes of everyone in court, and most particularly the judge's.

Most of the time Judge Goldstein was superhumanly long-suffering with Korkolis. Just now and then he allowed himself an impulsive crack of the whip along the lines of, 'My well-known patience is being sorely tried, Mr Korkolis.' Once, glancing away from the prisoner and up into a corner of the courtroom ceiling, he let slip, 'That is an outrageous comment.' A little light sarcasm might be employed: 'Mr Korkolis, address the jury later about whatever dreadful significance you see in that.' How careful did he have to be? I wondered. The bear-traps in the path of a judge trying someone who had chosen to defend himself – particularly a foreign someone, struggling with the language – are obvious even to a layman. The Court of Appeal stood less than a mile away.

Unlike her oldest brother, Marily tried never to look at Korkolis while he was cross-examining. Her face was set grimly most of the time, staring at the jury on the other side of the courtroom, though she would break into a huge, incredulous grin at some of Korkolis's suggestions. She thought carefully before answering each question, but not always. 'If you knew George was in on the plot . . .' he began on one occasion, but got no further. Marily gave a snort like a cornered wildcat. 'I find that outrageous and insulting,' she spat. Even Korkolis was momentarily silenced.

WIGS AND CIGS

Once most of the principal prosecution witnesses were out of the way, things began to speed up. Even Korkolis's meandering interrogations were noticeably abbreviated. Because jurors' notebooks may not be removed from the courtroom (we used to wonder whether the cleaners read them overnight), I would write up my own notes from memory and scraps of paper when I got home in the evenings. For the middle two weeks of January they veer between action and *aperçu*:

George's chauffeur, Dennis Banks, gives evidence. Looks like an ambassador: tall, greying, respectable, dressed in double-breasted suit. The best-spoken witness so far. Pity he has nothing interesting to say.

Today's batch of prison officers have shaven heads and torturers' faces. They make Moussaoui the French-Algerian and Mereu the wrestler look like cherubs. It must be hellishly dull for them spending whole days in court with nothing to do but suppress yawns. The clanking of keys heralds their arrival with the prisoners at the side-door which leads directly into the dock. From there, I imagine, there are cobwebby staircases down to the cells. Roy has said he will give us a tour of them one day.

There are fourteen people in the dock most days, including the jailers. The interpreters lean in towards their clients so they look like pairs of lovers, mouth to ear and ear to mouth.

Eureka! Our lottery syndicate has won ten pounds. A good omen. If the trial goes on for long enough we are sure to end up rich. It was decided the winnings would be re-invested in another ten lines of numbers. Stuart announced that if we won the big one he would spend his prize money buying a box for life at Ibrox Park, the Rangers' stadium.

The defendants have spent sizeable sums of money setting up the hit: hiring cars, renting Hogan Mews, etc. The contemporary kidnap kit includes the following: mobile phones, intercoms, chargers, transformers, transceivers, tape recorders, adaptors, binoculars, camcorder, Polaroid camera, syringes, gun, holster, stungun, wig (£95 from Selfridge's), masks, latex gloves, sticky tape, handcuffs, earplugs, false passports and false rubber stamps for same. We have examined the bill for a voice distorter, purchased at a West End shop which openly sells such things. By my reckoning, your well-planned kidnap or fake kidnap these days can cost you close on a quarter of a million pounds in capital outlay.

There were twelve people wearing wigs in Court 9 until Gale and his junior left. During a break, the usher gives an impromptu lecture on the subject. He says the newer, whiter ones are made of nylon, the older, yellower ones of horse hair. Old wigs are chic. If a young barrister is wearing one, it's sign that he or she has been favoured with it by a retiring silk. Wigs are said to provide the lawyers and judges not merely with an aura of impersonal authority but also a degree of anonymity, which is useful for their own protection. It is true: a QC looks quite different when you run into him outside the Fleet Street branch of Boots, bareheaded and wearing a raincoat.

Watching Joanna Korner grinding cigarette butts under the heel of her black court shoe, I wonder whether there might not be another explanation for the wig-yellowing phenomenon. The Old Bailey will be the last public building in Britain where smoking is banned, even under New Labour. Barristers, policemen, court officials – everyone puffs away as furiously as actors in rehearsal or squaddies off parade. It is also the last redoubt of the roll-up, much favoured by the older ushers and security men. All that messing about with Rizlas helps to pass the time, I suppose.

Several police witnesses get into a muddle when addressing the judge. In your run-of-the-mill Crown Court the correct form is Your Honour. But at the Old Bailey it is My Lord. Ahem. Also, judges dress like barristers when they are sitting in the Bailey and must dispense with their sashes. The top judge here is the Recorder of London, who has a flat in the Old Bailey itself. Novice ushers are schooled not to enter it by mistake, in case they should find Mrs Recorder in her curlers.

Miss Wendy Nunn, George's secretary, goes into the box. It was she who took the first call from George after the kidnap. Mr K insists on calling her Mrs Wendy the whole time, committing a double solecism. Miss

Nunn is forthright and helpful but her voice has the intonation of someone who spends much of her day saying 'How can I help you?' and 'Would you bear with me?', typical of a million London Wendys. We miss Marily's dazzling smile.

In the Gents' I ask the interpreter who looks like General Franco why Mr Fraghistas has an 's' on the end of his surname in some of the court documents and Mrs Fraghista (sic) does not. She is in the genitive, he says. Even though she is now a widow, she was once 'of' Mr Fraghistas Sr, her husband. Greek feminists have a sitting target there.

Petros Poulmentis takes the stand. He is George's partner at World Carrier (London) Ltd. They set up the business together. He is a big, good-looking, crinkly-haired man. He looks like an Englishman's idea of a Greek playboy: he has enormous white shirt-cuffs of the kind that pre-war dandies used to 'shoot' but Mr Poulmentis merely fiddles with. [In fact, I learnt later, he is a family man, who moved to England when he was only 19 and is married to an Englishwoman.] *He speaks calmly and confidently and grins a good deal. He swigs mineral water from a bottle out of the left-hand corner of his mouth with the regularity of a chain-smoker trying to kick the habit. He says he disapproves strongly of George's gambling. Mrs Fraghistas and Marily had both spoken warmly about Petros. 'He is like a brother to us,' said Marily. According to Korkolis, the reason he called himself 'Petros' during the kidnap was so that anyone listening to his telephone conversations would assume it was Poulmentis talking.*

The jury spent some time this morning calculating what all this is costing the tax-payer. One estimate was

£400 an hour. No, no: £25 a minute, more like it. That still sounds to me like an undershoot. Sarah, the clerk of the court, who sits at a desk beneath the judge's dais, spends much of her time totting up lawyers' fees: a sort of human taximeter. She is a big cheery young woman with a lovely face who looks like Dawn French and wears a red Aids ribbon under her gown. Maybe after the trial she'll help me put a price tag on it. Another of Sarah's jobs is to administer unpunctual jurors with wiggings – an appropriate term, since Old Bailey clerks do wear wigs. A clerk's reprimand is a good deal more serious than an usher's.

There is now a certain house-pride about other cases going on in the Bailey. Court 1 is occupied by the trial of a former Ukrainian prison guard. He is accused of war crimes. Stuart and I agree such retrospective legislation is a mistake, more than half a century later. He'll probably get off. [He did.] We note days when there are armed police and extra cameramen outside the front entrance. That usually means IRA, we inform nervous new jurors.

Great excitement this afternoon: Mike Gatting, the former England cricket captain, has been seen in the jury restaurant. Bob went up and got his autograph. Apparently Gatting had been called up three times before and managed to wangle deferrals – all right for some. On this occasion, however, not being wanted on voyage for the New Zealand test series, he had to give in. I telephoned The Times *and a nice little story duly appeared in the diary column, to Bob's wonder and astonishment. Even Roy the usher was impressed. The story prompted him to disclose that Edwina Currie had also been proscribed recently and would have been one of our own jury intake – had she not been an MP and therefore entitled to slip the net. Boo.*

The Juryman's Tale

A long morning with the jury out. We discussed the state of civilisation. Stuart had this to say: 'When I came down from Scotland, if I had an argument with someone I'd put him on the cobbles. Not any more. Now you never see anyone getting a straightener. You don't want to argue with young blokes for very long. They all carry knives. If a party candidate calls canvassing, I ask him if he's in favour of hanging. If not I tell him to bugger off.' Perhaps things aren't looking so bleak for the Tories after all.

We have just had two and a half days off because of an ailing juror, Pat. I had offered her some Anadin and the usher spotted me. Not allowed, he said firmly. In keeping with the general nannying, you are not permitted to take medicines from anyone else in court, only those prescribed by your own doctor. Otherwise it's a visit to the Old Bailey matron. Pat duly went off to see her, but with some trepidation. This was because I had slipped her two Anadins anyway when the usher left the room and she had taken them surreptitiously. Now she was about to be given more pills by matron. Should she risk suspicion by refusing them – or an overdose by taking them?

I was wondering whether we were about to start asserting that oldest of workplace rights, the right to throw a sickie once a month. Now Kate has come up with a variation on the theme: she has a family funeral to attend. That means another day off for everyone in court.

Korkolis tried bullying the bench this morning. His outburst began, 'Don't ask me to proof . . .' but he didn't get much further. His Lordship intervened sternly, but rather spoilt the effect by producing a stupendous mixed metaphor: 'If you want to put your horns against me, Mr Korkolis, you will find you're on a losing wicket.'

Mr K's upbringing might have helped him cope with the Minotaur image, but he must have been stumped by the cricketing allusion.

Kate: 'I'm bored. I'm dying of boredom. I couldn't bear another day off' (she having just requested one).

The judge, on being invited to re-estimate the trial's running-time: 'If I could predict that I would go out and buy the winning lottery ticket.'

Joanna Korner on her junior, Jeremy Benson, who had made a time-saving suggestion: 'Mr Benson is full of good ideas on a Friday afternoon.'
Judge: 'The best idea would be to stop now.'

POLICE MATTERS

I lost count of the number of police witnesses. There must have been at least thirty of them, from DCI Vanner to the humble beat bobbies who were hauled off the street to make up numbers for the raid on Hogan Mews.

There is no such thing as a typical policeman. They came in all shapes, sizes and colours, from PC Sylvester Hack from Paddington Green, a tiny black man, to more traditional bruisers who looked like they had spent their adult years in a fairground boxing booth. After they had taken the oath they would each launch straight into a soldierly recital of name, rank and station. The only thing they had in common was an Estuary accent, a painful inability to pronounce the names of suspects and victims correctly, and a sort of wooden self-confidence, which I imagine was the product of countless appearances in the witness box.

There was also a hint of truculence. No doubt this came from long experience of having their evidence challenged and disbelieved. Every notorious mis-trial, from the Guildford Four to the Carl Bridgewater case, blows a huge hole in the credibility of the police force. It did not require Korkolis to remind us of such instances (though he did): there cannot be a jury in the land whose judgement is unaffected by them.

Watching so many policemen and women go through their paces I noticed a couple of other characteristics which I think jurors must find irritating. One was their obsequiousness towards the judge, tagging 'My Lord' on to the end of every answer, when it was *us* they should have been addressing. The other was their reliance on notebooks and reports, some of them written up hours after the events concerned and often in concert with one or more colleagues. Fair enough, of course. But it had the odd effect of making it look as though they were cheating, bringing their cribs in with them, whereas ordinary mortals giving evidence had only their memories to rely on.

The upshot was that in some cases I found myself believing the police witnesses despite themselves. There was something not quite wholesome about a few of the detectives. They looked as though they spent too much of their days cooped up in cars smoking and eating Pot Noodles – which I suppose they do, poor things. The puffy eyes suggested long hours of *anthropos das nichtas* living and late-night report-concocting. Their worldliness was uneasy-making, though also quite glamorous. The blonde whom you'd have taken for the editor of a Sunday tabloid or possibly someone even less salubrious if you'd met her in the street came across as a tough and unflappable detective. She stood her ground admirably against Korkolis, refusing to join in his favourite hypothesising games.

One worried for these people, all the same. They must live their lives in constant fear of putting a foot wrong. They are obliged to take notes of everything they see or do: number-plates, street names, descriptions of suspects, stopping for a pizza, slipping into McDonald's to take a leak. Each entry is timed to the minute. The cautious copper probably writes down how many Weetabix he has for breakfast in the police canteen. Think what it would be like in one's own life, knowing that every few weeks one was liable to be minutely cross-examined by a trained interrogator about one's work six months earlier – and, to make matters worse, that this *viva voce* would take place in front of twelve sceptical strangers and a headline-hungry press corps.

Detective Sergeant Martin Hawkins ran the police operation in the field, reporting back to DCI Vanner at the Yard or Mrs Fraghistas's flat. He looked a little like a Photofit of John Cleese, complete with moustache. At first he did not cut an especially impressive figure. He had sad eyes and a mild, somewhat hesitant manner which belied his long experience on Scotland Yard murder squads and in the Organised Crime Group. But as he explained the sequence of events that led up to the arrests of the kidnappers and the release of George Fraghistas, there was something about his evidence that gave it an extra believability.

He himself had had to take some very difficult decisions very quickly on 2 April 1996. A man's life was in mortal danger. The police had no idea how many kidnappers they were dealing with, whether they were armed or what they would do to their hostage *in extremis*. DS Hawkins was also responsible for the welfare of the men and women under his command. Some of them were young and inexperienced – he did not even know their names. Yet he was modest about his own role and disarmingly frank about the risks he took and the mistakes he made. Despite that, one was left in little doubt that it had been a brilliant piece of detective work.

This did not stop Korkolis scavenging relentlessly for evidence of a police conspiracy. Was Mr Hawkins really telling the court that he had led the assault on Hogan Mews without thoroughly reconnoitring the premises, without knowing who was inside, without arming his men and without even a pair of handcuffs between them? Yes, said Hawkins candidly. He knew it was dangerous but in his judgement there was no time to do anything else. They were lucky. Apart from George it turned out there was only Mereu inside, although – Hawkins nodded ruefully in the direction of the wrestler in the dock – 'he's a big lad.'

MOBILE SECRETS

Sifting what was relevant from what was not was becoming impossibly hard. Hours and hours had been spent dissecting the competence of the police and questioning their honesty. Yet so far the defence had produced not a particle of evidence suggesting there had been a conspiracy. We jurors had to decide whether to clog our minds with all this stuff in anticipation that the evidence would eventually be provided and everything would slot into place – or simply switch off, leaving room in our overloaded memories for more telling material yet to come.

Whenever Korkolis was on his feet, he appeared to be leading us through a maze from which there was no discernible exit – although he always gave the impression he knew exactly where he was going himself. The court was not always helpful either, quite often talking to itself above our heads and plunging us into further mystification. 'Does Mr Korkolis realise that if he reads from this statement it may be made an exhibit?' interposed the judge at some point. What was so dangerous about that? We already had dozens of exhibits. And anyway, whom was he asking? Certainly not us. By three o'clock most afternoons the jurors were sighing like whales coming up for air.

Fortunately, there were comic interludes. Do judges have

special training which includes making laboured jokes? If so, Judge Goldstein must have graduated with bonus marks for self-mockery, since he would alert us to what was coming with an 'I know this sounds like a typical judge's remark . . .' before leading into his punchline: 'But what is a pair of intercoms?' Here is another good one, provoked by a mention of pre-programmed numbers on a mobile telephone: 'I must be the only person in England who doesn't have a mobile phone. Do you mean that if you press the number you get Auntie Ada?'

Not to be outdone, Miss Korner, who may have ambitions to be a judge herself one day, came up with her own rib-tickler: 'I've no idea,' she said in her best Grenfell-ese, 'what a transceiver *is*.' She was rewarded with murmurs of 'Nor do I' from around the court, in which I felt the jury should have joined out of politeness, though Eddie could probably have delivered a five-minute lecture on transceivers and their uses without a note.

The judge got an even better response when he was provoked by a piece of paper from which Korkolis had begun to read: 'This is all very cosy. Mr Korkolis has copies of this document. So does the witness. But neither I nor the jury know what on earth is going on.' By courtroom standards, the chorus of 'Nor do I' which greeted this sally was full-throated. This time the jury joined in.

On 6 February there was a mass diaspora: we were to move from Court 9 to Court 5. It was on a different floor. The lifts were clogged with junior barristers and solicitors manhandling luggage trolleys piled with boxes and binders. A roomful of exhibits had to be moved. The consequence of all this was – nothing. Court 5 was precisely the same as Court 9 in every characterless detail. Even our notebooks and water glasses looked as though they had never budged.

The only novelty was that for a day we had a different jury room. It was not just any old jury room but the one belonging to Court 1, the most famous courtroom in the building. It was a panelled room with a vaulted ceiling, a twelve-foot oak table and a splendid fireplace. There were marks on the wall where the gas-lamps had been. The elderly basin in the men's washroom was called The Bedford. It was easy to imagine moustachioed Edwardian tradesmen with their collar-studs showing peering gravely at the notice above the fireplace:

To members of the Jury: HM's judges remind you of the solemn obligation upon you not to reveal in any circumstances, to any person, either during the trial or after it is over, anything relating to it which has occurred in this room while you have been considering your verdict.

It was sobering to think that from this same room, sitting at this very table, juries just like ours sent fellow-citizens to the gallows.

Impressed by our surroundings, Stuart suggested that we might as well do something to live up to them and elect a foreman. This is not normally done until the jury is sent out to consider its verdict. But there is nothing to prevent its happening sooner and quite a lot to recommend it, especially in a long trial where the jury has to take a number of small decisions along the way. So we each put a name on a bit of paper and conducted a secret ballot. I got the job, with Pat and Bob runners-up.

Back in court, an expert witness gave us a lesson in digital telephone technology. This was a delicate subject, to be approached by counsel on tiptoe. By now the jury had worked out for itself that by some means or another the police had been able to use the kidnappers' ceaseless flow of mobile phone calls to get an idea of their movements. We also knew, which the judge and his Auntie Ada almost certainly did not, that it is impossible to tap digital phones, unlike their analogue predecessors. So they must have had some sort of tracking technique. However, the details were a secret – such an important secret that the whole matter was subject to Public Interest Immunity, as made famous in the arms-to-Iraq affair. (This did not stop the *Sunday Telegraph* of 2 April 1997 running a report on the subject headlined 'Mobile phones "tag" owners'.)

Miss Korner and the expert witness had to skirt carefully around the topic. This did not make for ease of understanding. I have a note which records that at some point the judge said engagingly, 'I have absolutely no idea, as always, what is going on.' He was probably referring to this evidence on advanced telephonics, made all the more obscure by the PII order he had himself approved.

Even so, we learnt enough to form a sketchy notion of what it was all about. Essentially, digital phone calls are relayed by a network of cell-sites spread across the whole country. Each cell-site covers an area about half-a-mile square, centred around a receiver-transmitter. In urban areas this will probably be located on top of a tall building such as the London Metropole Hotel on the Edgware Road or the YWCA in Earl's Court Road. So although the operating companies cannot pinpoint exactly where a call is coming from, their printouts do give a general idea of the area. It is not one hundred per cent accurate, because if a cell-site is overloaded it cunningly re-routes the call via one that is less busy. Nonetheless, a motorist making calls as he travelled across London could be tracked, at least to the extent of the direction he was taking.

This was fascinating stuff, as well as important evidence. One could sense the police unease that even the little that was being disclosed was now in the public domain. But I don't suppose there is a serious villain in the land who doesn't know all this already, and a good deal more. (Almost as interesting, though utterly irrelevant, was the information that the current rate of mobile telephone thefts was about fifteen thousand every month. Perhaps Judge Goldstein felt confirmed in the wisdom of not owning one.)

As St Valentine's Day approached – the date on which the judge once optimistically estimated we would retire – there was still no end in view. The prosecution case was not over yet. Korkolis, who had not once been hurried during his cross-examination of the Crown's witnesses, claimed he was being restricted by the court. Perhaps he hoped to benefit from public hostility to PIIs. The judge cracked down: 'I have given you so much latitude in this trial . . . I don't think any other judge in the land would have given you as much. I will give you ten minutes to question this witness.' The court silently applauded.

Now Korkolis wanted to question George Fraghistas himself, having had no chance when Mr Gale was still his counsel. The judge rolled his eyes: 'I am not having that gentleman back.'

Korkolis: 'How am I going to deal with this?'

Judge: 'I've no idea, Mr Korkolis.'

THE CROWN CONCLUDES

From my home-written notes . . .

Day 43. St Valentine's Eve. We sang happy birthday to one of the jurors in the green marble lobby outside Court 1. It was also Jennifer's birthday in Friends, *someone reminded us. One girl asked another, in the hearing of a disapproving statue of Elizabeth Fry, the Quaker prison reformer, 'Did you watch* Friends *last night or were you having sex?' She didn't watch* Friends. *Thinks: What about a docu-soap called* Jurors?

A nice young doctor was in the witness box. It was he who attended to George after his release. He explained that 'police surgeon' is an old-fashioned term. Nowadays the correct description is 'forensic medical examiner'. Patrick Curran asked him to define a bruise. And what was the definition of a scab? The forensic medical examiner got rattled. It was embarrassing to see his confidence and carefulness shaken. Could George's wounds have been false injuries, maybe self-inflicted? 'The pretence is consistent with the reality,' replied the doctor through clenched teeth.

Joanna Korner (aside): 'Everything in this case is disintegrating.'

Nicos Fraghistas was recalled all the way from Athens at Korkolis's request. He was invited to confess that the two of them, Nicos and Korkolis, were acquainted before the kidnap. 'The only Korkolis I know is a pop singer in Greece,' sighed Nicos.

Ah, said Korkolis, but in an allegedly inaudible bit of one of the taped ransom conversations, Nicos could be heard saying the name 'Korkolis'. He wanted the jury to listen to it. So we all donned headphones, looking like competitors in a 1950s radio panel game. What we heard was 'crackle mumble mumble phone calls mumble mumble crackle'. Not 'Korkolis' but 'phone calls', we told the court, seizing a unique opportunity to speak.

So Mr Fraghistas had been brought all the way from Athens for the sake of this one question about this one tape? The judge was not pleased. Nor would the British tax-payer have been.

Day 44. The super-alert jury spotted an inconsistency. One of the police tapes recording the ransom calls at Mrs Fraghistas's flat came out mysteriously blank. The *batteries were flat: they had not been checked, said the police. But the jury – Bob, in fact – had heard mention of a back-up tape recorder. Perhaps the missing conversations were on that? We sent a note to the judge, feeling very on-the-ball.*

Nudged into action by the jury Korkolis, ever the opportunist, asked for the detective sergeant who had been doing the tape recordings to be brought back into the box. Poor DS Don King. 'This witness has come back four times,' remarked the judge, 'just because he had the misfortune to be in charge of putting tapes in the machine.' Mr King explained what had happened regarding the tapes and why the back-up recorder was useless if the main machine was out of order. It was not reassuring. There had been a cock-up. On the best interpretation, the police looked startlingly improvisational.

Day 45. Today the judge said we were in 'the death-throes of the prosecution case'. Hooray.

Day 46. There should have been fireworks and dancing in the streets. Joanna Korner got to her feet and said, 'My Lord, I can hardly believe what I am going to say, but on the forty-sixth day, that concludes the case for the prosecution.'

SELF-EXAMINATION

At 12.48 p.m. on 19 February Korkolis stepped down from the dock and walked over to the witness box, accompanied by a cortège of two prison officers and his interpreter. The court watched him take the oath with some trepidation. Under normal circumstances, a defendant choosing to go into the witness box would be questioned by his own barrister, giving his evidence-in-chief, before submitting to cross-examination by the other defendants' lawyers and the Crown. Korkolis was to be both advocate and witness: a riderless horse liable to career in any direction, for limitless distances.

He began with a surprise: a graceful address to the jury, craving our patience and apologising for ill-treating the English language. By now we were familiar with the line he wanted to take. George Fraghistas, according to Korkolis, had been in financial difficulties. He concocted the fake kidnap in order to extort money from his family without revealing that it was to cover gambling debts. Once the ransom calls started, the family realised they were being duped but decided to play along so as to avoid a scandal. And the police, for reasons only hinted at so far, chose to play along too, pretending that it was a genuine kidnap. They would not bring charges because George would refuse to testify against his four 'kidnappers'. All of this he would prove, said Korkolis.

'I draw the conclusion that the family and the police knew from the evidence. For me this is the truth.'

Unlikely? Highly. Impossible? Well, no, not beyond reasonable doubt ... Apart from anything else, the very implausibility of his account suggested that only a fool or a madman would have fabricated it. It also had the virtue of originality. The only other case anyone could think of where kidnappers and their victim had made common cause was the Patty Hearst affair back in 1974 – and even then, it was only after the heiress had allegedly been raped and brainwashed that she sided with her captors, the Symbionese Liberation Army.

Best of all, this conspiracy theory allowed the defence to go along with most of the Crown's evidence – nearly all of it, in fact, except for George's and some of the police officers'. They could agree that the ransom calls, the arrests, the rescue all took place exactly as described. The only question was, were these events what they seemed? Or were they a charade, a charade in which first the family, and then the key police officers who were helping them, chose to take part?

Had I been asked that question at that moment, I would not have hesitated for a quarter of a second. I personally had no reason for doubting the main thrust of the prosecution case, nor for disbelieving the police. There were strong reasons for thinking Korkolis a liar. What happened over the next few weeks was that this relatively clear view became thoroughly obscured. The fog from Dickens's *Bleak House* rolled over us, stirred into maddening swirls by Korkolis, thickened with boredom and endlessly shaping itself into distracting shadows. The 'truth', assuming that was what I had been looking at, still gleamed fitfully through the murk. But it was now in competition with any number of flickering will-o'-the-wisps. The defence, after all, had no need to cast light on its own version of events, merely doubt on the prosecution's.

Korkolis took a risk. He became a character witness for himself. He wanted the jury to see photographs taken in better days. They showed him in various poses: with his dear old mother in Athens, with friends around a swimming pool, showing off a sports car, living the good life in Rio de Janeiro. They were indifferent snaps, which made him look exactly like a tawdry small-time crook. He must have thought otherwise. 'I was travelling around the world making business,' he said grandly. He was vague about what his business had been: playing the stock market, dealing in precious stones, foreign currency, insurance, real estate. He wished us to see a successful, industrious man of the world brought low by ill fortune. All his life, he said, he had been the victim of betrayals. Friends and partners had let him down ('When I trust people I trust them fully'). They had landed him in various scrapes, for example an unfair jail sentence in Greece which he refused to serve. Instead he fled the country, preferring exile to wrongful imprisonment. He escaped using a false passport. In fact he had several false passports, he admitted, although they were not really false since they had been issued by a genuine official whom he knew. This was a state of affairs that demanded our sympathy, he suggested. 'It was very inconvenient living with these different passports.' He also had three UK driving licences.

My brain was swimming. Did Korkolis imagine he was putting himself across as a dashing international wheeler-dealer in telling us all this, a lovable rascal? Or was he hoping to gain points for candour?

Perhaps a bit of both. 'I have my own morality,' he assured the court. It was this morality of his that had allowed him to go along with George Fraghistas's plan to terrorise his family into handing over several million dollars. George and he were not exactly friends, he explained, but as young men they used to frequent the same cafés in the Kolonakis quarter of Athens. They had both done their military service in the navy. Many years later they met at the Casanova Club in London. Then, Korkolis said, they had seen each other by chance in the Edgware Road one day, when their cars were stopped at traffic lights. They had driven to a nearby square and got out to talk. Korkolis had £100,000 worth of gambling debts at the time. George asked him if he would like to earn some easy money. The seeds of the fake kidnap plan were sown.

Korkolis told the court: 'What is true about Mediterranean people is we are more open. We find it more easy to discuss things which other people might find strange. We don't have exactly the same barrier to going to the limit of the law.' Ah, so this was what he called his own morality. 'Mr Fraghistas knew I was a man with passports, but not connected with him . . . And I was of a nice family.' In other words, he implied, an ideal co-conspirator.

The risk Korkolis was running in saying all this was that by parading his character before the court he was inviting the prosecution to do a hatchet job in return – something that would have been ruled out had he not made the first move. The outcome was long absences for the jury during which, I have since learned, Miss Korner's team sought, by every means possible in the time available, to bring Korkolis's true criminal record to the jury's attention. That proved impossible because, under English law, documentary records of prison sentences in other countries are not allowed as evidence unless supported by appropriate witnesses. Without them, Korkolis could simply deny that he was the Korkolis mentioned in the records. A Greek policeman was flown over, I gathered, courtesy of the UK tax-payer, and toyed with his worry-beads for a while outside the courtroom. But whatever it was he would have said, it seems it was not enough to pass muster with the judge. Home he went to Athens. And we were left completely in the dark about Korkolis's frauds, perjuries and extensive prison career.

How different things might have been had we not remained in ignorance. But then, how different almost *everything* would be if juries were routinely told about a defendant's past. The acquittal rate would slump overnight – and no doubt a few innocent people would go to jail as a consequence.

LIE DETECTION

It is a fundamental aspect of our law that a defendant must be judged only on the evidence relating to the charges before him, not his 'previous'. In contrast to what happens under the French inquisitorial system, in this country the accused must be assumed not to have form. Even in a re-trial, jurors are supposed to be ignorant of what has gone before. As Ronald Thwaites QC wrote in a letter to the *Telegraph* in February 1997, 'The fact that the defendant has been in trouble before is not evidence of his guilt in a later case.'

While anyone can understand the supremely fair-minded principle behind this practice, I have yet to meet a single former juror who does not feel mildly outraged that such significant information is withheld from juries until after the verdict. After all, witnesses frequently have their pasts raked over in order to discredit them, notoriously so in the case of rape victims. Only the defendant is allowed to obliterate history in this fashion and start his life story from Year Zero.

The consequence is that juries are required to judge the honesty of defendants without the aid of a vital bit of knowledge, an everyday tool we all use in weighing someone up: what is this person really like, what is his or her history? What was the character of the defendant *before* he or she allegedly committed this crime? Outside a courtroom, this would be considered a hazardous way to proceed. No one would take on a baby-minder or give a plasterer the house keys so casually. An honest appearance is not enough. One requires references. In the case of Korkolis, we had only those references he chose to give us, and no means of knowing if they were true.

How *does* a jury decide who is telling the truth and who is not? The courts give no guidance at all. We are supposed to draw on our own experiences of life. Maybe subconsciously every citizen builds up a kind of mental dentist's tray equipped with lie-detecting probes to test the truth of what emerges from other people's mouths. I doubt it. More likely it is a jumbled shoe-box of personal prejudices and half-remembered TV clips from *Poirot* or *Inspector Morse*. Liars sweat and twitch and never look you in the eye; truth-tellers are relaxed and don't contradict themselves: that is the conventional wisdom.

But a jury cannot always get a decent look at whoever is giving evidence: in Court 3 at the Old Bailey, for example, the witness box is alongside the jury, not facing it. Even where the jury is across the courtroom from the witness, you would need a telescope to spot that telltale drop of perspiration or flickering eyelid. Research and experience suggest that there are no reliable formulae to help a juror anyway. Professor Glanville Williams remarked in his 1955 Hamlyn Lecture, *The Proof of Guilt* (Stevens & Sons, 1955), that 'some liars are bold and some honest witnesses are hesitating and nervous. All who have experience of the criminal courts can testify to this, though the jury who have to try the case may unfortunately be quite unaware of it'.

In his excellent book *The Jury: Disorder in the Court* (Doubleday, 1995) the *Wall Street Journal*'s then legal editor, Stephen Adler, upturned the conventional wisdom regarding fibbers:

> Studies show that compared with truth-tellers, liars typically make fewer hand gestures, move their heads less, speak more slowly, and sit more rigidly, but that they betray their anxiety by shifting their feet or tapping their fingers. In addition, liars tend to relax their facial muscles and affect pleasant expressions, as if aware that observers will be watching their faces for signs of deceit.

In one experiment cited by Adler involving seven hundred and fifteen people, 'a truthful speaker was judged to be lying by 74.3 per cent of the subjects, and a lying witness was judged truthful by 73.7 per cent'. In other words, unless you were a trained observer, the witness were Pinocchio or the witness box had glass sides (to allow an uncensored view of foot-shifting and finger-tapping), a skilled liar would have the advantage over an honest bumbler every time.

The very day our jury was sent out to deliberate, a television programme ran a nationwide experiment called Megalab aimed at deducing whether jurors were influenced by the appearance of defendants. The millions-strong audience was given some skimpy evidence of a crime, then invited to consider which of two men was guilty: the agreeable-looking blond bloke with the wide-set eyes or the Neanderthal brute at his side. Had the two men had sacks over their heads, it would have been impossible to decide, so flimsy was the case. As it was the result was stunningly unsurprising: 40 per cent of those who phoned in their verdict found Mr Nasty guilty while only 29 per cent (Quasimodos to a man and woman, probably) gave the thumbs-down to Angelface.

I suppose the result should have been alarming, confirming the superficiality of people's perceptions. On the other hand, which of us doesn't privately trust our instincts about a person's looks? Our ancestors have passed down genes programmed to be suspicious of, say, close-set eyes, thin lips and angry expressions, in much the same way that rabbits know they had best avoid anything on four legs which pants, barks and slavers. Doesn't experience prove this to be common sense more often than not?

There is another difficulty to which there is really no solution, and that is the ease with which the memory can deceive itself. Any married person is familiar with the one story, two versions phenomenon, otherwise known as the 'No, darling, it was Tuesday' syndrome. A witness may be as honest as young George Washington yet still misremember an incident. Each individual's memory functions differently. Alistair Cooke recently told listeners to his *Letter from America* on Radio 4 the story of a Harvard law professor who regularly gave a lecture called 'What Is Evidence?'

At a certain point it was always interrupted by a woman bursting into the lecture theatre, threatening him with a gun, and rushing out again. He would then ask the students to recount what had happened. They could seldom agree, even on the sex of the assailant. My wife has a flawless recall of dates, names and quotations, but forgets where she has left her glasses a dozen times a day. I do places, faces and smells (and glasses, of course). Only as a team would we make a reliable witness.

It is also obvious that any account of an event can change with the telling. For example, a police interview might frighten you into an unintended falsehood, which you then persuade yourself was true rather than appear to vacillate. Or an inaccurate press report might seem more authoritative than one's own recollections, and so colour them significantly. In the United States, lawyers are permitted to rehearse their witnesses, a procedure which must make their testimony wide open to editing.

Stress can drastically distort the way you remember an event. There have been innumerable tests involving fake car accidents where eye-witnesses come up with astoundingly different versions of what happened. The terror induced by a weapon can be still more disorientating. During our own trial, a real-life drama occurred not far away at the Law Courts in the Strand, when an aggrieved woman burst into a courtroom and threatened the three judges on the bench with a gun. According to the Old Bailey gossip, hardly anyone present – mostly experienced lawyers – was able to give the police an accurate description of the woman after she had fled from the court. Their faculties had presumably been paralysed by adrenalin, their vision hypnotised by looking down a pistol barrel. It was a real-life version of the Harvard professor's little demonstration.

Jurors are instructed in none of these nuances of perception. I doubt if it would be very helpful if they were. The juryman's eagerness to play detective is already a bit of a liability. The chance to take on the twin role of behavioural psychologist would be irresistible. Anyway, even lie detector tests are fallible, as the Michael Douglas character explains in *Basic Instinct*. Best to make do with such knowledge and experience as we have – in other words, that old imperfect stand-by, common sense.

At least in our own case we had the benefit of many witnesses and many days' exposure to them. We could learn on the job. The trouble was that Korkolis's manner was so erratic, it was hard to judge what he was saying by normal criteria. In our desire to be fair, even common sense was willingly suspended. In a native English speaker, his garrulousness would have made us suspect he was muddling us on purpose. As it was, my fellow-jurors showed great charity and sophistication. Without any sort of discussion, I had the impression I was not alone in my view that much of Korkolis's outlandishness should be put down to linguistic handicaps rather than deliberate obfuscation.

This meant exercising great patience. Here is how Korkolis, in a passage admittedly rather more strangulated than usual, described an alleged meeting between himself and George Fraghistas to discuss the blackmail plot. My note, as near verbatim as I could manage, reads: 'So the losses going on till now, OK? I told him. When in this now also. I accepted. I told him. No I go later. I told him. No, he told me. He organise he had a debt. He elaborated. Then if now we wouldn't do it as kidnapping as connected with debt.'

Amazingly, we sat through long stretches of this sort of stuff without going insane. By sheer determination on his (and our) part, Korkolis usually made his meaning clear. At one point he addressed His Lordship: 'My problem is how I am to deal with all this without confusing the jury.' The judge responded, 'You are doing exceptionally well, if I may say so.' And so were we.

But His Lordship also pointed out something I had already noticed and maybe others had. 'Mr Korkolis,' he said, 'you rush in direct proportion to the importance of what you are talking about.'

It was true. Every time we seemed to be approaching a particularly crucial part of the evidence, the stream of Korkolis's fluency would become the Rogue River in spate. Was this just over-excitement – or a ploy to whisk us through dangerous stretches of water without striking a rock? Korkolis retorted with a good joke. He was so prone to gabble, he confessed, that 'even I don't understand what I am saying'.

Judge Goldstein picked him up on something else: 'Mr Korkolis, you have said the same thing over and over again. There is an English expression: "Methinks he doth protest too much." It is from Shakespeare. It means if you go on saying the same thing over and over again the jury might wonder why.'

HELLO, HUMPHREY BAIZE

The scene each morning in Court 5 resembled *Groundhog Day*. Only the prison officers and the jurors' clothes changed. Everyone and everything else was identical, often including the words tumbling from Korkolis's mouth and being impassively recorded by the court stenographer. Again and again he returned to the same themes and we to the same thumb-marked pages of our taped transcripts. There was the striking brusqueness of Nicos towards his brother during the ransom calls; the failure of the police to arm themselves before storming Hogan Mews; a significant inconsistency in George's evidence about what happened on the afternoon of the arrests. These matters were insistently returned to and re-examined.

But there was method in Korkolis's maddeningness. He was like a mountaineer climbing a difficult rockface. Wherever his sharp eyes found a fissure, he hammered in his pitons with a storm of blows. He was creating a route, however precarious, by which he could haul the jury's credulousness up behind him. Any handhold would do. Why would they have hidden George in a cupboard that had no lock if it was a real kidnap? Why use sex-shop handcuffs on him which could be undone by twisting a tiny lever and didn't need a key? Why, after he and Zografos had been arrested and the police had found a pair of mobile telephones in their car, hadn't the police closed down the line to Hogan Mews? Wasn't this so that George could hear what was going on and be alerted that the police were on their way?

All this showed the kidnap was fake, Korkolis insisted. What is more, it was a benign sort of conspiracy: 'I have my own morality and my own values. I cannot take advantage of a weak person. I cannot take money from people that they need money. I would never going to threet anybody.' Besides, the Fraghistas family had had dealings with the Greek Colonels and with the Soviet Union: so it was dirty money anyway.

This might have been a good moment for a lofty reference to Occam's Razor by the judge. To a detached eye, the web of assumptions and innuendos being woven by Korkolis would have looked increasingly absurd and flimsy. For us, who were entangled in it, scepticism came less easily. '*Honi Soit Qui Mal Y Pense*' said the motto above the judge's head.

So the benefit-of-the-doubt gauge continued to waver. The business of the handcuffs had definitely moved it a notch in Korkolis's favour. Why *wouldn't* real kidnappers use real handcuffs? Once you had been shown the lever, it looked easy to undo them. The judge had even suggested rather sportingly that we should take them into the jury room and toy around with them ourselves. Miss Korner had objected:

they might still have traces of forensic chemicals, which could harm us. Humph. The detective tendency among us was keenly disappointed.

(Unknown to the jury, the lawyers had been just as intrigued. During a break, one of the defence barristers tried the handcuffs on, undaunted by chemical hazards. He had then been unable to get them off, despite knowing about the lever. His colleagues tried to assist. A farcical scene ensued, in which the usher was sent for help, presumably the Old Bailey bolt-cutters. Eventually DS Hawkins came to the rescue and released the QC from his shackles. Now, that would have been a helpful piece of evidence for the Crown, had we been told about it. But of course we never were.)

It was now nearly the end of February, Day 48 of the trial, and a minor civil war had broken out in the jury. Apart from the Christmas break the court had already been adjourned for several days because of illness. There had been a day lost for Kate's family funeral. Then my own aunt died. ('We can call the film *A Trial and Two Funerals*,' said someone unfeelingly.) Now one of the jurors was insisting that she wanted three days off to take her mother to the country for a birthday treat. The hotel had been booked long ago. This seemed to some a frivolous reason for holding up the trial, especially to those who would be forced to go back to their ordinary jobs until we reconvened. A compromise was reached, clerk and usher tactfully combining the roles of court officers and tribunes of the people.

This was evidence that as a body we were becoming quite good at sorting ourselves out and reaching consensus. But even the tightest-knit group becomes separated in a hall of mirrors. My impression was that in the jury box itself at this stage we remained twelve more or less bewildered individuals, trying to discern which of a myriad wavering images might reflect the truth.

The conspirators' plan, Korkolis said, was that if the

fake kidnap went wrong and the family smelt a rat, then they would make it look as much like a real kidnap as possible. This would save George's face and avoid the family's having to admit he was a scoundrel. The police would find weapons, balaclava helmets and incriminating tapes galore. But – and this was to have been the plotters' trump card – George would refuse to press charges or be a witness. 'Fraghistas was the only one who could shoo [sue],' Korkolis explained. 'This is correct. I know from experience. He can be tied from the ceiling and it is not a kidnap [if he doesn't sue].'

In other words, members of the jury (he appeared to be saying), if you think it looks as though we kidnapped George Fraghistas, that is because we wanted it to look exactly as though we *had* kidnapped George Fraghistas. The more genuine it seems to you, the better we did our job. When you hear the tape of George weeping on the telephone to Marily, that is because 'he made a false sobbing when his sister tried to negotiate'. Why were there traces of the defendants' saliva on the 'fake' balaclavas? Because they had had to pull the hats over their heads to know where to cut out the eye- and mouth-holes. 'How you should do it otherwise: you have the eyes up here and the mouth here?' They flushed the bits of wool down the loo.

They even mopped the surfaces of the upper floors at Hogan Mews to wipe off George's fingerprints, so that it should look as though he had never strayed out of his cupboard except to visit the bathroom. Actually, of course, they were all having a whale of a time, said Korkolis: 'There was a lot of laughing in the house.' George strolled about as he pleased. He ate chicken, mushrooms, prosciutto . . . but no sweets because 'he had diabeet', though he was partial to Häagen-Dazs. Clever Mr Korkolis to throw in these mundane details – which just happened to coincide with George's own account of his prison fare.

It was a case of black is white. If a suicide chose to make his death look like murder, the outcome would not be in doubt. The question would be: who did the deed? If the men at Hogan Mews heard the other two being arrested in Golders Green down the open mobile-telephone line in the car, why didn't they make their escape before the police arrived? Or did they genuinely believe they ran no risk of being charged even if caught red-handed?

The mobile-phone set-up in the car was an ingenious wheeze, which baffled both the police and the experts. For a time everyone was perplexed. It seemed to involve a previously unnamed character whom Korkolis referred to as Humphrey Baize.

In order to avoid the source of the ransom calls being pinpointed, the kidnappers equipped each of their two Nokia telephones with what we eventually twigged was a hands-free base (or Humphrey Baize). They were placed side by side in the car, close enough to 'talk' to each other. A ransom call from Hogan Mews would be directed to phone A in the car and picked up by phone B next to it. Phone B would be connected to the Fraghistas household. The police therefore assumed that all the calls were being made from a car, which kept moving around London. They never imagined for a moment that the car was merely acting as a relay station.

This led to great difficulties on the Tuesday of the arrests, once the police had managed to spot Korkolis's car and started to tail it. Because the ransom calls were being made by George, DCI Vanner and his men naturally assumed that the kidnap victim was *in* the car that was being followed, when actually he was still back in the cupboard at Hogan Mews. If he was in the car with a gun at his head as they thought, one false move by the pursuing detectives could be fatal. It was only when they decided to take the risk of arresting the occupants of the Rover late that evening and

George was not with them that the ruse was discovered. That was when WDC Hills picked up Korkolis's phone and found herself talking to DI Peter Young at the Fraghistas flat. He must have been surprised at the situation. None of the police witnesses had ever come across a pair of mobile phones linked up like this before.

On Day 49 Korkolis made an ill-advised attack on the judge. 'My Lord,' he said angrily, 'I am interrupted continuously. How I can give my evidence in my own way?' He told the court he had been reading an Appeal Court judgement where Their Lordships had stressed the importance of a judge not interfering with the evidence of someone conducting his own defence.

The judge responded coolly, 'I look forward to reading what Their Lordships might have to say about this case. In the meantime I shall lose no sleep over it.'

There were signs that the chief witness-cum-advocate for the defence might be winding up. Just before he finished, however, the judge addressed him kindly: 'Mr Korkolis, if there is anything you feel you have not covered, you will be able to re-examine yourself.'

Korkolis beamed. 'So,' he said delightedly, 'I have the right to re-examine me?'

Sweet Heaven, give us patience.

RISING TO THE OCCASION

Korkolis sat down at 3 p.m. He had been in the witness box for four and a half days, speaking continuously almost without a note. It was an impressive performance. By comparison a Budget speech is a mere sound-bite. It was remarkable that neither tedium nor tiresomeness seemed to have had the effect one would have imagined on the jury. A disengaged observer exposed to Korkolis's mangled English and hectic delivery, his abrupt mood swings from self-pity to contempt, would not have got through four and a half hours, never mind days, without becoming enraged. Yet somehow our jury seemed to be managing to concentrate on what he was saying without being distracted by how he was saying it. We had become professionalised.

It would be glib to suggest that just being on a jury brings this about. Our own astounding fair-mindedness may simply have been a symptom of imminent brain-death. But they say the office helps to make the man. Even within the much briefer compass of most trials, jury membership does seem to summon up people's civic-mindedness – perhaps for the first and only time in their lives. Although this is a cynical age, honesty, fairness and justice are concepts nearly everyone believes in, even if they do not personally live up to them.

Those who oppose the jury system because it is too prone to acquit find this incredible. The tendency is to equate sound jurymanship with education and intelligence. This is understandable but not altogether rational. Former Conservative MP Peter Bruinvels complained in the *Daily Telegraph* a few years ago that there were too many acquittals by juries 'made up of the unemployed, the lower working classes, and housewives'. In the very limited experience of myself and other ex-jurors I have spoken to, such people are often the keenest to convict. Many of the *Sun*-reading classes have a positive zeal for punishment.

Professor Glanville Williams in *The Proof of Guilt* is also pretty scathing: 'There is no guarantee that members of a particular jury may not be quite unusually ignorant, credulous, slow-witted, narrow-minded, biased or temperamental.' Nor there is. But it would surely be easier to find a judge who exemplified at least the last three of those qualities than a dozen people on one jury who exemplified them all.

Of course it would be desirable if most jurors were

literate, reasonably well educated and capable of following an argument. It would be desirable if most of the population were, too. Professor Williams is only stating the obvious when he asserts thinly that:

> Persons whose ordinary occupations are of a humble character rarely qualify as first-rate intellectual machines. They are not accustomed to giving sustained attention to the spoken word, and many will have a narrow vocabulary and range of idea.

Quite so.

But I wonder how many criminal cases really require to be judged by 'a first-rate intellectual machine'. In Britain not all that many, I would guess, apart from frauds or those involving abstruse medical or technical evidence. (The monstrously complicated civil cases which juries try in the USA are another matter altogether.) Anyway, first-rate intellectual machines have a known tendency to be sopping wet liberals, hag-ridden by political correctness. I expect Mr Bruinvels would agree. Pack the juries with them and the acquittal rate would take off like a jump jet.

The professor would probably judge that the jury in *R. v Korkolis and Others* contained about as much intellectual machinery as the Tin Man in *The Wizard of Oz*. But besides being considered responsible enough to vote, drive cars and bear children, we also seemed to have common sense, good humour, scepticism and patience. These strike me as far more useful qualities for the task in hand than a wide vocabulary or 'range of idea'. And in my view it was the jury system itself – the fact that we were forced to act together in this rather daunting undertaking – that helped bring these qualities to the fore.

Perhaps the four juries I have served on, including this one, were unusually blessed: no mavericks, fanatics or mutineers, no race problems and no nobblings. There are plenty of horror stories. Policemen on the one hand and liberal lawyers on the other will roll their eyes if you are too fulsome, quoting terrible miscarriages of justice. There are experts in the United States who make millions of dollars a year advising lawyers on jury selection. So the composition of a jury must be important. I must be wrong in thinking that any old twelve good men and true will more often than not rise to the occasion, whatever their sex, race, class and education. What a terribly sentimental, populist, irrational view . . .

CROSS-EXAMINATION

It was Patrick Curran's turn to get to his feet. He was appearing for Thanassis Zografos, the youngest of the four men in the dock. His cross-examination of Korkolis was not going to be easy: would he go along with the defence line as it stood, or would he try to put some distance between his client and the older man? If he went too far in that direction, he risked undermining Korkolis's case. Not far enough and, should the jury find the latter guilty, Zografos and the other two would go down like skittles.

The strategy emerged pretty soon. Mr Curran's first questions concerned the Rose Court Hotel in Paddington, where Zografos had worked as a sort of super-receptionist after he dropped out of his computer course at the South Bank University. He was an amiable young man who had run errands and acted as interpreter for the hotel's residents. One of them, a man called Sidiropoulos, was singled out by Mr Curran: an elderly former millionaire who had spent a good deal of his fortune at the tables. Korkolis, who was also a regular customer, agreed that he and Mr Sidiropoulos had made something of a pet of Zografos and used to take him out on sprees to the Victoria Casino in the Edgware Road.

Mr Curran painted a rather cosy picture of the hotel as a microcosmic Athens-in-exile, peopled by companionable Greeks who smoked, drank coffee and gambled together, stayed up late and got up later. Zografos, we were to understand, had been dazzled by these knowing men of the world.

So that was to be the line: a nice young boy, tempted into a low-risk blackmail operation by an older man whom he admired. Korkolis had told Zografos it was not an illegal plan; it was morally justified: George was only seeking his due from his own family. And in any case, they could not be prosecuted if George refused to give evidence.

Day 50. Counsel for Mereu and Moussaoui had only a few questions for Korkolis. Their significance was hopelessly unclear. As so often, it was hard for the jury to see what counsel were driving at. Words were left hanging in the air from which nothing could be implied. Would they be resurrected during closing speeches? I tried to log them in my mind for future retrieval, but it was difficult to know what to file them under. How much simpler it would be if the defence lawyers were obliged to present the jury with an outline of their arguments from the very start. As it was, I had a strong feeling these were simply decoy tactics, intended to mislead and set us worrying.

(Later in 1997 new rules came into effect under the 1996 Criminal Procedures and Investigations Act, which do require some disclosure of the main thrust of the defence, especially those areas where there is a disagreement with the prosecution – but only to the judge, not the jury.)

At 11.18 a.m. the Crown began cross-examining Korkolis. Joanna Korner sauntered into action in the manner of a very confident matador confronting a very small bull. Hand on hip, she plainly aimed to show Korkolis up as an all-round poor specimen. He had presented himself as a respectable businessman with his own moral code (Korkolis, interrupting: 'My one. My own one . . .') who had never broken the law. Yet he had a library of false passports – in the names of Nikolau, Kaltezotis, Karpathakis, Rentzepis as well as his own. There was evidence on tape of his seeking to obtain yet another from someone called 'the Fat One' back in Greece.

Korkolis was indignant at the suggestion that owning so many false passports was any kind of misdemeanour. 'I didn't use these passports to harm somebody, to cheat somebody . . . I think there are many things more disgusting.'

These were the opening shots in a prolonged battle of wits. Miss Korner came at Korkolis from every angle, accusing him of having gambling debts of his own, giving a false name to rent the £600-a-week house in Hogan Mews, using Zografos as his front man to hide his own identity. Her opponent dodged and sidestepped every attack with extraordinary nimbleness.

Why, when they were renting cars and making other preparations for the plan, did he always get Zografos to do the talking, since his own English was so fluent?

'I have difficulty how people speaks,' Korkolis replied instantly, giving Miss Korner a disarming smile. 'You speak very clearly. But in prison some people sound like Chinese. Three months in court have improved my English.'

Why did he need a stungun? Because he feared for his own safety in Hogan Mews, he said. There had been burglaries there recently. 'Check please for the bugglers in Hogan Mews.' Then he offered to use the gun on himself in the witness box, a bravado gesture which the spoil-sport judge prevented him making.

Try as she might, Miss Korner seemed unable to land the killer blow. Korkolis simply would not give up.

Trial by Jury

Day 51. Should we get into March, the time-span of the trial will parallel the course of the kidnap plot a year earlier almost exactly. We are now into the closing days of February and there must still be at least a fortnight to go. The alleged conspiracy, like the trial, got under way in November. George was seized, genuinely or otherwise, on 24 March and freed on 2 April.

While waiting for the prisoners to arrive we were called into court to be asked how we could help end the trial before Easter. We returned to the jury room to discuss this. Suggestions ranged from offering to sit later in the afternoons to coming in on Saturdays. There were problems with train timetables, an ailing spouse and Bob's Saturday football matches. I proposed a vote. The hopelessly inconclusive result did not promise well for the future. Eventually we settled for working until 4.45 p.m. on weekdays. Kate was inconsolable: 'But I'll miss Pet Rescue,' she moaned.

Will the extra time in court lead to drowsiness problems? Apropos dozing jurors, John Mortimer has an anecdote concerning an indecency case. A woman witness was giving evidence and was asked what the man in the dock had said to her. She was too embarrassed to repeat it in court, so the judge asked her to write it down. She did, and what she wrote was: 'Would you care for a screw?' This document was passed around the jury until it reached Juror No. 12, an elderly gentleman who was fast asleep. Sitting next to him, Mortimer relates, 'was a fairly personable young lady. She read the note, nudged her neighbour and, when he was awake, handed it to him. He woke with a start, read it and, with apparent satisfaction, folded it and put it carefully away in his wallet. When the judge said: "Let that be handed up to me," the juryman shook his head and said, "Purely private matter, My Lord."'

The reason the prisoners were late was that they had been held up in traffic. 'It was not my fault, My Lord,' explained Korkolis in cheeky-chappie mode. 'I was not driving.'

Nor was it the only time the black Maria service held us up. For one reason or another, delays continued to dog the trial. Often we ground to a halt for what the judge called 'housekeeping': photocopying new documents, hole-punching, indexing, finding the right tape to play into our earphones. It seemed a terrible waste of everyone's time and weirdly inefficient.

We had now reached exhibit No. 99. DS Hawkins would leave the court for ten minutes at a time to forage for what he wanted in his glory-hole next door, where the exhibits were stored. I learned later that there had been a total of three thousand potential exhibits at the outset of the trial. Perhaps that included every single cigarette butt found at Hogan Mews. When Joanna Korner confessed at one point that she had lost a document she said: 'This trial has done things to my brain.' During the longer longueurs, boiled sweets and glasses of water provided our only distraction. 'There's only so much water you can drink,' Kate complained. The older males nodded, weak-bladdered to a man.

There were compensations, chiefly the challenge of trying to pin down Korkolis's elusive character as it flitted erratically from mood to mood. One moment he would be all self-mockery – 'Do I look like a kidnapper? Me? A Greek?' he asked, looking down at his scrawny, grey-sweatered chest. The next he would turn on the melodrama.

'The only truth they [the Fraghistas family] spoke was their names. It was all lies – under oath!'

Korkolis attacked. 'Miss Korner, I don't know whether you have met intelligent people in your life,' he scoffed.

The judge jumped in. 'Would you like to apologise for that last remark?'

Korkolis retreated. 'I apologise.'

Miss Korner asked him about something that had been bothering me. The vile leather mask which George said the kidnappers had struggled to pull over his head in the car-park was, according to Korkolis, meant for another purpose altogether. It was to be used in the Polaroid photograph which the conspirators would send the family should the 'ransom' money not materialise. The terrifying tableau would show the handcuffed and leather-masked George with his mouth zipped up and the gun at his head. But, Miss Korner (and I) wanted to know, what was the point of a photo in which the victim's face was completely hidden? Korkolis reacted with a tirade about how any family would recognise a son even if his face were covered. 'Who else would it be? Me?'

Well, yes. You.

Day 52. Korkolis's long upper lip was prominent today. He was in a truculent mood. He warned the Crown: 'Miss Korner, you are playing dangerously with the lives of four people.' When Mr K is pursuing one of his whirling hypotheses Miss JK screws up her face as in a sandstorm. He moves his hands like dolphins.

Miss JK asked: why the syringes? Mr K: 'Every house can have syringes without having to make a kidnap.' What about the bandages found in Hogan Mews? What were they for? 'For miscles.' What? 'For training for Mereu.' The Olympic wrestler and his comrade Moussaoui bandaged their 'miscles' to go jogging. 'Jogging?' said JK with a Lady Bracknell swoop, astonished that people go jogging in mid-kidnap. K says plenty of joggers use bandages, not just wrestlers. And then, in a triumphant ellipsis: 'Diana the Princess makes jogging. So she is a wrestler?'

Later Miss Korner asked about the mattress that the police found outside the kidnap cupboard at Hogan Mews. Korkolis poured scorn on this question. The judge moved in like a Dimbleby on an out-of-order panellist. It was *not* an irrelevant question, he said. What Miss Korner was likely to suggest was that the mattress was used by a guard sleeping outside the cupboard, since the door had no lock. At this Korkolis erupted, accusing the judge of asking the prosecution's questions on its behalf. The judge looked down sternly: 'You will say "what a stupid question" to Miss Korner once too often.'

Korkolis wanted us to know that three highly incriminating tapes which had been found at Hogan Mews, apparently referring to the planning and execution of the kidnap, had been *deliberately* recorded by him in order to mislead the police. The judge said very reasonably, 'You have just said that everything on this tape is a lie. How is the jury to know when you are telling the truth?'

Korkolis looked stung: 'Now you play with me, My Lord. When the prosecution says lies I didn't see any miscle on your face move.' There followed a pained outburst, culminating in an accusation that the judge had been conspiring with Miss Korner in private. Korkolis said he was 'thunderstrick' by what had taken place. The jury had not the smallest idea what he was talking about, but since this was a familiar experience we would have let it pass had not the judge responded. We were now about to have explained to us one of those points of law which so often required us to leave the court.

Judge Goldstein admitted to us that he had had a brief private meeting with Miss Korner that morning, to discuss a matter of procedure. This was probably unwise, in view of the nature of the case: it would have been better had other counsel and Mr Korkolis been present. But nothing at all improper had taken place. He had told Mr Korkolis about it himself and apologised.

The judge said all this with icy self-control. Inwardly he must have been seething that a matter already discussed and dealt with in the jury's absence had been flaunted in front of us by Korkolis, accompanied by a tremendous show of ersatz outrage. It was a hucksterish trick, although we missed its significance at the time and the judge scrupulously avoided pointing it out to us.

Court was abruptly adjourned for the day, a sovereign remedy for ill-temper. The jury reeled into the outside world rather earlier than the newly agreed time of 4.45 p.m.

TIME TO ROCK AND ROLL

Day 53. Kept waiting once again. Should prison vans have sirens like police cars and ambulances? It would save the tax-payer thousands of pounds a week in wasted court costs.

At the start of each day we now customarily assembled on the green leather benches in Grand Hall, the jury room not yet being unlocked. Here one could drink one's take-away espresso and read the papers in much more dignified surroundings than the fifth-floor restaurant.

The Grand Hall is certainly very grand: a multi-domed, many-alcoved vestibule of great size and splendour. Leading off it are the oldest courts in the building, including Court 1. The architect was Edward Mountford, who won the competition to design the new courthouse in 1898, after the City of London acquired the infamous Newgate Prison, demolished it and cleared the site. No longer did passers-by have to carry nosegays because of the sickening stench. The new building was completed in 1907, using some of the stones from that terrible jail. It was opened by King Edward VII. There were four courts and ninety cells.

Mountford was not the kind of architect nor the early 1900s an era to shy away from the grandiloquent gesture. The baroque portentousness of the façade, presided over by the Recording Angel and topped by Justice with her famous scales, has its inner counterpart in the Grand Hall. It seems to have been expressly designed to humble the mighty and obliterate the humble. It is impossible to imagine a modern-day civic edifice being built with such resounding confidence or to such numinous effect. If Edward Mountford had been commissioned by God to design a venue for the Last Judgement, this would have been it. He would merely have added a few tons of gold leaf and powdered pearl.

The budget of £400,000, enormous by contemporary standards, allowed for every kind of extravagance. Richly patterned marble was shipped in from Italy, Greece, Belgium, Scandinavia. There were mosaic ceilings and painted lunettes. Edifying texts were chiselled into the friezes, with dots the size of cricket balls between each word for emphasis:

THE . WELFARE . OF . THE . PEOPLE . IS . THE .
SUPREME . LAW.
THE . LAW . OF . THE . WISE . IS . A . FOUNTAIN .
OF . LIFE.

Sculpted reliefs representing Justice, Mercy, Charity and Temperance loom down virtuously. They are escorted by rather earthier figures among whom I counted four naked breasts, one bare bottom and eight willies. The lunettes were painted by Professor Gerald Moira. His depictions of great law-givers through the ages look like scenes from the Old

Testament. His brief may have been to equate man-made law with divine justice, an aspiration common among lawyers to this day.

To the juror patiently waiting to 'POISE . THE . CAUSE . IN . JUSTICE . EQUAL . SCALES' (and wondering what became of the genitive case) all this is rather daunting, which was clearly what the architect intended. But barristers must find it thoroughly uplifting to have their priest-like status confirmed in this basilica of English law. How glorious to cast your eyes ceilingwards and see your lucrative profession allegorised in a painting of *Time Protecting Truth From Falsehood*. (And how apt that the role of Time in the law's affairs should be so recognised.) How splendid to be a wing-collared QC gliding silkily across the glimmering marble floor, wig held high and black gown billowing, while mere mortals creep about its echoing vastness like beetles on the bottom of an empty swimming pool.

'Court 5!' Roy the usher broke into my reverie with his customary summons: 'Time to rock and roll.' And off we filed, no more than an hour behind schedule. Joanna Korner joshingly told the court that the timing of the trial would now depend on the efficiency of Belmarsh Prison.

Oh?

This was new information. The jury pounced on it. Hitherto we had had no idea where the defendants were being held. Bob the postman was able to tell us more in the coffee-break. Belmarsh was on his delivery route. It was a spanking-new, high-walled, top-security jail in Woolwich, he said, specially tailored for tough nuts. From this we could deduce that in the authorities' eyes these men were Category A prisoners and dangerous – though that, of course, was precisely one of the issues we were there to decide. Even if they were being held in the Tower of London, we had to think of them as innocent unless and until we found them guilty.

Miss Korner was approaching the end of her cross-examination. She had returned to the three incriminating tapes which Korkolis said he had secretly recorded to help make the kidnap look genuine. We had the translated transcripts in front of us. In one of them a man, a woman and Korkolis himself were chatting in a kitchen about their plans for some unspecified event. Someone was cooking spaghetti. Odd phrases stood out. The moment 'he' was alone they'd be waiting for 'him' . . . Once it was all over, the woman could look forward to getting her gold Rolex . . . 'In a month at most we will have finished and then we can dance at weekends,' said Korkolis's voice. In a telephone call on another tape, Korkolis could be heard asking someone if he was 'in a hurry to get the suitcase with the money'. This same someone warned that 'those in the tall hats have got involved . . .' ('tall hats': Greek-Cypriot slang for the British police).

This someone, the jury deduced, must be a man called Pantelides who had been mentioned from time to time without being, so to speak, formally introduced. What we did know, because Korkolis had let it slip, was that this Pantelides was on bail of £350,000, which was a lot of moolah. Our note to the judge asking who he was and what he was charged with yielded nothing. The jury was not allowed to have the answer to these questions. It was all wonderfully mystifying.

Even without knowing anything about Mr Pantelides, the contents of the tapes seemed pretty damning – as Korkolis claimed they were intended to be. But Miss Korner was aiming elsewhere. Wasn't it true, she asked, that he made a regular practice of secretly recording conversations with friends and associates in this fashion? It was. He did it for self-protection. In that case, why were there no tapes of his meetings with George Fraghistas to discuss the planning of the fake kidnap – precisely the sort of exchange of which he was normally so careful to keep a record? Pause. 'Because I never imagined he could lower himself so much to betray me.' He said it with conviction. And he sounded almost convincing.

Korkolis's re-examination of himself did not yield much other than that his father was a governor of the Athens stock exchange and his uncle a Greek air marshal. This didn't cut much ice, even if it was true. But he finished on a note of high passion, addressing the jury. 'At this crucial moment in my life I am proud to say I didn't lie. The only support I have is my faith.' He cleared the witness box of his things and descended, a small, defiant figure in jeans and sneakers, much shorter than his guards.

In the break Kate said, 'He's a little weasel.' Stuart: 'Come on, Kate, feel free to speak your mind.' Kate: 'All right, he's an effing prat.' Hubbub of objections from other jurors: 'Of course he isn't. He's as sharp as a monkey. He's cleverer than Korner. He ought to be a lawyer . . .' Etc, etc.

Korkolis now had his own witnesses to call. The first was a phonetics expert. He was on the board of a publication with the marvellously arcane title *Forensic Linguistics*. His evidence was that George could not have heard someone talking to him in a voice distorted by helium. Anyone doing that for any length of time would probably die.

The next defence witness was Mr Polymeropoulos, an Athenian Mr Toad. He was a plump, balding man, with heavy horn-rimmed glasses and a blubbery smile. He had come to London voluntarily when he had learnt of Korkolis's difficulties, he said. He had a remarkably vivid recollection of a meeting many years ago at a coffee shop in Kolonakis, when he had seen Korkolis shake hands with a young man. Who was this young man? Why, Korkolis had told him, it was George Fraghistas.

That was it. Just the one meeting a very long time ago – oh, and another a month or so later, maybe? Polymeropoulos smacked his lips and wobbled his head invitingly. He agreed that he had not clapped eyes on Korkolis for ten or possibly twelve years. Miss Korner asked him if he was what is known as a professional witness. He affected to be horrified, denied it, smiled ingratiatingly and trundled off to catch the next flight back to Athens.

Korkolis had finished dealing with himself and looked quite satisfied with his performance. The jurors were left to ponder why. Either he was a first-rate actor, or he genuinely believed he had shown the jury what he wanted them to see. We would not hear any more long perorations from him until his closing speech. That was sure to be a marathon performance.

A SUITABLE BOY

Thanassis Zografos had dressed smartly for his début in the witness box. This is what most defendants and witnesses do (unless of course one is Richard Branson, who remained resolutely tie-less in court throughout his victorious libel case against GTech lottery mogul Guy Snowden in January 1998). Obviously the intention is to convey respectability. It is a ploy that sometimes fails grotesquely when the younger, rougher element try it on. An earringed skinhead in a shiny-new, boxy-shouldered suit looks even more sinister than he would in a T-shirt and trainers. If not hoodlum black, the suit is often a sickening shade of green or brown.

There are usually a number of these slightly menacing characters in the morning queue to get into the Old Bailey. The white boys look like underfed bouncers, cupping cigarettes and jerking their shoulders in a hopeless attempt to look cool. Blacks who go in for the jacket-and-tie routine often draw the line at leather shoes or cutting off their dreadlocks and look even more uncomfortable. It is all rather odd when you consider that it is not the judge these people need to impress but the jury, whose male members are generally the worst-dressed people in the courtroom.

Perhaps that was why Korkolis, who said he used to be a snappy dresser, chose to stick to his prison garb. By contrast Zografos had metamorphosed into a tidy-looking young man in a brown blazer, blue shirt and mosaic-patterned yellow tie. His thick black hair was carefully combed and fluffed up at the back. His pale, handsome, big-jawed face looked newly shaved. He flashed the jury a smile as he took the stand. It was a smile aimed squarely at the mothers among us, I would say. There was no doubt of the role he was going to play. We had had a foretaste of it during Mr Curran's cross-examination of Korkolis. It was to be that of the wide-eyed innocent led astray in the big foreign city.

Between them, he and Mr Curran managed it very well. The story that emerged was methodically told. This in itself played in Zografos's favour, a blessed relief after the mad verbosity of Korkolis. His English was near-perfect, rather better in fact than some of the jurors'.

The young Thanassis was born in 1971 in Trikala, a small town in central Greece, and grew up as 'a country boy'. He would be 26 in April. His father worked for the Ministry of Agriculture. His mother and his brother had been to visit him in prison, Mr Curran was keen to let us know.

His education had been at the village school and then in Corinth. After school, he had worked as a labourer, managing to fit in English lessons. When he was 20 he went to Athens and enrolled in a crash course in science, maths and English, paying his way with part-time jobs. His ambition was to go to university in England – which would have the incidental benefit of getting him out of National Service.

He won a place at the Polytechnic of Central London, now the University of Westminster, to do a B. Eng. in computers.

He dropped out of the course because, he said, although he was good at lectures he was lazy at revising. He left his hall of residence in Streatham and moved into the Rose Court Hotel in Paddington, where he became a full-time receptionist and interpreter for the Greek residents, many of whom stayed there while on visits to the UK for medical treatment. He would accompany them to their consultations. In 1993 he returned to his studies, enrolling in a software engineering course at the South Bank University. In 1994, alas, he dropped out again.

Zografos explained all this with becoming modesty. He was rueful about his academic failures. Mr Curran skilfully brought out the boyish vulnerability of the young Greek far from home. 'Were you happy?' 'I was lonely, but I was all right,' replied Zografos, squaring his shoulders bravely.

It was at the Rose Court Hotel that he met Mr Sidiropoulos and his friend Mr Korkolis. He described Mr Sidiropoulos as an ex-millionaire. (Joanna Korner, *sotto voce*: 'Is that an occupation?' Patrick Curran: 'It is for some.') As for Korkolis, he was 'very different from now': he was well dressed, self-assured, much less excitable and had plenty of money. They chatted. 'Mr Korkolis discussed mainly business if I can say.' Zografos became involved in some of this business, in particular a somewhat shady property company.

Zografos's first day was a success. He had politely directed most of his remarks directly at the jury. We had had the full benefit of his smile. When he frowned with concentration, his eyebrows writhed like caterpillers, which demonstrated how very much in earnest he was being. He had come across as a good-hearted, homespun lad, perhaps a touch naive.

I began to see a new problem shaping itself – one which faces a great many juries these days because of the growing practice of trying several defendants together in one trial (partly because of the organised nature of modern crime, partly to save money). Until now everything had centred around Korkolis. For the first time I became fully aware of how tricky it was going to be to treat each of the defendants separately. So much would depend on what we made of their relationships with each other. For example, there had been a time when I thought Korkolis and Zografos might have been lovers, remembering the gay magazine at Hogan Mews. There was a general view by now that Korkolis might be homosexual (which the police confirmed after the trial). But Mr Curran had made a point of getting his client to tell us he had a girlfriend. Korkolis could be extraordinarily persuasive, as we knew. Was it possible that Zografos was so impressionable he had let himself *believe* it was a fake kidnap, even though it wasn't?

As we packed up for the day, someone said, 'Why can't we just be told the facts, and then judge?' If only it were that simple.

Day 54. Another late start. Zografos missed the Belmarsh bus. The judge said the prison governor had rung to explain that it was all due to a monumental unmentionable word – a cock-up, presumably. Or perhaps it was just that Z took longer to dress these days, now that he had become so respectable. He arrived looking apologetic. Cunning Mr Curran greeted him as if he were a valued acquaintance rather than a remand prisoner accused of a cruel crime. 'Mr Zografos, good morning,' he said warmly and enquired after his health.

Zografos had had no reason to doubt that George Fraghistas was the instigator of the fake kidnap plan. He was offered $70,000 to take part. Why should George be so keen to go ahead? Well, said Zografos, he had come across ex-millionaires of this kind before, ruined at the gaming tables. One, who had made masses of money in Nigeria and lost it all in a year at the London casinos, had died of a heart attack on the steps of the Rose Court Hotel itself. He assumed George was such a desperate figure.

'Tell the court in your own words, watching His Lordship's pen, what happened then,' proceeded Mr Curran. And Zografos took us back to the Lanark Road car-park, the drive to Hogan Mews, the purchasing of cigarettes for George, the shopping expeditions for prosciutto (from Selfridge's), steak, fried chicken ('not Kentucky but very like') and Häagen-Dazs: all exactly as George himself had told it but for the fact that in this version George was a willing participant, who had climbed into the car at Lanark Road entirely of his own free will. Korkolis had told them that if things went wrong and they were arrested they were to say nothing. George would not prefer charges nor help the prosecution. It was easy money, safe money.

When Korkolis cross-examined him from the dock, Zografos did not look at him. This was interesting. How much clear water was Zografos trying to put between himself and his ex-Svengali? I tried to imagine Korkolis as he had been described in his glory days: dapper, confident, reassuring. Zografos called him 'sir'. Was that indicative of their real relationship or just a ruse to suggest he was still in the thrall of the older man?

Mereu's counsel, Michael Corkery QC, had not got much to put to Zografos: 'Did Mereu have any English?' Zografos said, 'Only one word.' Mr Corkery: 'I won't ask you what that word is.'

The ruddy-faced David Owen Thomas QC, for Moussaoui, was of the Rumpolian school of advocacy. For some unexplained reason he wanted to know if his client and Mr Mereu did press-ups and 'other unpleasant things of the kind that went on in the army'. 'They jogged,' Zografos replied. 'You can do too many exercises without special equipment.'

Mr Owen Thomas: 'I think Mr Zografos means you can

do a *great* many exercises without equipment – though for me it *would* be too many.' There was laughter in court, as the reporters say.

VIOLENT THOUGHTS

There had been surprisingly few language problems in the trial. The only interpreters who were continuously at work were the pair who whispered a running commentary to the two Frenchmen. But as the world shrinks and frontiers crumble, they and their colleagues are bound to be required in court more and more frequently. On my way out to lunch I checked what was going on elsewhere in the Old Bailey.

These were some of the people appearing in court that day:

Court 1:   Nadeem Janjua, Mayur Divecha, Mifta Chodhury
Court 5:   Konstantine Korkolis, Athanasios Zografos, Jean-Marc Mereu, Djemel Moussaoui
Court 6:   Demitru Vadineanu
Court 7:   Mustafa Tunc
Court 8:   Serge Tarpinian
Court 10: Malik Khan
Court 14: Dele Ogboma
Court 17: Anthony Zomparelli
Court 18: Jerry Agyemang. Bail application for Ravi Ilangaraja.

Even allowing for the List Office's misspellings, it was striking that half the courts were dealing with people whose names, at any rate, were resoundingly foreign. Was this a trend? What did it tell us? Perhaps it was no more than a reflection of the internationalisation of any big modern city. After all, here was I heading off for lunch at a delicious dim sum restaurant which made the purlieus of St Paul's Cathedral smell like Kowloon – and where the waiters were South African. Over the previous three and a half months my solitary lunch excursions had led me to Japanese sushi, Indian korma, Spanish tapas, Italian ravioli, salade Niçoise and Loch Fyne oysters, all within a half-mile radius of the Old Bailey – and the pub across the road was as Irish as potato cakes. Still, I found it interesting that when I looked in at Highgate Magistrates' Court on a Monday morning early in 1998, three out of seven defendants needed an interpreter.

I was digesting crispy Szechwan lamb when the Crown started cross-examining Zografos. Joanna Korner's first ball was a bouncer: was it true that the prisoners had been able to discuss the case together in prison over Christmas? This was a question the jury had been burning to ask but which, as with a good many queries that we feared might stray into the mysterious zone marked 'inadmissible evidence', we had been too timid to write a note about. Yes, came the answer. So they would have been able to co-ordinate their story . . . That was certainly something to think about.

We were now into the first week of March. The newspapers were excited by the news that the Labour Party wanted to hold child criminals responsible for their own evil-doing. This would be a vote-catcher among the jury-serving classes, I thought. There was not a lot of sympathy around for teenagers who terrorise housing estates and mug pensioners. For years the British middle classes have been in a funk about the tide of yobbishness supposedly swamping the country, egged on by stubble-chinned pop stars and the tabloid press. They would find an hour's conversation in the jury restaurant at the Old Bailey quite reassuring.

I told my juror friends what had happened to me the night before. I had been driving through Camden Town with my wife. It was around midnight. In a garage forecourt we suddenly saw what looked like a murder taking place: one man lay on the ground while another was beating him furiously over the head with an iron bar. I stopped and began hooting, hoping to scare the attacker off. Within seconds other cars had stopped too. A taxi manoeuvred to block the escape route. A man shouted that he had telephoned the police on his mobile. One motorist jumped out of his car and my wife joined him. They ran towards the two men.

The iron bar turned out to be a length of rubber hose and the victim shaken but uninjured. It appeared to be a case of road rage. What interested me was that so many passers-by had been prepared to intervene. It was not the sort of good-citizen behaviour one is led to expect these days. Some people have equally low expectations of the jury system.

With reference to violence, it struck me that one of the matters we would have to decide was whether Korkolis and the others were violent types. Would they have killed George? We had heard Miss Korner say to Zografos, 'You were the man in the garage with the gun.' And it was his fingerprint on the ammunition. She sounded a bit like a triumphant Cluedo-player. There was evidence of the syringes, with which they threatened to kill George by lethal injection. A younger juror reminded us that Mereu the wrestler worked as a security guard at rock concerts, a type pretty prone to get heavy. But were these guys a threat to the general public? Hard to tell but probably not, I reckoned.

Magnus had heard from a friend who had been in the prison service that, were our defendants found guilty, they could be looking at up to seventeen years each. This led to some thoughtful talk of the kind juries are not supposed to bother their heads about. There was something uneasy-making about the idea that a kidnapper who had not actually hurt his victim physically might go to jail for longer than a violent rapist or mugger. Jurors are meant to concentrate on their verdicts, not speculate on sentences. But of course they do and they would scarcely be human if they did not. For neither the first nor last time, I wondered how we would all be feeling were ours a murder case and capital punishment still in force.

The general view was that Judge Simon Goldstein would be a lenient sentencer.

THE LAST WITNESS

The judge reminded me more and more of Nigel Hawthorne as the sane version of George III. One day his patience was tried not by Korkolis but by counsel. Miss Korner was asking Zografos why he had remained silent after his arrest. Once he realised that George Fraghistas was helping the police, contrary to his undertaking, why hadn't Zografos simply come clean about the plot?

Because that was not the plan.

But he had spoken to his solicitor, hadn't he?

At this point Mr Curran leapt to his feet. 'My learned friend knows the rules. I don't know what things are coming to,' he expostulated, shaking his head in sorrow and astonishment.

Joanna Korner jumped up. She had not broken the rules.

Mr Curran jumped up. Yes she had.

Hadn't. Had. You rotter. Yaroo.

What on earth was going on? We had no more idea of 'the rules' than of quantum mechanics. The judge took on the expression of a long-suffering schoolmaster and asked us to withdraw from this unedifying spectacle. 'I have no idea what will happen next.' No more did we, and things were no clearer when we were allowed back into court, though it was Mr Curran who got on his feet to be conciliatory. It was one of those occasions when I felt that the jury was being treated as a mere adjunct of the law, necessary idiots who could not be trusted with an explanation of the scene we had just witnessed.

And something like it happened again. Miss Korner had sought to penetrate the shroud that surrounds a defendant's dealings with his solicitor and seemed to have got away with it – though the significance of this achievement was entirely lost on the jury. Now she wished to scale the walls of the prisons where the defendants had been held. To begin with, we were told, they had all been incarcerated at Highdown in Surrey, though they were held in different blocks. 'There was no communication. It was not a playground,' Zografos asserted. But later, when they were moved to Belmarsh, they were able to meet and talk. Aha.

Although the Crown had touched on this the day before, now the judge looked worried. 'You know what I am concerned about,' he said meaningfully, which was irritating: he must have known the jury had not the foggiest notion what he was concerned about. He was ostentatiously addressing counsel over our heads in his not-in-front-of-the-children manner. So out we had to go again, speculating madly and feeling rather betrayed by His Lordship, on whom we relied to treat us like grown-ups.

My advice to the judiciary is never to leave conundrums hanging in the air like this: all sorts of mischief might ensue. We cooked up a bit of mischief, though I am not saying that the one thing led to the other. Postman Bob had been agitating for some time about wanting to see whether it really was possible to get two men into the boot of a Rover 416. My own killjoy view was that this would be a waste of time, since I was sure it *was* possible, recollecting 1960s happenings in which improbable numbers of people had crammed into Minis. Eventually, we agreed to send a note asking merely if we could look at the car.

Why of course, said the judge when he had read our note. He would even try to get us the kidnap car itself, provided it was not sitting in an auctioneer's warehouse by now. We would be able to hold an inspection first thing on Tuesday morning.

Day 57 – Heinz Day, said Magnus waggishly. Today's pastimes included Kate reading out passages from a book called Weird Sex; *Sophie saying, 'Hey, if Korkolis had planned his kidnap a bit later he'd have got his second Orange phone for free,' and Magnus producing the first of the day's jokes: A girl went to a fancy-dress party all in black with a red feather in her hair. 'I'm a dying ember,' she explained. 'And if someone doesn't give me a quick poke I'm off home.'*

This was the day we were to look at a – or maybe even the – Rover 416. We assembled in court. The usher said, 'Silence, please,' and took the special oath required for juries going on walkabout: 'I will well and truly keep this jury as directed by the court . . .'

Unfortunately, while we were gathering to set off on our inspection someone made a lighthearted suggestion that two of us might seize the chance to leap into the car boot. The usher scuttled off and, unbeknownst to us, told the judge. We waited for nearly an hour, wondering what was going on. Eventually, the judge called us back into court. With excessive courtesy he thanked us for alerting him to what we had in mind. Not only were he and counsel agreed that we could not stage a reconstruction to determine whether a Greek shipping agent and a French Olympic wrestler could fit in the boot of a Rover; he had now decided we should not even see the car.

This was very deflating. We felt we had been misunderstood and unfairly reprimanded. It had been a joke . . .

Mr Curran called a witness from the gaming demi-monde, a casino manager from the Ritz. He did not help Zografos's case. True, he produced records of the astonishing sums George had laid out at the tables. Between 1992 and 1995 his 'drop' at just this one club had been a cool £5,632,600. That sum represented what he had staked, of course, not his net losses. But who could question that risking such sums might bankrupt a man and drive him to desperate measures? However, the manager rather spoilt the effect from the defence's point of view by explaining that although George's cheques had occasionally bounced, they were usually honoured within a few days. What is more, he added, Mr George Fraghistas would still be a welcome guest at the Ritz. I should think so, too, spending that kind of money.

Zografos's case was wound up at midday. Now the question was: would Moussaoui and Mereu take the stand? They would not.

Until recently, the jury would have been instructed not to draw adverse conclusions about their refusal either to talk to the police after their arrest or testify in court. Under present law, however, the judge was obliged to go through the rigmarole of informing the jury that it might draw what inferences it wished from their silence. Frankly, I cannot think many juries need reminding of what they would do quite naturally anyway. But this was what the great row about the Tories' 'abolition' of the right to silence amounted to, so naturally I paid close attention as each of the defence counsel in turn formally acknowledged the judge's words. We could infer away to our hearts' content.

It was a slight shock to realise that we had now come to the end of the evidence in this case. No new witnesses would be brought before us, no new facts that might illuminate or confuse the issues any further. All the pieces of the gigantic jigsaw had been laid out. Now it was up to Miss Korner, Mr Korkolis and the other three barristers to try to persuade us how to assemble it. Miss Korner had had her hair done for the big day. She would shortly begin her closing speech.

BARRISTERS

I have never been anywhere that made me feel as class-conscious as the Old Bailey. The place itself has a lot to do with it. It is as though a gentleman's club had amalgamated with a police station. The rough and the smooth mingle in awkward proximity. Crudely speaking, judges and barristers are toffs, whereas almost everyone else is a prole. That is not literally true. There are scores of QCs who never went near a public school and speak in all manner of accents. Our own judge had come up the hard way from humble beginnings. But that is how it will strike the eye of a novice juryman at the Central Criminal Court, be his own blood never so blue.

It is partly the air of self-assurance with which the barristers saunter round the place, as though they were the guardians of mysteries unfathomable to the rest of us. This of course is exactly what they are: members of a powerful and secretive profession with its own language and arcane rules.

It is partly the subfusc uniform, with its touches of starchy white – as forbidding as a Grand Inquisitor's yet understatedly glamorous, especially as worn by one dandyish woman barrister who favoured pin-striped trousers. Jurors, solicitors, interpreters, witnesses are mere starlings beside these glossy magpies.

It is partly the way they drawl and peer condescendingly over the tops of their specs and write their notes with fat black Parker fountain pens. It is the unavoidable arrogance that comes of being licensed to interrogate strangers about their most private affairs and call them liars to their faces. 'Of course this is all nonsense, isn't it?' they will say. 'The truth is, and you know it, that it was you who blah blah blah blah . . . *Didn't you?*'

If the barristers are the officer class and the judges are the generals, the policemen, ushers and other court officials are the NCOs, deferential to those above them, bossy to those below. While we of course, the jurors, defendants, and most of those who appear in the witness box, are the poor bloody infantry: kept waiting, chivvied, expected to obey orders and hold our tongues. I once had the temerity to address Mr Curran directly regarding some documents he had said the jury were to have. We were in court, but the judge had risen and general chitchat had broken out. 'Mr Curran,' I said, 'Mr Curran.' He was only about five feet away. He looked at me aghast, as though I were threatening him with a hand grenade, then turned to the usher: 'Is that juror trying to *speak* to me?' It was a moment worthy of a Bateman cartoon. The usher looked mortified that one of his flock had bleated out of turn and shooed us from the court.

So although these highly educated, highly paid men and women may not actually *be* toffs, that is how they behave; and although juries are not drawn exclusively from the *hoi polloi*, that is how they are treated. I imagine most barristers give barely a thought to this immense divide between Them and Us. It probably does not matter a great deal anyway. To the first-time juryman or witness, the majesty of the law is pretty majestic whether the attorneys are in wigs and waistcoats in the Old Bailey or schmoozing an American courtroom in a button-down shirt and loafers.

But there is this danger, I imagine: that the average juror in this country will feel he has a great deal more in common with the average defendant than he does with the average barrister and m'learned friends (who, by the way, really do seem to be his friends, which must alarm the prisoner in the dock just as it intrigues the jurors: the minute the judge has risen, there they all are, prosecutors and defenders, chuckling conspiratorially and calling each other by first names).

There is no way of knowing whether fellow-feeling for the accused and resentment towards the accuser ever do sway a jury's verdict. But it is hard to believe they have no influence. Put it this way: it would have been easier to imagine the Archbishop of Canterbury sitting on an Old Bailey jury than to picture any of the counsel in Court 5 being comfortable in that role.

Inevitably, however, when it comes to doing what they are primarily there for, barristers must communicate with ordinary mortals. They must curb their erudition and tailor their eloquence to their audience: Them must talk to Us. This is one of the strongest reasons for supporting the jury system. It ensures that the defendant understands what is going on. He is judged according to arguments and in language both he and the jury can follow.

That is the theory. In practice, of course, a barrister could talk in baby language and still leave his listeners perplexed. The adversarial procedure has many virtues, chiefly that of giving the defence the widest scope for making its case. Its drawback is that by more or less forcing counsel to take extreme positions and magnify every conflict of evidence, it can make it hard to judge the truth. One side says black, the other white. Not surprisingly, the outcome in the juror's mind is often a throbbing grey.

In *Members of the Jury* (Wildwood House, 1976), a collection of jurors' experiences edited by Dulan Barber and Giles Gordon, one contributor, Jeremy Brooks, put it like this:

The fog which obscures the minds of a large proportion
of the general public is not sufficiently allowed for . . .
They rely on Authority to tell them what to think, and
when two representatives of Authority, wearing identical
wigs and gowns and speaking with equal certainty, tell
them to think two utterly opposed things, their minds,
unable to cope with the conflict, simply shut up shop
for the day.

The fog cannot be as impenetrable or the shop so quick to
bring its shutters down as Mr Brooks believes, otherwise
we would have hung juries every week. The problems are
slightly different. The first is that jurors must face the fact
that not all these grandees in their court finery can be telling
the truth. The public is dimly aware that defence barristers
are merely mouthpieces for their clients and that their job is
to present not The Truth, but the truth as those clients relate
it. Even so, it is a sophisticated concept. There is not a lawyer
in the land who has not been asked how he or she can take
on a case if they believe in their hearts that the defendant is
guilty. There cannot be one who has not replied that it is
a fundamental right to have one's defence put forward as
professionally as possible, so long as one insists that it is
true. Yet this corner-stone of British legal practice is never
explained to juries, so far as I know. Maybe it would be
helpful if it were.

The second problem for the jury is that, having come to
terms with the idea that the Crown and the defence cannot
both be right merely because they look suave and talk BBC
English, they must decide which of them to believe. The
jurors' minds will ultimately be made up not solely according
to the evidence they have heard and the witnesses they have
seen. The final pitch for their votes will come in the closing
speeches. This is each barrister's final chance to plead his
or her case. Apart from the judge's summing-up, these

will be the last words the jurors take with them into the jury room.

THE CLOSING SPEECHES

Joanna Korner QC

It was 2.20 p.m. on the fifty-seventh day of the trial, 11 March 1997. Joanna Korner unfolded herself like an anglepoise lamp and turned herself sideways to face the jury. In American courts, the lawyers are free to roam about as theatrically as Peter Snow on election night. Here we are more restrained and our learned friends are confined to their places. This means there is little room for gesticulation, or they will knock their junior's wig off. Nor can they eyeball the jury at close quarters unless, like Mr Curran, they happen to be sitting next to it. So all the art must go into the words. And so as to ensure that the words sink in, members of the jury, rhetorical devices are employed to hold the jury's attention, such as saying 'members of the jury' at every opportunity.

Miss Korner began by reminding us that the anniversary of 24 March, the day of George Fraghistas's kidnap, was approaching. This was largely because a case due to last six weeks had been immensely prolonged by Mr Korkolis's decision to defend himself – which he had a perfect right to do. 'Professional and personal lives have been disrupted.' The length of the trial had had 'a tendency to emphasise the minutiae over the whole'. The role of the other defendants had been blurred and filtered through Korkolis, on whom the focus had concentrated. There had been too many subsidiary issues: George's gambling debts, the finances of his shipping company, the role of the police. The case was not about any of these, she said. What it was about was

whether George set out to defraud his family or whether
he was the victim of a carefully planned kidnap. Few of
the facts were in doubt. It was the explanation for them
that was in dispute.

Korkolis had put up a great many arguments and
allegations. 'When you're on a sticky losing wicket, if
you throw enough mud, some of it will stick,' said Miss
Korner, sending a humdinger of a mixed metaphor towards
the stumps. But we should concentrate on the evidence:
Zografos's fingerprint on the gun's ammunition; the saliva
traces on the balaclavas; the strand of George's hair found
in the leather mask; the syringes; the mattress in the kitchen.
There was the testimony of the police doctor who had
thought the handcuff wounds on George's wrists were
several days old, not self-inflicted just before the arrest.
Above all, there were those incriminating tapes, which
Korkolis claimed were deliberately recorded to make the
kidnap look authentic. 'Members of the jury, you may think
that if ever there was an explanation that defied credulity, it
was this one.'

There was 'not an iota of evidence' against the police,
despite Korkolis's promises to provide it. No one had once
suggested that the police had planted evidence. If there were
inconsistencies among the police witnesses, they were the
result of human frailty, not a deep-laid plot.

The next morning, Day 58, Miss Korner resumed vig-
orously, suggesting that the whole defence case had been
concocted *after* seeing the evidence disclosed by the Crown.
This seemed to me a very telling point. Apart from the
mentions of discussions in Belmarsh Prison, this was not
a notion that had occurred to the jury, since the rules on
prosecution disclosure had never been explained to us. It
suddenly became pretty plain, in retrospect, that Korkolis
& Co had had a chance to match their defence with great
cunning to what they knew would be the main thrust of the

Crown's argument. On top of that, Korkolis had been clever enough to make up some of his case on the hoof, responding to prosecution evidence produced in court and coming up with the odd ambush – introducing documents that not even the other defence counsel had seen, for example. He had also been quick enough to exploit one or two of the jury's questions with impressive dexterity.

'Members of the jury,' said Miss Korner, folding her arms in a confident manner that seemed to invite the agreement of all reasonable persons, 'doesn't this case stand or fall on what you have seen of the two protagonists?' Mr Korkolis used false identities: almost no document in the case would lead the police to him. And was his personality really that of a man taking orders (i.e. from George)?

Korkolis had told us he was a man continually taken advantage of by people whom he had trusted. Despite all this, 'He was prepared to place complete trust and confidence in a man he hardly knew.' He was a great recorder of business conversations. There were plenty of unexhibited tapes to prove it. 'Why, in view of his own history of being betrayed, did he not tape any of his conversations with Mr Fraghistas before and during those nine days?

'You have had an unrivalled opportunity, not given to many juries, to assess this defendant,' she went on. He was plainly an extremely gifted, highly intelligent man, with a remarkable memory. But he was a manipulative man. He was not on trial for his personality, or for being insulting: he was abrasive, to use a neutral or semi-neutral term. But he became more so in the face of difficult questions . . .

As for Zografos, one had to regret seeing a young man led into perdition. He was not stupid. But he became 'bound up' with Mr Korkolis.

She turned to Mereu and Moussaoui. 'Despite their builds, they are shadowy figures in this trial. They have always remained in the background. They were there as the bodyguards.' Yet the few brief words Mereu had said to the police when he was captured were important. Not only did he ask how many days in prison he might face; he also wanted the police to know he had been kind to George, and had given him cigarettes and fruit. Wasn't this one of the most significant remarks in the whole case?

'Sit back and consider the unchallenged evidence. Appearances can be deceptive ... Consider what the evidence discloses from men caught in the act who have mounted a defence out of desperation ...

'If the defence is to be believed, Mr Fraghistas was a man devoid of all moral scruple ... determined to put his family through hell on earth and to submit his mother to mental torture ...'

Joanna Korner sat down at eleven-twenty. She seemed to me to have done a thoroughly skilled job of pulling together the most important strands in her case and disentangling the red herrings. She made us cast our minds back to those distant weeks in the winter of '96 when George had occupied the witness box for a punishing eleven days and when his family and his business partner had taken his place one after another. Despite having endured all manner of insults from Korkolis, she had been dispassionate. And by giving the other three defendants only the most glancing attention, she had astutely left the spotlight on their leader, where it surely belonged, and who was now about to make his own closing speech.

Constantinos Korkolis

Shortly after midday, Korkolis stood up in the dock. He had not had his hair done for the big day. He looked as scrawny and scruffy as ever, a bravura act of gamesmanship which one secretly quite admired. But then came his opening words: 'I will be much longer than the prosecution.' Oh Lord. 'I am going to fight this case on the prosecution evidence.' He invited the judge and counsel to object to anything factually incorrect about the evidence he would mention.

There followed a very polished little address to the jury, the gist of which was: 'I didn't come here to be liked or disliked.' It was well judged. 'I am presented by the prosecution as a very intelligent man. I am flattered.' That is what he meant to say, but it sounded, rather sweetly, like 'I am fluttered'.

Then he got into his stride, accelerating with his customary unstoppability. Could we accept that a genuine kidnap victim would be fed on steak, prosciutto, and use a hair dryer? The whole Fraghistas family had lied. They were guilty of 'flagrant perjury. They tell the biggest lies ever said in this court'. They were 'ruthless persons, who think they have a divine right to do anything that serves their purpose – a *Dallas/Dynasty* family'. From 1991 to 1996 George had put down £8,400,000 worth of chips gambling at Crockford's; yet at the time of the kidnap he had just £63.81 in his current account at the Alpha Bank in the Haymarket.

'You think Mrs Fraghistas is a respectable woman? Ha. She is ruthless like the rest of them. For this family their biggest ordeal was to explain themselves to ordinary people like you, members of the jury.'

This was shrewd. He had been losing us, I felt, with his intemperate attacks. But the appeal to class solidarity probably made an impact with the jury. He proceeded at tremendous, relentless, mind-numbing speed, riffling through documents, criss-crossing the enormous area that the evidence had covered, sowing little landmines of doubt. Why would real kidnappers have chosen Hogan Mews given the proximity of neighbours? Why a cupboard with no lock? Why handcuffs with no key?

It was all familiar, over-familiar stuff. I spotted several

snoozers, including two prison officers. One of the barristers looked as though he was slipping into siesta mode but suddenly popped his eyes open wide and stared at me hard, daring me to doubt he ever closed his eyes except in thought. The judge and Mr Curran also seemed to keep looking at us in the most unnerving way. Was this just to make sure we were not nodding off or were they wondering what was going on in our pedestrian minds?

Under such close examination I began to feel like a part of some unwieldy, imperfect mechanism which could not be trusted to perform its function yet which, lamentably, was the only instrument at the court's disposal. They, the lawyers, were the trained marksmen. We, alas, were their blunderbuss.

Korkolis droned on doughtily. People in the public gallery came, gaped, dozed and went away. One of them fell off her chair. When Korkolis thoughtfully suggested that the jury might be tired and want a break, the judge agreed eagerly, adding that 'probably none of it is going in' . . .

'Draw near and give your attendance,' boomed the usher. 'God save the Queen.' It was the fifty-ninth day of the trial, 13 March, the anniversary of the Dunblane massacre. (Now there was a case it would have been hard to try dispassionately, had the killer lived.) Korkolis was still in mid-speech, reading out transcripts of the demand tapes at a gallop. The first eyelids in the public gallery closed at 10.35 a.m. It felt as though he were winnowing the evidence like corn, but finding only the chaff. Come to think of it, wasn't 'chaff' what the wartime RAF called those clouds of tinfoil which they released to confuse the enemy radar?

Korkolis spoke on, apparently without a note, remembering each police witness in extraordinary detail: names, ranks and contradictions in the evidence. He drew attention to the Public Interest Immunity orders that had blocked our knowing if and how the police had traced the mobile telephone calls.

After several false starts he started to wind up. 'In my life I never cease to be surprised at the depths to which people will lower themselves just to achieve their objectives . . . Can you fit any of us as criminals?' He swept his hand like an impresario towards his colleagues. 'Mr Hawkins was ready to travel in the North Pole to find if there was anything against me . . . Our picture does not fit to pictures of criminals. Is it possible by common sense to believe such a thing?

'The truth doesn't matter in some cases. When the police have gone so far, a conviction must be secured by any means. I came to this trial expecting everything to be fair . . . But Miss Korner was throwing mud.'

And then it was back to us, the target of his pleas. 'For me being tried by a jury is the best guarantee. A British jury. This is the pillar of your justice system: twelve independent people, sober in your vote, accountable only to your conscience. It's your view that counts. Your legislation is very wise in this. Just you will decide. Nobody else. Members of the jury: the only thing that counts – and we have hopes – is you. Your verdict, if not guilty, would be a strong message that a British jury cannot be cheated.' He ended this rather fine eulogy to the jury by reminding us that other victims of police fit-ups such as the Guildford Four would be looking to us.

It would have been quite an affecting coda to Korkolis's maiden closing speech, had he not then turned on Judge Goldstein with an ill-judged attack on the bench's integrity. 'Very wisely,' said Korkolis, 'senior judges in this land have said it is most undesirable for a judge to interrupt the evidence-in-chief of a defendant . . . The judge is not allowed to show any disbelief even if the defence is laughable . . . The judge can show his disbelief by facial expressions. It cannot be written down if it's by facial expressions. The other defendants and I turn our eyes to you for an impartial trial. So far as I am concerned you are not impartial in this trial.'

Mr Curran swivelled his eyes skywards. The usher looked astounded. The judge turned slightly pink and adopted his sunbathing lizard look, but let him finish. At twelve-thirty Korkolis sat down. Chatting casually afterwards, some jurors seemed amazed at Korkolis's nerve. 'It doesn't matter what the verdict is for the kidnapping,' said one. 'Surely he'll get twenty years for contempt.' While he was about it, why didn't Korkolis accuse the judge of having a numbered Swiss bank account of his own, joked another. Stuart's comment was succinct: 'If the galleys were still around he'd have the biggest effing oar in the boat.'

All the same, Korkolis had done what I presumed he had set out to do. Where Korner had seemed to clear the air and sort things out, Korkolis had succeeded in talking up a sandstorm. As Sir Louis Blom-Cooper QC, one of the jury system's most constant critics, told me when I interviewed him for this book: 'I always used to say, if you were a defending counsel, the prime duty you had was to throw up a smoke-screen in front of the jury. You weren't there to help them; indeed quite the contrary. Your best chance of getting your client off was to so confuse the jury that they'd say at the end of the day, "I can't say beyond reasonable doubt that this case has been proved." ' Sir Louis might have given this novice advocate a sardonic pat on the back.

Patrick Curran QC

Mr Curran did not waste a second before stressing to the jury that he represented Mr Zografos, not Mr Korkolis. He gave us one of his stares. Then he said forcefully, 'As regards the concluding part of Mr Korkolis's speech, insofar as I understood it I do not adopt it.' He backed this up with another stare.

Evidently he wanted to keep something of a gulf between his client and Korkolis. But not so great as to cause the entire defence case to topple into the void. We the jury had to consider one single question, said Mr Curran, steering a careful course: did we accept, so as to be sure, that George Fraghistas had told the truth, the whole truth and nothing but the truth? 'You have heard those words more than any other jury in this court this year.' If we were not sure, the verdict must be not guilty.

Miss Korner had asked the jury to consider whether George was the sort of man who could have helped send four innocent men to jail. 'If it's his neck or their neck,' said Mr Curran, 'he would, wouldn't he?'

The mention of Miss Korner brought home the fact that her place was empty. Her capable junior, Jeremy Benson, had apologised for her absence. She had had to appear elsewhere. But still, it seemed odd for her not to be there during her opponents' closing speeches, as though she were either over-confident of her case or careless of the outcome.

Mr Curran was scornful of Miss Korner's airy dismissal of the tax-dodging allegations made against George. Smiling and wagging his thumb at his vacant seat, he reminded us of the absurd moment when Mr Gale had asked George if he had laughed at something he said. George had said no and covered his mouth. But this was *a lie*, Mr Curran almost shouted. 'Those who can be trusted in small things can be trusted in large things.' It was an incident we all remembered – but an utterly piffling point. Was Mr Curran scraping the barrel?

His goal was clearly to discredit the Crown's principal witnesses: 'There is no case for reverence towards the Fraghistas family. [He misread our jury's very mixed feelings in that regard.] You as a jury are judges and judges cannot be respecters of persons. Each witness must be looked at coldly, making allowances for eccentricities, mercurial temperament . . .' We should be aware of George's 'acting ability': could someone who had been through such an 'unimaginably terrifying experience' have been so cool in the early telephone calls? Wouldn't he be a mental wreck after his ordeal? 'Do you know the feeling when you're particularly nervous? It's certainly a feeling familiar to members of the bar . . .'

This was needlessly ingratiating. We had listened again and again to the tapes of George talking to his secretary Wendy on the first day after his capture. Whatever Mr Curran maintained about their coolness, I for one had already decided there was a distinct quaver in George's tones.

When George had broken down in the witness box on being shown the leather mask, 'within seconds *the strong voice came back*,' Mr Curran bellowed. 'Are you prepared to rule out some dark and murky corners in that man's life?'

This was a plot that required great nerve. 'Does George have that kind of nerve? How many people do you know who would be prepared to risk £200,000 on the turn of a roulette wheel? This takes nerve, real nerve, doesn't it? This is a world where one day someone can be a millionaire, the next living in the Rose Court Hotel.' What if he'd gone to the well once too often to beg the family for funds?

One had to hand it to Mr Curran. He was really singing for his supper. He quoted Dickens (*Bleak House*), the Bible (George was Nicos's 'prodigal brother'), the Duke of Wellington ('If you believe that, you'll believe anything') and Lewis Carroll's Humpty Dumpty ('When *I* use a word, it means just what I choose it to mean – neither more nor less'). Some of these allusions, I fear, may not have hit their target, given the state of English education. Nevertheless, seeds of doubt had definitely taken root.

'Compare Zografos as a witness with George Fraghistas. Was he evasive? Was he arrogant? Was he rude? Was he argumentative?' (Would he add, in the famous words of the late Mr Justice Caulfield, referring to Jeffrey Archer's wife Mary, 'Has he not fragrance?') 'Young men can do foolish things; that's as old as the world. It's foolish to get involved in the schemes of older men . . . He's lazy. He doesn't stick to his books. But, oh, who should cast the first stone? [The Bible again.]

'We only have the weak weapon of the spoken word to defend Mr Zografos. I ask you to take up that weapon.'

Michael Corkery QC

As soon as Mr Curran sat down, Mr Corkery stood up. His wig was slightly askew and he had a watch-chain looped across his tummy. He wanted us, the jury, to know that we were the inheritors of an eight-hundred-year-old tradition that went back to Henry II. Juries then as now had to give due attention to the evidence, 'without fear or favour, without affection or ill-will . . . The facts are for you.'

This was flattery and flummery. Then came humour: 'We are all a bundle of prejudices. Remember W.C. Fields: "I'm not prejudiced: I hate everybody equally." ' And then – I am not sure what came then except that as the afternoon wound to a close, I recall Mr Corkery – who incidentally prosecuted the renegade Labour MP John Stonehouse – somewhat improbably saying, 'Some of you may have been brought up as I was on Kipling. Do you remember the *Just So Stories*?'

The next morning, Day 60, Mr Corkery took us on a little etymological excursion. The word 'kidnapping', he said, derived from the eighteenth-century 'kidnabbing', the practice of grabbing little boys and shipping them off to America as slaves. Then we got down to business. He told us that it was our question early in the trial, when the jury had sent up a note asking if Mr Fraghistas had any gambling debts, that had gone to the very heart of the case. The implication was that, but for us, the Crown would have skimmed past it. I dare say there was an outbreak of silent preening in the jury box.

Mr Corkery enjoyed his little jokes. How would George have gone about recruiting his henchmen? 'There is no job centre for kidnappers.' Ah, well, as Mr Korkolis had said, Greeks and Mediterraneans in general are more open than some to shady propositions. This was not meant to be a racist remark, but 'in some parts of the world you can't cross the road without crossing someone's palm with silver'. Fraghistas and Korkolis might have had quite a lot in common: a streak of quasi-dishonesty. 'George is a fake. If you have such a suspicion, your suspicion should be changed from a suspicion into a firm belief.'

It was unsettling to hear George being called a heartless liar by this pleasant, fluent man. (I noticed Mrs Fraghistas get up and leave the court, looking distressed.) If all the kidnap paraphernalia suggested a kidnap, Mr Corkery continued, it also suggested a completely bogus set-up, 'with everything you need to fake a kidnap – handcuffs, masks – you know the drill'.

He drew a heart-rending picture of Monsieur Mereu being strip-searched, hustled about by non-French-speaking coppers at Notting Hill, spending a night in the cells in his police-issue paper suit and blurting out: 'I was nice to George. I gave him cigarettes and fruit.' Miss Korner, he sneered, had had a nerve to say that this was the most telling remark in the whole case. (Well, wasn't it?)

Otherwise, of course, his client had remained almost completely silent. 'There is a right to maintain silence,' said Mr Corkery. 'Let us consider this historically. History is not a bad thing . . .' In Mr Corkery's mother's own lifetime a defendant was not even allowed into the witness box, for fear he might incriminate himself under the stiletto-like questions of clever barristers. Now the Criminal Justice and Public Order Act 1994 allowed the jury to draw such inferences as appear proper from the accused's silence. 'It is a matter for you whether you hold his silence against him.'

What were we to make of Mr Korkolis? 'Mr Korkolis feels everyone is against him. He is eccentric. But in this country we are accustomed to eccentrics. He has made lots of points – good, bad and indifferent. So many good points got lost in the fog of telling. Mr Korkolis is clearly wrong about some of his accusations. But he is what he is. Make allowances. He has chosen to defend himself. That is not easy in a foreign country. The court is a strange environment.'

As for Mereu, he had no criminal record. He was a Graeco-Roman wrestler, a lover of sport. His fingerprints were on *L'Equipe*, the French sports paper found at Hogan Mews. Anyway, he had had nothing to do with renting the house or the cars; he had made none of the telephone calls; he had not bought the Sten gun – 'sorry, ha ha, stungun . . .' George had said that one of the men in the garage looked like a giant. 'Who is this giant?' boomed Mr Corkery, leaning towards the dock. 'Any giants back there?' It was an absurd bit of pantomime.

The key words in the charges of kidnapping and false imprisonment were 'against his will', we were reminded. If George Fraghistas *might* have faked his own kidnap, it would not be against his will. 'Have the Crown made you sure and certain? We have made it clear to you, beyond peradventure, that there is the greatest doubt.' The same three words applied to the count of false imprisonment: against his will. If Fraghistas *might* have faked it, the verdict would have to be not guilty.

Mr Corkery invited the jury to send Monsieur Mereu back to France as he had arrived in this country, a man without a blemish on his character.

David Owen Thomas QC

'Words, words, words, words. Is that all you blighters can do?' From Kipling we had moved on to Shaw; but it was a good beginning and summed up the jury's feelings very satisfyingly. 'You, members of the jury, have already sat in this courtroom for half as long again as Noah was sloshing about in the Ark.' This was an excellent point: we were setting new, positively biblical endurance records. Go on, Mr Owen Thomas.

Mr Owen Thomas reminded us we must not 'dump' all our verdicts together, something which had indeed been worrying us. He said he had no complaints about Detective Sergeant Hawkins. (Mr Hawkins's face looked not a jot less stony: it must be hard for police officers to sit through this sort of thing trial after trial and hear themselves labelled as incompetents and perjurers.) 'It is very bad advocacy to repeat things,' he went on, and the jury's faces lit up with hope. He peered amiably at us over his half-moon spectacles, blinking like the Dormouse at the Mad-Hatter's tea party. 'In order to liven things up, I have tried throughout this trial to find a different way of saying "No questions" from time to time . . .' Loud laughter drowned the rest of the sentence. Small furry models of Mr Owen Thomas should be sold to tourists at the entrance of the Old Bailey.

There were some lively moments. He adopted a West Country burr to mock the suggestion that the city was a better place for a kidnap hideaway than the country, ooh-arrr. He sought our sympathy for Moussaoui, banged up in a London police station, by asking us to imagine ourselves imprisoned in Spain by those chaps with hats that turn up at the front which they don't wear any more. He scored with the jury by saying that our proposed experiment with the car boot *should* have been carried out – by the Crown and before the trial began. Losing his thread at one point, he said, 'I

know you are sufficiently alert to spot any deliberate – I
mean accidental – mistakes I make ... There, I nearly made
another one: Zográfos, not Zógrafos: I keep making him a
Russian.'

One reason why he had not put Mr Moussaoui into the
box was that he had seen Mr Korkolis being 'badgered about'
by Miss Korner under cross-examination. He reminded us of
one dispute: 'She would not let go of the bone. It was like
having an Alsatian at one end and a terrier at the other.
Yet the following morning the Alsatian sat down, put out
its paw and apologised.'

In short, it was all knockabout stuff. The judge scribbled
away placidly – perhaps he was preparing his summing-up.
He raised his eyes when Mr Owen Thomas said, 'In March
1966 ... Did I say 1966 ...?' and the judge muttered, 'It
just seems like that.'

It was around three o'clock when Mr Owen Thomas
dropped anchor. 'Members of the jury, I have finished.
When you retire, do please remember the points which I
and Mr Corkery have made, and consider the case against
each accused quite separately. Remember where the burden
of proof lies. If it may be that George Fraghistas entered
into this matter knowing full well what it was all about,
you cannot convict.' He sat down.

The judge beamed. 'Members of the jury: another mile-
stone is reached.'

There was only his summing-up to come. We took an illicit
photograph of ourselves back in the jury room. 'Thumbs
up or down,' I suggested jovially. The others were not
amused.

I tried to pull together in my mind the four very different
closing speeches we had heard. One thing stuck out: the
only really successful defence tactic had been to impugn
the honesty of George and his evidence – given so many
months ago we had almost forgotten what he looked like.

Nevertheless, doubts there were and, as we had repeatedly been reminded by defence counsel, we had to be sure beyond reasonable doubt.

But it was significant that no one besides Korkolis had seriously questioned the honesty of either the police or the Fraghistas family. And I was left with several insoluble conundrums. First, if the kidnap had been faked, why was it necessary for George to have *four* accomplices when he could almost have managed it on his own? Second, once the gang knew the police were on to them, why didn't the wily George order them all to make a run for it, leaving him to explain that he had 'escaped'? Third, would the family really have been so forgiving and so obsessed with their good name as to give evidence on George's behalf if they knew he was to blame? Finally, if George really was the ringleader and knew everything that had gone on, why on earth didn't he give watertight evidence? He need never have mentioned the 'helium' voice changer; he could have got over the unlockable cupboard door problem by saying he knew there was someone sleeping outside it; he could have claimed to have been moved to other rooms in Hogan Mews, just in case he had left fingerprints there. No, the conspiracy theory just did not make sense. And yet, and yet . . .

THE SUMMING-UP

We were approaching the climax of the trial. Very soon now the jury would be on its own and everything would turn on us. Once we were sent out, nothing anyone outside the jury room could do could alter our minds or gainsay our decision. We were the ultimate fact-finders in this case. The majesty of the law was about to abdicate and cede the throne to the man on the Clapham omnibus. It was a mad notion, an awesome act of faith in the reasonableness of the common man and woman. Now there was only the judge to give us a last chance to make sense of it all and avoid some catastrophic blunder.

The accused, their guards and their interpreters peered over the edge of the dock looking like the relics of a Chinese beheading. There was an item of housekeeping: a last-minute exhibit was given an official number – 103. It was a photograph of the ground-floor lavatory window at Hogan Mews, from which the defence claimed a really determined George Fraghistas might have escaped, had he not been implicated in his own kidnap. It looked barely big enough for a child chimney sweep to fit through.

The judge launched his summing-up with a great outburst of flattery: 'I agree with Mr Korkolis: you are the backbone of the British justice system . . . Everyone in this courtroom has noticed the intelligence and perspicacity of the jury.' Even Mr Korkolis, who had questioned the integrity of almost everyone else involved, had said he was satisfied with the fairness of the jury.

We must bring an open mind and common sense to bear 'so as to follow a path through the trees', he went on. 'You will accept my directions as regards the law. But you and you alone are the judges of the facts. I am not the thirteenth juror . . . I am only going to remind you of a minute portion of the hundreds of hours of evidence you have heard – much of it irrelevant.'

The judge sounded measured and reassuring, working his way steadily through a large ring-binder containing his hand-written notes of the trial. One felt like a horse that had been indifferently ridden and even mistreated for the past four months, suddenly in the hands of an expert horseman.

He spent time explaining how the burden of proof lay solely with the Crown, with such thoroughness that one began to wonder how it is that an English jury ever returns a guilty verdict. He told us what we might infer from a defendant's silence. He told us (again) to apply our common sense. He allowed himself a lighthearted reflection: 'When this case is long over and memory fades, we will remember Mrs Fraghistas's remark: "My husband played poker with half of Athens." '

Then he picked his way back along the tortuous route we had travelled together, mapping its twists and turns. 'This case,' he said, 'is all about money and greed. Every approach . . . brings you back to the same starting point: are you satisfied so that you are sure that George Fraghistas was not involved?

'The Old Bailey has heard in its history some of the greatest liars that ever existed. The defence says George was up there with them, that he was one of the great hypocrites of all time.' He pretended to love his family but in reality he was prepared to extort money from them and torture his mother. Most despicable of all, he had sold his partners down the river.

'George must have been a very good actor. Remember how the police said he behaved on his release, all those kisses. There was the occasional tear, the refusal to discuss his private money, a collapse. Was this all part and parcel of the act?' In court, 'Was George caught out in any obvious lie?'

The contradictions were laid out before us, with meticulous fairness. On the one hand, on the other: 'You must decide.' What did Mereu's famous remark about cigarettes and fruit mean? 'It is entirely a matter for you.' (Every time he said 'It is entirely a matter for you' I felt the hair on the back of my neck prickle with alarm: the buck was about to stop – with us.) We should not allow ourselves to be sidetracked by small anomalies but concentrate on the big issues.

'Finally,' he said, 'there are one or two matters you may find odd about this case. You may think they cry out for consideration.' There was the matter of the syringes and 'all that talk about lethal injections'. There was the puzzle of why the men had not made a run for it once they knew the police were closing in. There were those incriminating tapes. What did it all mean? It was, of course, for us to decide.

Then we were given our final instructions. We had already picked a foreman, so that was done. We must now retire to consider our verdict – our unanimous verdict. We should not even contemplate a majority verdict until he told us we might. 'You must not feel under any pressure at all. If there is no verdict tomorrow, you will go home.' (Ah, so there would be no luxury hotel for Bob after all.)

And that, members of the jury, was that. The ushers solemnly swore to keep us secluded from the world in a 'private and convenient place'. We gathered armfuls of binders and were led back to our cheerless jury room. Mobile phones were confiscated. We were shown the bell which was our only link to the outside world. We were to ring it to order food and drinks, to ask for an exhibit, to send a note to the judge and, once the moment came, to let the usher know we had reached our verdicts. Then the ushers withdrew and locked the door.

DELIBERATION

Friday 21 March. We were on our own. For about ten minutes we did our best to avoid confronting the fact. We passed around sweets, lit cigarettes, made frivolous remarks. I suppose we were mildly hysterical. We agreed that we would start only when we had all finished our coffees. We drank very slowly.

Trial by Jury

The law says that jurors may never tell a soul what they discussed in the jury room during their deliberations and I do not propose to break it. However, I think it is both legitimate and possibly useful to describe what our confinement was like and what we did, as opposed to what we said, during the three and a half days that we were out.

There is no guidance as to how juries should reach a verdict. They must make up the rules as they go along. Since the deliberations are entirely secret, there is literally nothing to stop the decision being made on the toss of a coin. I was foreman, so it was up to me to suggest how we might proceed. Stuart and I swapped places so that I was now at the head of the table, with the window behind me. First of all, we agreed that whoever was talking should try to address their remarks through the chair and should be allowed to speak without interruption. And no one would be allowed to stay totally silent. That was easy enough.

Then we had to tackle the problem of dealing with four different defendants, each with three charges against him. We thought the sensible thing would be to discuss the case in general and plough through whatever bits of evidence people were concerned about before taking each defendant one by one and charge by charge.

I was not keen to have an outright vote at this early stage. I wanted no one to be committed to a view he or she would later feel bound to defend, an approach which, I have since learned, is known as verdict-driven deliberation: you identify the minority, then the rest of the jury concentrate on persuading them to change their minds. Not only might such a procedure lead to bullying, I thought. It could easily provoke exactly the kind of stubbornness one would want to avoid.

Evidence-driven deliberation, by contrast, is what we planned to do: going back over all the main points made by the Crown and the defence, before eventually focusing on the accused and the indictments. All the same, I felt it would help to get us going if we could gauge, very roughly, which way each of us was leaning: however cautiously, was it towards guilty, towards not guilty or in neither direction at this stage? We went round the table. All I can say is that the outcome was absolutely inconclusive. In other words, there was a lot of work for everyone to do. For the rest of that Friday we were hard at it.

No two jury deliberations can be the same. But the accounts in *Members of the Jury* suggest that there are some common features. Anthony Barker, for example, found jurors reluctant to give even a provisional view until they had heard what others thought. He noted a strong feeling that the jury wanted to prolong the discussion to let people know they had done their duty fully and so as 'to get their psychological money's worth from being on the jury'. He also wrote about the difficulties presented by 'the binary system of British justice', where everything seemed to boil down to 'Did he or didn't he?'

The phrase 'beyond reasonable doubt' was not an easy idea for many people to grasp. As John Mellors said in the same book: 'There must be reasonable doubt if you can construct another theory' for what happened – which is exactly what the defence normally sets out to do. (I was struck with a related thought: our system allows majority verdicts, yet a majority verdict is one which by definition has raised a reasonable doubt ... 'I'm not asking anyone to accept it,' argues the 8th Juror in the most famous of all jury dramas, Reginald Rose's *Twelve Angry Men*. 'I'm just saying that it's possible.')

Another ex-juror, Harry Cohen, reflected on the reluctance of some jurors to reach a judgement. One of the strongest reasons for people wanting to get off jury service, he found, was 'a deep-rooted feeling of inadequacy' and 'resentment that they were being forced to ... decide whether a man should go to prison or remain free'. He summed up their feelings as 'It shouldn't be left to the likes of us to make decisions of this kind.' Or as the 6th Juror in *Twelve Angry Men* puts it, 'I'm not used to supposing. I'm just a working man. My boss does the supposing.'

Anthony Barker also mentioned a dilemma which I had to cope with myself. He did not want to be chosen foreman 'because he might be expected by the others to be only an impartial chairman and counter of heads, whereas I wanted to be in on any arguments'. I reasoned that while the foreman should be impartial so far as conducting the discussion was concerned, he was as entitled to express his view as the next juror – indeed was obliged to do so, while making it clear that his view carried no more weight than anybody else's.

That evening we were sent home for the weekend, button-lipped, verdictless and unusually despondent.

We met again in Jury Room J on Monday morning. It was 24 March – the anniversary of George Fraghistas's alleged kidnap. We had all found it impossible not to brood about the trial over the weekend. I had gone so far as to spend Sunday morning typing out a detailed checklist of points in the Crown's favour, set against those in the defence's. My plan had been to print out a copy for each of my colleagues, but I became worried that this might be some sort of breach of the rules. What *were* the rules for a jury sent home for the weekend in mid-deliberation? I rang a friend who is a judge. The minute I mentioned the word 'jury' he snapped as tight-shut as an oyster. He simply could not talk to me about anything to do with a deliberating jury, however innocuous – and he put the phone down. I decided not to take my list into court. I memorised it instead.

Outside the sun shone. Inside, our room had now become thoroughly squalid. No cleaners would be allowed in until we had reached our verdicts. The ashtrays were full. The wastepaper baskets spilt over with plastic cups and empty Coke cans. Binders rose in heaps all over the table and floor. A century or so earlier we might have been starved into hastening our verdicts. Things were not much better now. One might have thought the tax-payer would lay on a decent lunch for twelve citizens selflessly performing their public duty. Not a bit of it. The only available victuals were sandwiches fetched from the jury restaurant by the ushers, for which we had to pay cash in advance. One day there were no cheese-and-pickle sarnies, another no apples. They even ran out of milk.

Our only proper break was a ten-minute stroll inside the high walls of a yard at the rear of the Old Bailey where the Sheriff of London parks his Rolls. Guarded by two ushers, we walked around in a glum circle, like exercising prisoners.

At the end of the day we were taken back into the courtroom. I watched the faces as I told the judge that we had not reached a verdict. Joanna Korner looked astonished. The defence counsel appeared relieved. I did not look at the men in the dock.

Tuesday: somehow we remained good-tempered. The excitement of our first day's deliberations had quite vanished. The discussion was extraordinarily tiring. We went back over certain items of evidence again and again, with a patience I think we all found surprising. Nerves frayed but did not snap. No one said, oh to hell with it, let's take a vote and get out of here. There was an unspoken agreement that the moment had not yet arrived.

On Wednesday we ate slices of my daughter's twenty-first birthday cake, drank proper coffee from the thermoses we had learned to bring in with us, and sent for a new exhibit to examine. By now we had been instructed by the judge that we could return a majority verdict. Oddly enough, that did not really relieve the pressure. I think by this time we had all inwardly decided that we owed it to everyone concerned, not least ourselves, to try to be unanimous. That morning we experienced our first – and only – outbreak of inter-juror anger. There were heated words. Quite soon, however, tempers cooled and those concerned apologised to each other.

We sent a question in to the judge, seeking clarification about the exact meaning of the indictments. He was at lunch. We were allowed to parade around the yard while we awaited his answer. Just after two o'clock we were hustled back into the courtroom where to our relief the judge spelt out exactly what we wanted to know.

We returned to our room. There was no further conversation. By a sort of murmured accord we agreed to vote. Very solemnly I went round the table asking each juror in turn for his or her verdict on each of the three indictments against each of the four defendants. They answered quietly, almost breathlessly. The whole procedure must have taken a quarter of an hour at least. Eventually, everyone had spoken. After deliberating for fifteen hours and fifty-five minutes we were unanimous on every count.

We sat back in silence, overawed by what had just occurred. Then the tension suddenly ebbed. Someone joked that we should withhold our decision and pretend to be deadlocked until after Easter, so that we could earn a few extra quid. We spent a few moments planning what to do after the verdict – drinks at McGovern's across the road. We agreed, also unanimously, that we should invite Roy the usher. We had already clubbed together to buy him a present. I wrote a note to the judge, saying that we had reached our verdicts, and asked someone to press the bell.

THE VERDICT

Shortly after three in the afternoon, we entered the jury box in Court 5 for the last time, with our hearts pounding. The clerk of the court was on her feet, turned sideways in her place to look directly at me. Behind and above her, the judge looked narrowly down at us. I was asked to stand.

Twelve times Sarah stared hard into my eyes and asked me for our verdict, prisoner by prisoner, count by count. Twelve times I stared back and heard my answer – 'Guilty' – ring eerily around the court, silent but for the sound of George Fraghistas sobbing on his mother's shoulder.

And were these the verdicts of us all?

They were.

Once the verdicts were delivered, the atmosphere changed dramatically. The moment of truth for a jury that has delivered a guilty verdict is when the prosecuting counsel tells the court about the defendant's antecedents – the 'previous' which under English law is normally hidden from the jury and had certainly been kept from us. Were we right? Was Korkolis really the criminal that we had decided, beyond reasonable doubt, he was?

Joanna Korner got lankily to her feet and put the missing bits of the jigsaw into place. Constantinos Korkolis was not the innocent businessman he had tried to lead us to believe. He was not the dupe of another man's betrayal. He had a long and murky criminal record in his home country.

The judge intervened. The jury, he said ringingly, had been the victims of a monstrous deception about Korkolis's true character. It was a moment of the most intense relief, a vindication. We could breathe again.

Even the defence barristers suddenly sounded matter-of-fact about their clients' guilt, merely asking for their previously unblemished records to be reflected in the sentences. But My Lord was in no mood for leniency. He looked thunderous. The transfiguration was extraordinary. Gone was the tolerant and courteous figure, joking about the courtroom being hot enough to grow grapes in. He addressed the four prisoners with a sudden, steely ferocity, in tones of pent-up condemnation. 'The crime of kidnapping for ransom is, after murder, the vilest, foulest crime known to the English criminal law . . . None of you can expect any mercy whatsoever.'

He stared hard at Korkolis. 'You are probably the most evil and dreadful man I have ever met. I have the gravest doubts whether Mr Fraghistas would ever have got out of this alive.' The defendants deserved no mercy, he said chillingly. He would show them none.

He sentenced Korkolis to prison for twenty-five years. It was the longest sentence ever imposed for such a crime in this country. The other three men would each serve sixteen.

'*Take them down!*'

The drama that had engrossed us for so long had reached its climax. The seriousness of our role had been underlined by the severity of the sentences. Our part was now complete. Again there was that sense of an enormous tension suddenly released.

Judge Goldstein put off his frown. He turned to the jury. He was his benign lordship once again. He thanked us warmly, saying that what we had done was overwhelmingly worthwhile. Then he gave us a reward for our diligence: it was a fifteen-year exemption from having to do jury service again. We smiled back at him, feeling proud and pleased. Some of the jurors, I think, might have been just as happy with a shorter sentence. Fifteen years seemed a long time to wait.

THE DOUGHTY DOZEN

The group of strangers who sat down next to each other in an Old Bailey courtroom one day in November 1996 might not have struck an observer as the epitome of 'twelve good men and true'. They would have looked a pretty unimpressive lot: ill-at-ease, slightly dazed, a good deal more cowed than the four men in the dock. They did not have many A-levels among them. One or two had never passed an exam in their lives. They were there to perform an extremely demanding task. You would not have entrusted it to any single member of this group in a million years.

On-duty, they did their best to take in hundreds of hours and hundreds of thousands of words of complicated, contradictory evidence. They suppressed yawns, sucked sweets and watched the courtroom clock. Off-duty, the men talked about football and played cards. The women did quizzes in magazines and discussed the merits of leather sofas. The smokers got up the non-smokers' noses. The men got up the women's. Yet they all seemed to rub along rather well together. You could even say, were you to insist, that they *bonded*.

Surprisingly quickly, it was no longer a group of a dozen strangers. It was a jury: Judge Goldstein's, Mr Korkolis's and Roy the usher's jury. During the months that followed it began to seem that this ungainly twelve-headed creature operated really rather well. Everyone in some way made a contribution: the young GPO sorter, Sophie, who proved a whiz at Greek names; Eddie the Anglo-Spaniard who understood mobile-phone technology; Anna, our London-born Italian, who knew about Mediterranean family loyalties; Bob the postman who was hot on cars; Rangers-supporting Stuart who had a remarkable knowledge of previous trials. We had a trained psychologist among us, which was a bonus.

And when we wanted to take a look at a Rover just like the kidnappers' which happened to be parked outside the jury room window one day, we had a plane-spotter with a pair of binoculars in a carrier bag.

The body that eventually decided to find Constantinos Korkolis and his fellow-defendants guilty was not a voting panel of twelve individuals. It was an English jury. Its character was formed by class, culture, nationality, education, experience, prejudice, the judge, the court, the case and a host of other influences – but the most important of these was simply luck.

Researchers beware. A jury is a random construct with a dynamic of its own, 'a strange potion' as a Labour QC once told the House of Commons. No two juries can be the same. Yet for the system to function we have to assume that every jury *is* the same. Because the jury is not so much a tool, as an idea. It is an admirable idea. But it will continue to work only so long as we continue to have faith in it.

AFTERMATH

It was fairly late in the evening when the last juror left McGovern's. Some of us overshot our stations on the way home. We had exchanged addresses, vowed to keep in touch, talked about a grand reunion. Apparently a lot of juries behave like this after a long trial.

During the following summer we telephoned each other quite frequently. I had a card from Terrie in Spain. Pat faxed from Auckland, where she was busy looking for a house. Magnus rang to say that by an extraordinary coincidence one of his fellow package tourists on a visit to Moscow had been Commander Niall Mulvihill, head of Scotland Yard's Organised Crime Group and Laurie Vanner's boss. He knew all about our case, and described Korkolis as a sociopath. Stuart telephoned with his opinion of the new government, whom he thought a load of right plonkers.

Sophie and I had lunch together when she had a day off from her sorting office. Like the rest of us, she was still excited about the trial. 'I do miss it,' she said. 'It was the most interesting experience of my life. I'd love to do it again.' She had two improvements to suggest. First, judges should make it clear at the outset not only that juries may take notes but that they *should* do. Second, counsel should explain the purpose of a particular line of questioning or the calling of a particular witness *before* they embark on it: then jurors would know what to listen out for.

Sophie told me that some time after the trial she had gone along to George Fraghistas's offices in Albemarle Street. She did not know exactly why she went except that she wanted to know that George was all right. She had stood outside the office but had not known what to do next. So she didn't go in, and after a while she left. When I met George some weeks later and told him this story he was immensely touched.

I did not visit Albemarle Street. But I did re-visit Hogan Mews. This time I noticed that Westway, the elevated extension of the M40 into central London, was no more than a couple of hundred yards away from the mews. The traffic emitted a low, unceasing roar even at four o'clock in the afternoon: it would have blanketed any but the loudest cries from a frightened man imprisoned in a windowless room.

Then I drove from the mews to Lanark Road, timing myself. Despite the speed bumps and the beginnings of the rush-hour, the journey took me just over four minutes door to door. To those unfamiliar with the kidnapper's rule-book, this might seem eerily close. It did to me. It gave me a moment's post-verdict anxiety. True, Hizbollah hid hostages like Terry Waite and John McCarthy right in the heart of Beirut, a busy modern city being the best kind of haystack in which to conceal a needle. But still, a mere four-minutes' drive from seizure to incarceration struck me as unprecedentedly cheeky.

DCI Laurie Vanner, a man with huge experience of this kind of crime, eventually set my mind at rest. Hogan Mews was the ideal place to hide George Fraghistas, he explained. The most dangerous time for kidnappers is when they are transporting their victim to wherever he is to be held. They are vulnerable to traffic accidents or a police search. The captive might shout or kick to attract the attention of passers-by, or even escape. The shorter the time he is in motion, the better. These people, I gathered, had known what they were doing.

I was also curious to take a look at the Rose Court Hotel, that hotbed of gambling Greeks where Thanassis Zografos had fallen into bad company. So one day I did.

The Rose Court Hotel was not quite the raffish place I had imagined. It is one of those dispiriting establishments that cluster around Paddington Station offering succour to the friendless and far-from-home. There are whole Victorian terraces of them, their improbably grand names proclaimed in nasty italic lettering. The Rose Court has chosen a cerise typeface with which to disfigure its white-painted façade. It overlooks a small, oblong square shaded in summer by plane trees. There is an air of seedy gentility about the whole area.

A tousle-haired man eyed me impassively from the reception desk and nodded when I asked if I could look around. Once upon a time this would have been Zografos's job. There was nothing much to see. The place felt as though it were striving for anonymity: two small reception rooms, claustrophobically gloomy, a bar, a narrow staircase leading up to the bedrooms. The ambience was 1950s provincial. Listening to Zografos describing the hotel as a home-from-home for expatriate Greeks, I had pictured something cheerier. I had imagined I would have an ouzo in the smoky, taverna-style bar, and chat up one or two of the long-term guests over a dish of mezze. Instead the place was deathly quiet.

I wondered if the Rose Court clients had followed the trial in their newspapers. The Greek press had been full of the story. And it wasn't over yet. A fifth man had been charged with taking part in the kidnap of George Fraghistas: Kyriakos Pantelides, the mysterious figure who had been on bail during our trial and whose voice we had heard on Korkolis's secret tapes. His trial was coming up soon. Kate and I arranged to go together.

THE VIEW FROM THE GALLERY

The Pantelides trial was listed for 28 July. There are two entrances to the public galleries at the Old Bailey. The one to which tourists are directed is in the newer part of the building. The Pantelides case was to be heard in one of the Edwardian courtrooms, Court 3, so we had to go in by a side-door on Newgate Street, where the notorious prison once stood. On the pavement outside a score of unhappy-looking people were waiting for the door to open at ten o'clock. We were body-searched on the way in and warned that no one could bring a mobile phone or tape recorder into the court. There was nowhere to leave such a thing, which meant at least one perplexed visitor being turned away. I told her that for the price of a coffee she might be able to leave it at Shamus O'Donnell's pub across the road – information which the security people could just as easily have given her themselves, though of course they never do.

I climbed six gloomy flights of stairs up to the waiting room. It was a dispiriting place: a large, high-ceilinged room, bare except for two small leatherette settees, a table and a single ashtray. White-tiled walls and, in one corner, an old-fashioned sink the size of a horse trough (which has since been removed) gave the place an air of menace. It made me think of a Third World police station, where the sink might have some hideous role in interrogations and the tiles could easily be mopped clean of blood. This impression grew as the morning wore on and the room filled up. Since there was sitting room for only six people, the rest sat, squatted, or lay on the floor, smoking.

What appeared to be the population of an entire Turkish-Cypriot village took up most of the space. There were eighteen of them: short-legged moustachioed men, several old women in black headscarves, and a pair of sharp-faced young girls who seemed to be the only fluent English speakers among them. There were also two Spaniards, two Greeks and a Chinese youth. Later this disconsolate crowd was joined by some ostentatiously British Brits: an earringed man with a shaved head, a scar-faced girl with a terrifying cough who never stopped smoking and a gigantic middle-aged Hell's Angel with a blond pigtail and tattooed arms.

The Turks were waiting for a verdict. There was a noisy mêlée at the security guards' desk when it was discovered that none of them would be let in to court unless they had their passports with them. Passports? Yes, said the guard gruffly and refused to explain why. One of the girls burst into tears.

Later there was another commotion. The earringed tough, the scar-faced girl and the Hell's Angel had been joined by an angry-looking woman and two fat, crop-haired teenage boys. They all filed in to the Court 2 gallery where I was told a young man was being tried for murder. Ten minutes later the Hell's Angel was escorted forcefully out of Court 2 leaning on the woman. He was alternately sobbing and shouting incoherently about the 'poor fucking little bastard' and 'this fucking court' and 'all the fucking lies'. He was prodded towards the street, roaring like a lion.

Another five minutes passed while the Turkish-Cypriots gossiped excitedly about what they had just seen. Then the repellent teenagers were hauled out of the gallery too. A police officer propelled them towards the door and told them that if they did whatever they had done again they would not be allowed back in court ever. As it was they were banned for the rest of the day. Later on I saw the whole gang of them sitting outside a nearby pub, their table tottering with empty pint glasses and full ashtrays.

Eventually Kate and I were allowed to slip into the Court 3 gallery. The courtroom was restful and pretty after the disagreeableness outside. It had a graceful vaulted roof with arched skylights that let in the July sunshine. It was odd to be sitting in court as mere spectators. There were several familiar figures below us lolling on oak pews upholstered in green leather, waiting for the judge. Jeremy Benson, Miss Korner's junior, was leading for the Crown. Near him was Martin Hawkins. George Fraghistas was there too. In the well of the court sat our old friend Roy the usher. They all looked up at Kate and me and Roy asked cheerily how we were. It was quite like old times. Then he commanded everyone to be upstanding in court and in came the judge: it was Simon Goldstein. Roy told us later that His Lordship had winked at us, though it must have been so judicious a wink that neither of us spotted it.

The defendant, Kyriakos Pantelides, was led into the dock and sat in a chair immediately below us. All we could see was a tanned bald head with about twenty hairs strung across it, wire-framed specs, a squashy nose and the outline of a thin Arthur English moustache beneath it. He wore a grey suit and polished black shoes. The woman with blowsy orange hair and silver fingernails slumped in a corner of the court was his wife. The judge agreed to prolong Pantelides' bail on sureties of £300,000 while the trial lasted – so long as someone went and checked that the sureties had indeed been lodged.

The jury panel marched in and were called into the box by name. Kate and I examined them with professional curiosity. None of them made any attempt to be excused. They were a much younger lot than we had been. Only one of them, a man in blazer and tie, was over thirty, I guessed. He would probably be the foreman. The rest were a clean-cut lot who looked only slightly apprehensive, swore their oaths by Almighty God and sat bolt upright in their antique, cruelly narrow seats. As with us there were six men and six women, though unlike us one of these was a young black girl in a brimless leather hat which she wore every day of the trial. One juror, a handsome young man, asked the usher to guide him through the oath as he had trouble reading. The red-faced clerk, who seemed to be suffering from the same affliction, stumbled abominably as he read the indictment.

Mr Benson presented the case against Mr Pantelides. It was bizarre to hear the long, complex story of the Fraghistas kidnap, which had cost us so many weeks to unravel, briskly and dispassionately encapsulated into a morning's narrative. It was clear the Crown was going to rely chiefly on those two tapes of conversations with Pantelides that Korkolis had secretly recorded. 'Members of the jury,' said Mr Benson, 'you may be wondering what happened to the other four men. They were convicted . . .'

George took the stand. It was as though we had gone on to fast rewind. There he was again, dark-suited, white-shirted, clutching his mineral water bottle, just as he had done eight months earlier. Mr Benson asked him about what happened at the Lanark Road car-park at about six o'clock on the evening of Sunday 24 March 1996. George began to re-tell his story, how he had parked his car and was getting out of it when – he faltered. He turned away from the court and fell silent. His body began heaving with suppressed sobs. There was a long pause during which no one in court said a word. Then a halt was called to the proceedings. The jury was sent out. What would they make of this, I wondered. It was exactly the same as when we had seen George confronted with the leather hood. They could have only the sketchiest idea of the double ordeal he had already been through. The judge was concerned that they should be put in the picture.

Surprisingly, that was the last they heard from George. From then on he was present merely as a spectator: the judge and both counsel rather suddenly agreed that his testimony was not really necessary. The polished young barrister acting for Mr Pantelides, Mr Fulford, explained to the jury that thanks to their decision, 'this unfortunate gentleman will not have to go through the horror of living through his experiences again'.

Without the victim's evidence, the rest of this short four-day trial seemed to lack a centre of gravity: it was not so much *Hamlet* without the prince as *Macbeth* without Duncan. When Jeremy Benson asked DS Hawkins to help him read the tape transcripts ('Can I ask you to play the part of Mr Korkolis? And I will be Mr Pantelides'), the proceedings took on a surreal air. Pantelides warned Korkolis in the middle of the kidnap that 'the tall hats have been involved'. He was asked by Korkolis at one point whether he was 'in a hurry to get the suitcase with the money'. The jury must have been thoroughly perplexed. What was a 67-year-old Greek-Cypriot dressmaker of unblemished character doing having such conversations with a man he suspected of being the kidnapper of George Fraghistas? It was all tremendously confusing.

After barely an hour's deliberation, the jury found the defendant not guilty. The oldest of the jurors was, as I had anticipated, the foreman. He and his colleagues looked quite confident that they had reached the right decision. I was not altogether surprised. Mr Fulford's closing speech had been persuasive. While he admitted that Mr Pantelides' failure to alert the police of what he knew about the kidnap had been ignominious, there were serious doubts about his being a participant in the plot itself. Those doubts were evidently enough to persuade the jury that they could not be sure of the defendant's guilt. Only an hour earlier the judge had summed up with immaculate fairness, stressing that word, '*sure*', just as he had with us. It had echoed loudly in my own head as I went off to have a coffee and await the verdict. I wasn't sure I would have been sure of the defendant's complicity.

George Fraghistas met me outside to say goodbye: he was off back to Athens the next day. Was he disappointed? He shrugged. Perhaps the evidence *was* too slight and muddling. Besides, the man had already endured three weeks in prison as well as many months on bail.

We shook hands. The next time I was likely to see him would be at Korkolis's appeal hearing, whenever that was likely to be. George would not need to be involved, except as a spectator. Nevertheless, he thought he would want to be there, perhaps to complete the catharsis. It was sobering to reflect that the drama into which he had been pitched on a quiet Sunday evening back in March nearly a year and half earlier was not over yet.

I strolled along Fleet Street and down to the Embankment. Every other person I passed seemed to be a tourist. It was the last week of July. The concentration of foreigners was nearly as remarkable as at the Old Bailey – where that day's trials had included the usual numbers of African, Mediterranean, Asian and East European names. How many eager sightseers, I wondered, visited the most famous courthouse in the world only to discover a compatriot of theirs sitting hauntedly in the dock, charged with some unspeakable crime? That would give a certain *frisson* to their London sojourn.

The woebegone Turkish-Cypriots whom I had encountered in the public-gallery waiting room had spent three days in that dismal place while the jury was out. I had got into conversation with a white-haired old man who could barely speak English. We were sharing an ashtray. He told me that the case concerned a murder. And what was his relationship to the defendant, I asked. 'He is my grandson,' he said sadly. I spoke to one of the young girls. She had spent some of the long hours sitting on the floor with her head in the lap of an old woman, perhaps her grandmother, the old man's wife. Was she also related to the man in the dock? 'Yes,' she said with an exhausted smile. 'He is my husband.' Good luck, I said automatically, without knowing any of the details of the case.

By the last day of the Pantelides trial they had all disappeared. Hung jury, a policeman told me: there would be a re-trial. What sort of a murder was it? 'Contract killing,' he thought. 'Nasty business. The victim was beheaded.'

And I'd said good luck to that anguished young girl – and meant it. Perhaps it was the camaraderie of the courtroom that had prompted me. I suppose that is a danger in hanging around a place like the Old Bailey for too long. Defendants, lawyers, court officials – even jurors and spectators after a while – must become almost blasé about the banality of human awfulness. It could make one both too cynical – and too forgiving.

I bought a coffee at one of the floating bars along the Embankment and sat out on the deck, eyed by greedy seagulls. It was low tide. The river smelt pleasantly of mud. I thought of George's shipping business. He had told me that afternoon that he felt unable to go on living in London. The city that had been his home for nearly fifteen years had become a hostile place, liable to ambush him with unsettling recollections. He was selling his house. Crime disrupts a victim's life in ways the criminal can barely imagine. For the professional villain a crime is a finite action with no after-effects – unless he is unlucky enough to get caught. For the victim it can be more traumatising than a bad car accident. Some years ago I was attacked by three men not far from the Old Bailey, just the other side of Ludgate Hill. I was knocked to the ground and given a kicking and ended up having my face stitched in the A and E department at Bart's. Ever since then the sight of a group of young men walking along a pavement towards me turns my pulse-rate up a notch. I am sure my attackers never gave the matter another thought.

Korkolis had brutally damaged not just one man's peace of mind but that of his whole family. The most shocking aspect of the Pantelides trial so far as I was concerned was to hear discussed in court the full extent of Korkolis's previous record. He had been a relentless crook. He had been in prison twice in Greece. He had been sentenced to a third term which he had fled the country to avoid, using one of his false passports to get away. Interpol had issued an extradition warrant for his arrest.

In order to paint his client, Mr Pantelides, in a better light, Mr Fulford made the most of Korkolis's villainy. 'They do not come much worse in this world than Mr Korkolis,' he told the jury grimly. 'The prosecution and the defence stand shoulder to shoulder on this man: kidnapper, blackmailer, extortionist, fraudster ...' This was the full, no-holds-barred *curriculum vitae* which had been concealed from our jury, quite properly, but was now being dissected as dispassionately as a corpse in an anatomy lesson.

No wonder Judge Goldstein had told us we were the victims of a monstrous deception. What a relief that we had managed not to be deceived.

POSTSCRIPT

It was a dull Thursday morning in late February 1998. Almost a year had passed since our jury delivered its verdict, nearly two since George Fraghistas was kidnapped. London was preparing itself for the great Countryside March that would bring hundreds of thousands of rural folk to Hyde Park to protest that the new Labour government was threatening their way of life. In the holding cells at the Royal Courts of Justice in the Strand a few dozen of Her Majesty's prisoners were preparing to make their own protests about their way of life – by appealing against the length of their sentences or the verdicts that had sent them to jail in the first place. Among them were Constantinos Korkolis, Thanassis Zografos, Jean-Marc Mereu and Djemel Moussaoui.

This was the final act of George's personal drama. He had told me he would be there for the appeals and so he was, sitting in the well of the small oak-panelled courtroom. He had flown in from Athens the night before. He looked anxious, plainly perplexed at a system of justice that allowed his convicted kidnappers a second ride on the judicial carousel at the tax-payer's expense. There were other familiar faces in Court 6: George's faithful partner Petros Poulmentis, DS Martin Hawkins, Mr Curran, Mr Corkery, two junior defence barristers from the Old Bailey saga, Korkolis's solicitor. We sat and watched as several other appeals were speedily and humanely dealt with: a school security guard convicted of theft, a pair of road-rage toughs, a fresh-faced boy who had crashed the car he was driving when just 15, killing the young girl who was his passenger. Then came Korkolis & Co.

The two Frenchmen sat in the well of the court, bull-necked and shaven-headed, with an interpreter between them. Korkolis and Zografos were in the dock, crushed between six prison officers – the heaviest guard we had seen all day. Zografos was wearing his witness-box blazer. Korkolis was looking unprecedentedly spruce, in a jacket and tie and with his hair combed.

In the absence of a jury the proceedings were wonderfully swift. Hearing the appeals were Lord Justice Swinton Thomas, Mr Justice Jowitt and Mr Justice Astill. They each sat behind a green-shaded desk-lamp and a rack of legal reference books, into whose pages they occasionally made a synchronised foray. Lord Justice Swinton Thomas had a rather unfortunate wig which looked like a woolly tea-cosy. Perhaps this was because he was a Lord Justice rather than a mere Mr. They listened calmly to the pleas on the four men's behalf, occasionally interrupting counsel with brisk questions.

We heard Mr Curran say on Zografos's behalf that 'he was completely mesmerised' by Korkolis – as our jury had suspected. We heard Mr Corkery describe Mereu the former wrestler as a simple man who even now had barely mastered 'prison English'. We learnt that he and Moussaoui were being held on the Isle of Sheppey so that they could be as near as possible to their relatives in France, which showed a nice touch of consideration by the authorities. Moussaoui was behaving so well in jail that he had been made 'a hot-plate attendant' at meal-times, his counsel said. As for Korkolis, who was appealing against verdict as well as sentence, his barrister's argument was that Judge Goldstein had been unfairly sceptical throughout the trial and had undermined Korkolis's role as defendant/advocate. Furthermore, in the tongue-lashing he had given the prisoner prior to sentencing him ('one of the most evil and dangerous men I have ever met') the judge went over the top.

The trio on the bench retired to consider their judgements. George paced the corridor and smoked a cigarette. Was it really possible that Korkolis might get a re-trial and the whole horror would have to be lived through once again?

Eventually the judges returned. They concluded that the trial had been conducted entirely correctly. The jury's verdict – our verdict – was not unsafe. Korkolis was therefore refused leave to appeal against it. As for Judge Goldstein's remarks about him, said Lord Justice Swinton Thomas, 'A judge may be forgiven, after a trial of this length, if he lets off a little steam.'

But the four men did get their sentences reduced. The clinching argument seemed to be that Korkolis's twenty-five-year sentence had been the benchmark by which the others' terms were set. The only way to shorten the time that Zografos, Mereu and Moussaoui were to serve – for which there was a reasonable case, given their previous clean records – was to lower Korkolis's sentence too. That may not actually have been the reasoning, but it was how it appeared.

So the original sentences were quashed. Sixteen years became thirteen. Korkolis's twenty-five would now be twenty.

George Fraghistas and DS Hawkins did not seem too dismayed. My own feeling remained that the judge who had sat through all four months of the original trial, listened to every syllable of the evidence and watched every nuance of the defendants' behaviour had probably got it right in the first place. But my reaction was only to be expected. Once a jury has seen a case through to its climax, any tampering with the outcome is bound to be something of a let-down.

The fact remained that Korkolis would be in jail for a very long time. Twenty years was still one of the severest sentences ever imposed for the crime of kidnapping for ransom in this country.

JUDGING THE JURY

THE SACRED BULWARK

The jury system is often under attack. How is it surviving in this post-Thatcher era, when so many institutions have been shaken to their foundations? What is its future? Is it safe? Does it deserve to be?

Here is a dispassionate description of how it works by John Baldwin and Michael McConville in *Jury Trials*:

> Twelve individuals, often with no prior contact with the courts, are chosen at random to listen to evidence (sometimes of a highly technical nature) and to decide upon matters affecting the reputation and liberty of those charged with criminal offences. They are given no training for this task, they deliberate in secret, they return a verdict without giving reasons, and they are responsible to their own conscience and to no one else. After the trial they melt away into the community from which they are drawn.

Or as Professor Glanville Williams puts it:

> There is no other comparable activity in life in which experience is not regarded as an asset, no other social institution with such haphazard and fleeting membership.

On reading that, a German or a Spaniard might shake his head in disbelief at our devotion to such an amateur means of doing justice. Yet in Britain in the 1990s you are far more likely to run across a critic of the monarchy than someone prepared to say hard things about the jury system. Both are semi-mystical institutions. Both are the product of centuries-old tradition. And both are riddled with imperfections. But whereas even ardent supporters of the monarchy admit that it is founded on anachronistic principles, endearingly out of keeping with modern times, the jury remains a totem of the people. Although heavily criticised in some circles, it is as firmly rooted in the national psyche now as it was a hundred or two hundred years ago.

Furthermore, in an age dogged by relativism and uncertainty, its function is admirably clear-cut: 'The jury just says yes or no,' observed Lord Devlin. 'It is the oracle deprived of the right of being ambiguous.'

Reactionaries and republicans can admire it equally. As an institution it is not only very old and very English; it can also be said to be gloriously democratic, uniquely classless, disinterested, down-to-earth and fair. As an instrument of justice, its efficiency might be questionable: too soft-headed, too prone to acquit, too expensive, say some. Too prejudiced, say others – against the police, for example. But in principle we approve of the jury as a check on oppressive or outdated laws. We like the idea of a lay tribunal standing between the polished professionals of the legal establishment and mere mortals in the dock. The population is raised in its own estimation knowing ordinary people have this role to perform. If the monarchy defines the public as subjects, the jury defines them as citizens – which has a sweeter ring to most ears nowadays.

In other words, the British are deeply sentimental in their attachment to trial by jury. No British government in its right mind would abolish it.

But that does not mean the jury system is sure to survive

in its present form for ever and a day. It has some thoughtful enemies and a great many would-be reformers. They are chiefly to be found among the legal profession and in university law departments. They have produced quantities of literature on the subject. In the United States, where the jury is even more revered than in the United Kingdom, up there with the Constitution and the Declaration of Independence, there has been a prodigious amount of investigation. Some of its results have been disturbing. Others have had regrettable side-effects. The cumbersome and often distasteful process of jury selection, for example, has been strongly influenced by studies of how jurors of different backgrounds are likely to vote in certain kinds of case. The O.J. Simpson trial was not the first to give the impression that the composition of the jury was a more important factor than the evidence.

In some respects, the jury system appears more vulnerable to attack in America than in this country. That is partly because we have been less hidebound and quicker to innovate. But it is also because over here the jury has been beating a quiet tactical retreat for decades. The public has a vague idea that trial by jury is the template for any case bigger than an unpaid parking fine. That is wildly inaccurate. Juries here have long since been dispensed with for most civil cases other than libel (unlike in the USA, where billions of dollars hang on jury decisions). Juries are hardly ever used in Coroners' Courts any more. As for criminal cases, the overwhelming majority are dealt with not by juries but by magistrates. The estimated figure varies rather unsatisfactorily between 93 and 98 per cent, about two million cases a year. That leaves at most 7 per cent of cases to be tried by juries – more than half of which never even reach that stage, because the defendants get cold feet and plead guilty before they ever come to trial. In short, jury trial is very far from being the norm.

In its dying months the last Conservative government was

planning to reduce the number of cases heard by juries still further. The intention was to remove the accused's right to opt for jury trial in what are known as 'either-way' cases – cases which may be tried either summarily or in a Crown Court. In future the magistrates, not the defendant, would take this decision. Jury trials cost a lot more and take much longer, and since the great majority of cases that come before the Crown Courts concern 'either-way' offences (70 per cent of them ending in guilty pleas), the savings in time and money would have been substantial.

The proposal was actually based on a key recommendation of the Royal Commission on Criminal Justice under Lord Runciman, which reported in 1993. Geoffrey Robertson was one of many barristers who condemned this recommendation for threatening to destroy a valued right. But it might well have been implemented despite such resistance, had it not been that the government was unpopular and the then Home Secretary even more so. Newspapers thundered, the great British jury was reconsecrated and Michael Howard was cast as an enemy of the people, bent on removing the Englishman's sacred right to trial by his peers. Even the *Daily Telegraph* opined: 'Mr Howard's admirable concern for efficiency, economy and speed risks running up against the requirement of justice in a wider sense.'

Astonishingly, the present Labour Home Secretary, Jack Straw, despite his own vituperative attacks on the Howard proposals, wasted very little time in taking up exactly where his predecessor left off, relying on his party's massive majority to brush aside accusations of hypocrisy. Lawyers right across the political spectrum opposed Straw's Treasury-driven measure. 'So much for human rights under new Labour!' lamented Conservative barrister Sir Ivan Lawrence QC in a letter to the *Times* in October 1999. He might have invoked the famous words of the eighteenth-century judge and jurist Sir William Blackstone about the lure of new and arbitrary methods of trial:

However convenient these may appear at first . . . let it again be remembered that delays and inconvenience in the forms of justice are the price that all free nations must pay for their liberty in more substantial matters; that these inroads upon this sacred bulwark of the nation are fundamentally opposite to the spirit of our constitution; and that, though begun in trifles, the precedent may gradually increase and spread, to the utter disuse of juries in questions of the most momentous concern.

Those who know the jury system best do not always love it most. There are some serious indictments against it. The Louise Woodward trial was merely the latest case to have brought the system into contention. Hiller Zobel, the urbane judge who was in charge of those proceedings, might himself be counted as a pretty sardonic critic. After the 1992 O.J. Simpson trial he expressed this view of juries: 'It is asking the ignorant to use the incomprehensible to decide the unknowable.'

How would our own jury system fare if it were itself on trial, and we were to assemble a notional court to hear the case?

PROSECUTING COUNSEL

One of the jury system's most outspoken opponents is Sir Louis Blom-Cooper QC. Oddly enough, he is not especially concerned about the competence of juries, which is where most critics stick their darts. His view, which is supported by American findings, is that generally speaking juries are as good at reaching acceptable verdicts as magistrates and judges sitting alone. What he objects to is the cost and cumbersomeness that juries entail, and the fact that they do not have to reach reasoned judgements for which they are accountable. One day juries will simply wither away, he thinks, 'driven to it by virtue of the economics'.

He is a highly civilised man, a member of numerous public inquiries, a former *Guardian* and *Observer* legal correspondent, an author and, as ex-chairman of the Howard League for Penal Reform, hardly an illiberal figure. But he is sceptical about the mythology that attaches to the jury system. There is 'a purely gut feeling that somehow trial by our peers is better' – when it is not even truly by our peers, as so many people are excluded from jury service. It is not really democratic either, since jurors are not elected.

'My rooted objection in a democratic society is that juries are unaccountable,' he said. He had just finished a new book, *The Birmingham Six and Other Cases: Victims of Circumstance* (Duckworth), published in the winter of 1997. It draws attention to the difficulty of dealing with perverse acquittals and wrongful convictions when the decision-makers are absolved from explaining their actions. Yet 'insistence on reasoned verdicts would lead to the demise of trial by jury', he writes. 'No twelve good men and women could compose proper, adequate and intelligent reasons this side of Doomsday . . .' As things stand, if a jury acquits, they are answerable to nobody: there is no appeal against an acquittal as there is on the Continent, only against a conviction. (Senior policemen make the same point, arguing that it is unjust to rule out an appeal supposing new evidence of guilt or even a post-acquittal confession should come to light.)

Sir Louis also disapproves of the jury's famous freedom to ignore the judge's instructions and reach a verdict according to its conscience – the very thing that sets it so high in the eyes of its champions. He told me how back in the 1970s he defended one of a group of people led by the peace campaigner Pat Arrowsmith, who had been charged under the 1934 Disaffection Act for leafleting troops at

Aldershot. The evidence against them was overwhelming. The trial lasted fifty-one days. Afterwards, some of the jurors revealed – as they were allowed to in those days – that the majority had decided to acquit after just five days.

Not only was this a colossal waste of money, said Sir Louis wryly. 'It was a perverse verdict, because they hated the Act. I personally object to that. If Parliament has passed a law and if they were true to their oath, they were bound to find them guilty . . . I don't think it is right that twelve ordinary people who are not appointed or elected by anybody should come along and refuse to give effect to the will of Parliament.'

Sir Louis would prefer the trial process and the weighing of evidence to be done by professionals. 'You wouldn't want a butcher to take out your appendix.'

There are many objections to this view. But one of the strongest is that judges sitting alone would become 'case-hardened', which is another way of saying more inclined to take a dim view of mankind and less prone to give the accused the benefit of the doubt. (The problem with judges, wrote G.K. Chesterton, 'is simply that they have got used to it . . . They do not see the awful court of judgement; they only see their own workshop'.) Sir Louis scoffed at the suggestion. Ninety-nine per cent of crime is in effect tried by judges and magistrates without juries, he said, exaggerating only slightly. Are they case-hardened? And then there are the Diplock courts in Northern Ireland, where judges sitting alone have been trying terrorist-related cases since 1973 (the equivalent court in the Republic of Ireland also sits without a jury, though with three judges on the bench, not one). Sir Louis had been doing a lot of work in Northern Ireland recently and had been able to observe what was going on at close quarters. 'The Diplock courts have been a huge success, absolutely huge,' he argued, thrusting into my hands a book called *Judge Without Jury*, by John Jackson and Sean Doran of Queen's University, Belfast (Clarendon Press, 1995).

'I think judges have increasingly come to regard the jury system as expendable. People would say "Oh God help us if we had to appear before Judge So-and-so who's thoroughly prejudiced." ' But that was not the right conclusion, Sir Louis explained. Being a summing-up judge and being a decision-making judge were very different functions. 'Once you are the decision-maker and you are answerable for your decision and have to give your reasons, you breed a very different kind of judge. The Diplock courts have shown that. The judge has to sit down and give his reasons: that is *such* a discipline.

'The real objection I have to the proponents of jury trials is their claim that this is a fundamental freedom,' he reflected, alluding to the absence of British-style jury trials in the rest of Europe. 'If you go to Strasbourg and say "I was deprived of trial by jury, a breach of my fundamental freedom", they'd laugh at you.

'It may be that it is a system that suits the English, deeply rooted in our culture and valuable for that. The Americans are worse about it than we are. They are besotted with it.' But an advanced society, Sir Louis believed, did not need the safeguard of the jury system. It was better-suited to illiterate societies, where you did not have the spotlight of the media to keep an eye on the judiciary.

Just before I left, he stood over me chuckling as I copied out a line from the philosopher and jurist Jeremy Bentham, writing in 1843. The jury, wrote Bentham pithily, was 'an institution admirable in barbarous times, not fit for enlightened times, necessary as matters stand in England'.

Sir Louis's new book refers trenchantly to the Morris Committee's report on the jury system in 1965 which, while stressing that the system of trial by jury needed to be maintained as 'fair, sensible and workable', did not wish to prejudice any future inquiry into its merits, 'as to which we realise that there is room for divergent views'.

Sir Louis thinks this invitation to review the workings of the system was too lightly cast aside. His last words as he saw me out into his pretty Islington street were about the 'inscrutability' of the jury. He would be in favour of allowing research into its workings, he grinned wolfishly. 'Then the whole thing would collapse.'

DEFENDING COUNSEL

Helena Kennedy has almost no qualms about juries. She is an engaging, energetic, much admired QC who has made something of a speciality of defending alleged IRA terrorists. She was preparing to do so in a forthcoming case the week I saw her. Despite the notorious miscarriages of justice in which men had been wrongly convicted of terrorist offences, she did not feel it was juries that were to blame.

'I believe juries do a tremendous job,' she shouted. We were eating pizza in a noisy basement near her Doughty Street chambers. She was about to be ennobled as a Labour baroness, and was off to see Garter King of Arms that very afternoon, so she refused a glass of wine. Her car had been clamped that morning which meant that she had arrived late, beaming apologies: we had to talk and eat fast. This is probably an habitual condition for the ultra-busy Helena Kennedy.

'I think juries are very good. Their sixth sense is working, their sense of smell. They sniff the air and get a feeling about whether people are truthful or reliable. They may go in with a whole set of prejudices one way or the other but what always impresses me is that they can filter them out. They can make distinctions which are really very subtle.

'You can see the effect in the verdict, when they find a defendant guilty on some counts of the indictment but not on others. Collectively this group of people are better than the sum of their parts. They do rise above their prejudices.

I believe people are perfectly capable of taking on that enormous sense of responsibility which comes with jury service. I think they are wonderful.'

I remembered Helena saying to Ruby Wax, on the latter's TV chat show in June, 'Juries feel a pride in what they are doing. I have to bring out their better selves.'

But was there nothing she could suggest to improve the way jury trials work? There was. 'I am very cynical about what goes on in the US,' she said. 'I think it is all ghastly. But one of the things we could learn from them in longish trials is the swearing-in of a thirteenth juror.' This would clearly be a sensible reform. The idea is that the extra man or woman sits in on the whole trial, just as the other jurors do, but only steps into the box should one of them fall ill. This would avoid the problem that arises when for one reason or another several people drop out of a jury, making a majority verdict impossible.

I wanted to know what she thought of the Roskill Committee's proposal in 1986 that 'for complex fraud trials . . . trial by a judge and two lay members should replace trial by judge and jury'. The committee took the view that in such cases many jurors were out of their depth. The recommendation was not implemented. Opponents argued that the evidence on which it was based was sparse and that if implemented it would be used to pry the jury away from other types of 'complex' cases. Nevertheless, of all the proposed reforms of the jury system, it is the one most commonly advanced. Non-lawyers share the feeling that randomly picked, unqualified juries should not be burdened with such cases – and potential jurors live in fear of being assigned to one. Helena Kennedy takes a robust line: 'The truth is that fraud trials are not about fine-line accountancy. They are about whether somebody was on the fiddle, somebody was being dishonest' – matters on which juries are quite capable of making up their minds.

The frequent sight of armed policemen at the Old Bailey had set me wondering about juries hearing terrorism cases on the mainland. Surely it must be very alarming to be a juror in those circumstances?

She agreed that there was a scary element for the jury in such trials. 'They are given all sorts of special directions about phone calls, noticing anything untoward or being approached by a member of the public. They are told to use a back door into the Bailey. It means, I always feel, they are all too conscious that the State feels these people who are on trial are dangerous, whereas that is the issue that is in fact being tried. It all adds to their tension.' But she knew of no case where a juror had cried off out of fear.

At the Old Bailey terrorism trials are generally held in Court 2, where the jury cannot be seen from the public gallery. In other courts 'you're terribly conscious of being looked at all the time'. Jury panels for terrorist trials are usually questioned by the judge more closely than is normal so that people with Irish connections can ask to be – and often are – let off. All the same, it seemed to me admirable that so many ordinary men and women are prepared to undertake the task so unflinchingly.

Helena Kennedy had a different worry. 'The temptation could be – I have no proof of it – that there would be anxieties about letting such defendants go.' On the contrary, I thought: there must be a very strong temptation for nervous jurors to play safe and let them off. (Bruce Houlder QC, who is the Bar Council's vice-chairman of public affairs, told me, 'Even in IRA cases my impression is that juries are determined not to be intimidated. The more the threat, the more likely an English jury is to get cussed and be affected against the defendant.')

In the 1970s, when Helena Kennedy came down from Scotland to practise at the English bar, each counsel could exercise seven peremptory challenges, which meant that up to that number of potential jurors could be rejected without a reason being given. That was later reduced to three. Now there are none. It is very nearly a pure lottery, in striking contrast to the massively time-consuming and expensive process of jury selection in the United States. But many lawyers here would like to see the return of their three peremptory challenges. Helena Kennedy does not seem to feel as strongly as others on this issue. She recalled that they often used to drop jurors and get worse in their place. Once she had been very worried about a man wearing a shirt with epaulettes. Was he a security guard, or a member of a fascist group? Eventually she had learnt that he was a fireman – who went on to become an excellent jury foreman.

All the same, she said, 'I am very unhappy at the idea that randomness might throw up an all-white jury in the case of a black man being tried. The black community could feel very aggrieved. Age might be an issue, too. In a case about drugs, for example. What if you get a jury of people like my mother? She's terrified of drugs. And I'd be very unhappy if a mother was on trial for killing a baby, for example, shaking her baby to death, if the jury was too young. I don't believe in juries of all one gender, either.'

Under the present set-up, the only way to rectify such situations is for the Crown to agree to use its right to 'stand by' a juror in the hope that the next name called will be more suitable. Possibly, Miss Kennedy thought, such an approach could be more formalised and judges could be instructed to encourage it. But she is definitely not of the school of defence lawyers who think the only good juror is a dumb juror.

She admits she once nearly threw Hans Eysenck, the controversial psychology professor, off a jury, having recognised him on the panel, 'not because of his views on race: I was concerned that he was quite a powerful personality and would absolutely dominate in a controversy'. Anyway, she thought better of it and let him stay. Now, she said, 'What I want in a jury is some intelligent people. I don't want a lumpen jury. There are some people who do. I want them to think hard about what the burden of proof really means.' Sometimes juries are called upon to do quite difficult things, she said, where the evidence is just not good enough. And for that you want people on the jury who are going to keep reminding the others of what the standard of proof requires.

Hmm, I thought, as I saw her off to see Garter King of Arms: Helena Kennedy thinks the intelligent juror is an antidote to careless convictions; others are convinced that more intelligent jurors would mean fewer perverse acquittals. Come to think of it, there is no reason why both views should not be right.

THE JUDGES

No head of an Oxford college can have seen the inside of a jail as often as the ex-Principal of my alma mater, St Edmund Hall. In his pre-academic role as Her Majesty's Chief Inspector of Prisons for England and Wales, former judge Sir Stephen Tumim became a great deal better acquainted with the living conditions of convicted criminals than any of his fellow members of the judiciary ever was or is ever likely to be. His liberal views on prison reform are famous. So could I assume that he was also a supporter of the jury system?

'I am basically in favour,' he told me, 'though I must say that from the judge's point of view it is frightfully irritating. You listen to a case and, as the judge, you want to decide it. It is much more fun trying civil cases. In civil cases you decide what happened. In criminal cases you have to sit there without interrupting – and you can't even write your letters, as you have to keep at least one ear open on what is going on.' The amiable Sir Stephen is much better than most judges at cracking jokes. In his academic corduroys and bow tie it was hard to imagine him on the bench, bewigged and beetle-browed. As he got up to pour us sherry I noticed his footwear: a pair of espadrilles in Oxford blue.

In the vast majority of cases he reckoned that a judge can guide the jury to some extent during a trial, without risking an appeal. 'Indeed, I think that is part of the judge's job.' Nonetheless, he said ruefully, 'Very often you don't agree with the jury – maybe one in ten cases. There is nothing you can do about that. And I think it is improper for a judge to indicate to a jury, even just by a bit of body language, that he thinks they are mistaken.' But there it was. The jury served a worthy political purpose and it was inconceivable that it could be done away with. 'The jury system,' he beamed contentedly, 'is one of the necessary irritations of life.'

We talked a good deal about the composition of juries. Juries aren't always as dense as they appear, in Sir Stephen's experience. Sitting as a recorder in Oxford many years ago, he remembered an occasion when counsel had objected to a particularly unimpressive-looking panel. They had been especially worried about one old man who came on to the jury with his collar all over the place, looking terribly scruffy. 'He was challenged – because he hadn't shaved for about a week. But I recognised him,' Sir Stephen chortled. 'He was a professor of theology – a man of great distinction.'

He did not seem over-regretful that peremptory challenges had been abolished. Although an all-white jury judging a black defendant might look bad, 'I actually don't think I believe in using a challenge to choose whites and blacks. I think you have got to go on the basis that people are going to act fairly . . .' But he would go along with the idea of encouraging judges to get together with the prosecution to exercise its stand-by in cases where the composition of the jury seemed unsuitable. 'The Lord Chief Justice could do that.'

He was pretty sure that judges deciding cases alone would not give more satisfaction to members of the public. Judges vary enormously. When you have a judge such as the late Sir Bernard Caulfield who went on about Jeffrey Archer's wife Mary being 'fragrant' it is very difficult to say that jurors are any more out of touch than the judiciary.

Sir Stephen's particular gripe was about the way in which the judicial process seems to have been tilted away from straightforwardness. 'The thing that has really transformed jury trials for the worse in my lifetime is photocopying. Photostats are the real disaster of the jury system. In my childhood, indictments were much shorter because it all had to be copied by hand. My father was Clerk of Assize of the old Oxford circuit: he wouldn't have a typewriter within hearing. All the indictments were prepared by hand: that meant you didn't put many counts in. It had a very healthy effect in keeping charge sheets short. You didn't chuck in a dozen extra counts in order just to catch the defendant out. You had one count and got on with it.' It was far easier now to fox a jury with piles of paper, especially in fraud trials.

One means of simplifying trials would be to follow the example of the civil courts. 'I have always had a theory of judging, especially in civil cases, that it is terrifically worthwhile for the judge to get there early. He then reads the papers before he goes into court.' Sir Stephen was referring in particular to the written 'pleadings' submitted in advance by both sides in a civil trial – outlines of the plaintiff's and the defendant's cases. He saw no reason why a similar practice should not be applied in the criminal courts where, as things stand, only the prosecution must give a detailed account of its arguments. Since 1997 the defence must also let the judge know its intentions, but need submit only an outline of its case.

Sir Stephen supported the idea of swearing in replacement jurors for long cases. But he was firmly against the State's having a right to appeal against jury acquittals. 'There must be an end to it. Somebody who has been acquitted by a jury ought to be able to say "Right, that's it." ' Otherwise, he thought, the police would never stop grubbing around trying to prove themselves right. And anyway, if someone was wrongly acquitted, that was not the end of the world.

The day after I visited Sir Stephen and we had strolled about my old college's endearing little quad, I called on a high court judge in the forbidding surroundings of the Law Courts in the Strand. 'Mr Justice Popplewell' it said in large letters on the door of his room. Sir Oliver was sitting at a smallish desk in front of a wall of bookshelves, filled from floor to ceiling with handsomely bound legal tomes. The first thing he did was to hand me a scrap of paper on which he had written down Mark Twain's scornful remarks about the jury system: 'We have a criminal system which is superior to any in the world and its efficiency is only marred by the difficulty of finding twelve men every day who don't know anything and can't read.'

Sir Oliver said he would not weep if juries were abolished, though of course that was wholly unlikely to happen in our lifetimes. Apart from the cost of jury trials, they too often led to the wrong result. In his experience as a judge, between 40 and 50 per cent of acquittals (and a minute proportion of convictions) he regarded as perverse. It was all very well to shrug off such verdicts as a regrettable flaw in the system, but, as he said more than once, 'You cannot regard this as a game.' Sometimes the consequences were horrendous. He recalled one case, for example, where an East End villain had been charged with a particularly horrible murder (he had used a sword). The two key prosecution witnesses had been so frightened that their evidence was shaky. Even so, the jury's decision to acquit had astonished the court. The result was that this extremely dangerous man, with a long record of criminal activity (which of course the judge, though not the jury, knew all about), had been released back into the community. Worse, because he had got off on this high-profile occasion, it would be very difficult for the police ever to mount a successful prosecution against him again, even if they could find witnesses brave enough to come forward.

'We don't know what goes on in the jury room,' said Sir Oliver, though he admitted that as a young barrister he and his colleagues had occasionally overheard snatches of juries deliberating when the walls of their room were thin enough: the level of debate was not edifying. Juries could vary strikingly. He always made a point as a judge of addressing juries at the start of a trial and noticed very quickly which were going to be bloody-minded and which were eager and interested – like the jury which, having found a defendant guilty in Maidstone, voluntarily turned up en masse in Lewes to watch him being tried for a second offence.

It was obvious that verdicts were not always reached in a sensible way. He remembered a case where a woman caught stealing an improbable quantity of tins of cat food had been acquitted. The reason, it appeared, was that the jury felt it would be wrong to convict her, when only that day another jury had found a man charged with a very violent offence not guilty. Sauce for the violent goose, they reasoned, should be sauce for the cat-food-thieving gander.

Certainly, he thought, complex fraud cases should be heard by a tribunal rather than a jury. He was also in favour of magistrates rather than defendants deciding whether to send 'either-way' cases to the Crown Court. At present, too many such cases ended in guilty pleas anyway. But he seemed to agree with Sir Stephen Tumim that shoplifting was 'very often a jury case'. Like Sir Stephen, he had sat as a recorder in Oxford from time to time, where the genteel shoplifter is a familiar figure.

Sir Stephen recalled such people trembling before him in the dock. 'Members of the upper middle classes: dons and dons' wives from North Oxford. Magistrates nearly always convicted them – unless they happened to know them socially,' he joked. 'Juries would be much more tolerant. I was all in favour of acquittals, even if they'd got it wrong. A guilty verdict was just too damaging to their reputations. A lot of these people were probably accused of no more than walking out of a shop with a box of chocolates under their arm. But a box of chocolates can be a serious matter if you are an elderly clergyman.'

The point about juries is that, unlike magistrates, they have not seen it all before and are therefore disposed to be open-minded. 'If you were charged with shoplifting and you hadn't done it, what would you do?' Sir Stephen asked me. 'It's a very interesting question. I'd rather be judged by a jury than by magistrates. I think in the end serious problems of dishonesty should be heard by a jury.'

THE EXPERT WITNESS

Michael Zander is a leading expert on jury trials and was a member of the Runciman Commission on Criminal Justice. We met in his small office at the London School of Economics, where he was Professor of Law. He is a strong supporter of the jury system for serious criminal offences. But he was also in favour of the Commission's controversial recommendation to end the defendant's right to opt for jury trial in 'either-way' cases.

There were administrative and financial advantages. More importantly, he believed, there was also a matter of principle involved, namely that it is more appropriate that the court should select the trial venue than that the defendant should, just as it is the court and not the defendant that decides which judge should preside over a Crown Court trial. In 80 per cent of 'either-way' cases defendants themselves choose to appear before a magistrates' court, since they tend to impose lower sentences. Of the cases that are sent up, more than 60 per cent go up at the magistrates' insistence anyway. And of those defendants who make that decision themselves, more than 70 per cent subsequently plead guilty.

Professor Zander was less firm on the subject of peremptory challenges, but did rather favour their restoration. The three peremptory challenges were useful as a sop which allowed defendants to feel that not everything was stacked against them or out of their control – though of course, even after a challenge, one had no guarantee who the next person from the panel would be. The defence can still challenge a juror 'for cause'. The Catch 22 is that no questions may be asked to establish what the cause might be. You have somehow to know it in advance. Professor Zander recalled that in a recent case in New Zealand, a rather *non-compos*-looking juror struck both the judge and the defence as unsuitable. So they asked the prosecution to use its 'stand-by', which is what happened.

Oddly enough, the Home Office had embarked on a study of the effects of peremptory challenges just before their abolition under the Criminal Justice Act 1988. The results of the study appeared contemporaneously. Ironically, they showed that there was no evidence to support the belief that men in suits and blue-rinsed matrons were being stood down in droves. Nor were there marked differences in acquittal rates between unchallenged juries and those where challenges had been exercised. Under Runciman, Professor Zander was in charge of a study of his own, anatomising three thousand Crown Court cases over a two-week period. Asked whether they thought peremptory challenges should be restored, 56 per cent of defence barristers said yes, 56 per cent of prosecutors said no, and 86 per cent of judges also said no.

Put the bench's preferences on the matter alongside the notorious abuses of the system in the USA and I would say it was a fair bet that peremptory challenges are not due to make an imminent reappearance in this country.

In any event, Professor Zander remains a staunch proponent of the random selection of juries. 'I like the idea of picking twelve people, as it were, from the streets,' he said. His own researches show that if you analyse juries in terms of their class and background, the proportions closely mirror those in the population as a whole, contrary to the received wisdom. All the same, he was enthusiastic about the system in Massachussetts, New York and Arizona: in these states it is now mandatory that no one (except in the direst circumstances) should be excused jury service. He had been amused to learn that in the spring of 1997 the presiding judge in the New York Court of Appeals had himself been summoned. So was the professor's own father-in-law, who was not only at attorney himself but also 94 years old.

For all his academic thoroughness and quickness with statistics, I had the impression that Michael Zander remains a defender of the jury system for reasons that Louis Blom-Cooper would find sentimental. One of the Runciman Commission's recommendations was that more research on juries should be allowed. Professor Zander supported the idea in principle, but was still slightly worried by it. There were two dangers in finding out too much about how juries actually go about their task. One, it would give opponents a useful stick. Two, it would threaten the mystique. Perhaps these were not the most appropriate sentiments for a cool-headed Professor of Law. But this made his candour all the more telling.

POLICE EVIDENCE

Some months after our trial I got the go-ahead to talk to the three key Scotland Yard men involved in the Korkolis case: DCI Laurie Vanner, DS Martin Hawkins, and DC Ian Slade. We met at a former police station in Aldgate which I had a little trouble finding. It was a dingy 1960s block with an abandoned air, looking more like a derelict polytechnic college than a nerve centre of criminal investigation. Traffic wardens had moved in on the ground floor while the Organised Crime Group had offices upstairs. Someone had punched a ragged hole in the plywood wall of the reception area.

DCI Vanner is a tall, trim man approaching 50. He had been twenty-nine years in the police force and was with the Organised Crime Group from its foundation. He specialised in kidnapping and sieges, and had long experience of hostage negotiations. He spent weeks every year scooting around the globe sharing his expertise with overseas police forces – advising, lecturing and sometimes in the thick of action.

DS Martin Hawkins is another peripatetic policeman. He arrived late at our meeting wearing lightweight clothes, having just flown in from Germany. Before that he had been in St Lucia. Forty-seven years old, he had been with the Met since 1971. After long experience on murder squads, he moved across to hostage-takings and kidnaps. He and Laurie Vanner had worked together before, and were both involved in a guerrilla siege in Sierra Leone not long before the 1997 rebellion. (Evidently the Yard is a valuable invisible exporter – more invisible than most.)

DC Ian Slade was Martin Hawkins' chief lieutenant on the Korkolis case. He was 35 and had been in the Met for seventeen years, the last two of them with the OCG; before that on murder squads around London. An impressive young man with Gary Lineker looks, he struck me as an obvious high flyer.

I formed the impression that these three were admirable policemen: thoughtful, highly skilled and enormously dedicated. No wonder the Fraghistas family felt they were in good hands. When I interviewed George Fraghistas after the trial he was bursting with admiration for his rescuers. 'People have an image of the police as a stereotype. I got a culture shock. I realised they were no different from you and me.' He told the *Guardian*'s Duncan Campbell: 'They love their job. When they released me you'd have thought they had just had sex – they were smiling, they were so happy they had succeeded.'

Of course, as Helena Kennedy says, 'At the serious end of crime you get used to a very sophisticated form of policing . . . you are getting the crack end of the police service.' These men seemed to bear that out. Martin Hawkins demonstrated a small but telling example of their professionalism when he said that, although they had felt a warm affection for the Fraghistas family, he had had to warn George that their relationship before and during the trial would have to be strictly arm's-length. When he was in Athens to pursue his investigations he took care that he always met George in the office, never at any of the family's homes.

(It is a minor irony that expertise actually misled DS Hawkins the night he burst into Hogan Mews. He ran upstairs first, because 'in all my experience kidnappers always hold their victims in an upstairs bedroom'. Had there been someone with a gun at George's head downstairs in the kitchen, that could have been a fatal error.)

DCI Vanner and his colleagues talked animatedly about the jury system, while making it clear that these were their personal views and did not necessarily reflect the official line. Generally speaking, the police do not love juries, though they know perfectly well they must live with them.

It is easy enough to understand their scepticism. Most of Laurie Vanner's early service was in south London. 'I saw an awful lot of trials as a divisional detective,' he said. 'Defence lawyers always worked on the basis that it was best to opt for jury trial – even if you'd just got caught with your hand in the till. The villains always said go for a jury trial. Snaresbrook Crown Court used to be famous – infamous – for acquittals. It was because of the jury catchment area.' (In the early 1990s, figures from the Lord Chancellor's department showed a 29 per cent acquittal rate at Snaresbrook, compared with 16 per cent nationally.) Now all that had changed, he added: catchment areas have been made much more diffuse.

He told the story of a case back in the 1980s. A gang of skinheads were accused of beating up some black boys, one of whom was appallingly injured. 'The evidence against them was overwhelming.' But after a month's trial, they were acquitted. Some time later a juror wrote to Laurie Vanner saying that the verdict had been clear from day one: four of the jurors were either friends of the accused or actually related to them.

Nobbling still happens now and then, the detectives said, even though the introduction of majority verdicts thirty years ago made it pretty ineffectual. In organised crime cases, families and friends regularly sit in the public gallery to see if they can identify a juror, who can then be leaned on. 'They can follow him home, threaten him or bribe him,' said Laurie Vanner. 'Just staring hard at a juror can be deeply disconcerting.' Usually they pick on the person they think has the strongest personality and is most likely to sway the others. Old Bailey jurors are better protected than some against this sort of thing as the juries are drawn from a hugely dispersed area.

Martin Hawkins said that a major fault in the layout of most courts is that the public can get a good look at the jury, which they cannot in Court 2 at the Old Bailey. 'Juries should be hidden,' he said. 'And jurors' names should not be disclosed. They should be referred to by their numbers.' (This has happened on occasion, though of course it virtually rules out a challenge 'for cause'.)

Every detective spends a good deal of his or her career in court, observing juries at close quarters. If there was a single strong criticism emerging from our conversation it was that juries were not always up to the job. As Martin Hawkins put it, 'Juries should be more balanced with professional people. They are not representative. There are too many people who get off doing jury service too easily.' There should be more jurors with brains and qualifications and different experiences of life. 'Then I think you would get a fair selection of the community. That is not what's happening.'

'Our perception of juries, especially in long cases, is that the good guys go,' said Ian Slade, echoing the view widely shared among the chattering (and jury-avoiding) classes. He proposed a simple device for making it harder for people to get off: they should be allowed as far as possible to pick their own preferred fortnight in which to serve. Potential jurors would be told that they would have to do their duty some time in the next twelve months but could choose when to do it. Once the dates had been confirmed, there would be no excuse for failing to be available, except in cases of real hardship. This seemed to me a first-rate idea.

Despite the drawbacks, Laurie Vanner and his colleagues felt that in major cases, juries could be relied on to behave responsibly. There was a common appreciation of the seriousness of murder, rape and so forth. But in minor cases, tribal loyalties could take over. 'So what if he nicked a few quid?' jurors might be inclined to say. 'There but for the grace of God, etc.' (Paul Johnson made the same point in a *Daily Mail* article in February 1997, observing that juries in such cases were often frivolous or bloody-minded.) As for complex cases, there was a notable tendency for jurors to 'shut off'. Even those taking notes would stop doing so – and incidentally, why didn't judges insist that all jurors make the effort to take notes?

DS Hawkins said he thought fraud trials should be heard by specially able jurors – accountants, for example. But then, even as he was speaking, he admitted that he had always been against having police fraud squads manned by specialists. If an ordinary policeman couldn't understand what was afoot, he had argued, how would the court?

I said I had the impression that most jurors were able to rise to the occasion of a trial. Martin Hawkins agreed, but made a point that had not occurred to me. He said he wondered whether, when it came to ordinary people who had never taken a big decision in their lives before, the feeling of power might not go to their heads. It might make them behave irrationally. 'You take them out of their natural environment, put them in a position of authority . . .' There might be a strong temptation to put one over on the establishment, by disbelieving the police, for example. After a few jury experiences the juror would recognise that calling police evidence into question is a routine defence gambit. 'But not many get the chance to learn that.'

DCI Vanner had left by now and it was lunchtime. I took detectives Hawkins and Slade to the next-door pub for a drink. Ian Slade was already involved in another case. Martin Hawkins was investigating war criminals. They seemed cheerfully undismayed by the knowledge that, however hard they worked on their new tasks, however strong their evidence, the ultimate judgement on their toils would come not from a judge or their own superiors but from twelve ordinary, unqualified, randomly selected members of the public. How many of us could bear to operate under such conditions?

In January 1998 Laurie Vanner, Martin Hawkins, Ian

Slade, Graham Clemence and Don King were all awarded Commissioner's Commendations for their initiative and bravery in solving the Fraghistas kidnap case.

THE VICTIM'S VIEW

I called on George Fraghistas at his brother's flat in Maida Vale on a rainy day in June. He was looking healthier than he had in court, crisply dressed in a green shirt and slacks. He seemed to be pleased that he was putting on weight again, after losing 20 lbs during the kidnap and more during the trial. We drank coffee and ate ginger nuts while he talked about the police.

He said to me, 'You would have thought they would be tough and arrogant. But they were so kind. They gave us a hell of a lot of support after it was all over. Real concern. They kept calling me to ask how I was, if I wanted to see an expert at the Maudsley Hospital. It has a unit which specialises in helping kidnap victims and hostages.'

But he preferred to get over his ordeal by himself. He did not want that sort of help. Instead he devised a more positive form of therapy. Early in the summer he threw a dinner for every single policeman and policewoman who had been involved in the operation. He and his mother and the rest of his family, including six of his seven nephews and nieces flown in from Athens, hosted a great feast at The Belfry, London's most exclusive dining club. Some thirty-odd coppers, from the DCI to the most junior PC, sat down to Anton Mosimann's famous food and had a memorable evening. According to Laurie Vanner and his team, no one in living memory had ever given the police such a generous thank-you for doing their duty.

It was harder for George to be dispassionate about what he had gone through in the witness box. Under our adversarial system the court had allowed the victim of a violent kidnap to be treated as though he were a blackmailer, a liar and a heartless traitor to his own family. 'The worst time was the trial,' he said ruefully. 'The cupboard was extremely nasty – imagine being in the dark for nine days. But it was like a mugging. I can live with it. What it was impossible to get used to, and was extremely hurtful, was eleven days in the witness box being insulted in this vulgar and barbaric way. That was the bad part. One of the defence counsel said "You are a cheat with a T and cheap with a P." That was much worse than being in the cupboard.'

It was almost as lonely, too. 'The police repeatedly told me and my family we should not talk about the case before the others had given evidence. It was very difficult. We all became paranoiac about it, to the extent that I couldn't speak to my mother at all. Everybody in Greece said we were stupid. They thought we should have sat down and talked about it. But we took it seriously. I know it showed, because it would have been obvious if we had all talked among ourselves.'

He was right about that. I remembered being struck by how plain it was that the family witnesses had *not* co-ordinated their stories. That is the sort of thing an alert jury picks up quite quickly. So what had he thought about the jury? Were we alert? What had he made of our role in his courtroom ordeal?

'I must say that it is a very good system,' he answered. 'In order to be able to judge a system you must test it to extremes.' Whether he intended to compliment us for sorting out an extremely complicated case or meant that it was an extremely close-run thing, I wasn't sure.

'During the trial I got very scared,' he said. 'You see someone hammering the same point over and over again . . . Everything depends on twelve people you have never met before, whose background you don't know, whose mental capacity you don't know: you don't know the experiences they have had in the past. The outcome is based on what these twelve people are going to think. God knows, it is extremely frustrating. The defence would not let me stay in court in case I put psychological pressure on the jury.'

He could not make out which way the jury's sympathies were going. Our faces were like stone, he said. Every now and then he would see one of us apparently fast asleep. The uncertainty became even more acute while the jury was deliberating. Martin Hawkins had become concerned when we went into a second day. The Crown had begun to worry about a hung jury. Poor George had comforted himself with the thought that, if indeed we failed to reach a verdict and there was a re-trial, he would at least know the defence case inside out.

I was rather pleased to learn that we had been so inscrutable. Not even that high-rolling gambler George Fraghistas had had a feel for which way the dice were falling.

THE VICTIM'S MOTHER

Mrs Rhea Fraghistas looked round her small, pretty flat and laughed. She was telling me how every day during her son's kidnap the little living room we were sitting in had been crammed with policemen. With Nicos and Marily there as well, it had been a fearful squash. An officer had slept there every night, on the pink sofa under the window which looked out over Rotten Row.

'The jury? I was scared stiff. Not at the beginning of the trial. But when I heard all those lies being told. I never knew lawyers could tell so many lies – though one of the Crown Prosecution Service girls told me that if they take off their wigs and their robes they're lovely people.' She snorted delicately.

'The jury had such blank faces. I hoped there would be a few learned people among you, who could make the others understand. Because it was a very difficult case. The prosecution was blind about what the defence would be. If only you had known he was a crook, which you could not know . . .

'If I had been on the jury I would have been confused too. All I hoped was that the jurors would see the truth. This was my prayer.'

THE COURT OFFICIALS

The usher and the clerk looked oddly out of context sitting in a corner of the Old London pub on Ludgate Hill with drinks in front of them and no gowns. It was like meeting one's tour guides back in England after returning from a package holiday. It was a Friday evening in early July. We greeted each other as old friends.

Roy became an usher because he had so enjoyed a stint as a juror at Middlesex Crown Court. He was nearing 50 and had been a butcher all his working life until then. There was no difficulty about this mid-life career change: he simply went along to the Job Centre. He had been at the Old Bailey for four years and loved the place.

Sarah joined the court service as an administrative officer when she was just 16. Born and brought up near Glasgow, she had worked at seven different courts in England and was now a Higher Executive Officer, which meant regular spells as a clerk of the court. One of her tasks as clerk was to ensure that her court sat for at least four and a half hours a day in order to justify the running costs – approximately £7,500 per diem. She preferred long cases because everyone involved, including the jury, could develop a rapport. Our trial pleased her greatly on that score.

Roy and Sarah had watched hundreds of juries at close quarters and on the whole thought highly of them. 'You can't beat having twelve ordinary, utterly different people taking the decision,' said Roy. 'It is the most unlikely thing, but it is the fairest. I think that, even though I have seen dozens of weird verdicts. People say it's better that ten guilty men go free than that an innocent man should suffer. That was certainly true when there was capital punishment' – which there was, of course, when Blackstone made that famous remark.

Apparently a lot of jurors get so hooked that they ask if they can do it again. But Roy thought the ideal juror was a first-time innocent. A little knowledge is a dangerous thing in the jury box, he said. He would disqualify himself as a juror now, having seen what he'd seen: he would be too cynical.

Sarah bore him out. She had often seen jurors looking absolutely stunned when, having found a defendant guilty on a minor count but not on the graver one, they then heard his appalling antecedents read out by the Crown. That was enough to harden anyone's heart next time they heard a barrister put the case for the defence. She had seen a few men she thought innocent found guilty, especially of rape. But she had also seen obviously guilty men acquitted.

Sarah said she made a point of smiling at jurors to put them at their ease, which she thought was important. 'If a juror loses it in the first few days, he loses it for keeps.' Roy agreed: 'I've seen a juror physically shaking with nerves at the responsibility of it all.' But on the whole, juries were hard-working, good-tempered and well-behaved, they thought. You did get the occasional pain in the neck, said Roy, but it was rare – and he had never had a mutiny. He did once have a gruff-voiced transvestite on a jury; but he/she was an excellent juror and was only discovered because of an outbreak of afternoon stubble.

On the very rare occasion that there was any trouble and his gown was insufficiently intimidating, Roy would send for the clerk: the wig usually did the trick. Besides, wigs and gowns served another purpose: they raised people's expectations of what was wanted of them.

Roy and Sarah made an excellent double act. On the one hand they sang the praises of the jury system with genuine enthusiasm. On the other they did a good job of demystifying it in a thoroughly down-to-earth manner. Our jury would have been tremendously reassured had we had a half-hour chat with these two before we took our places in the jury box. Come to think of it, every jury should have a Roy and Sarah to give them a pep talk before going into action.

THE COURTS CORRESPONDENT

The London *Evening Standard* had its correspondent in court for the beginning and end of *R. v Korkolis and Others*. A South American-style kidnap in the middle of London was a big story. Like other newspapers, it had observed a blackout during the nine days of the kidnap itself, at the request of the police. Once the four men had been charged, the contempt of court laws had meant that the *Standard* could do no more than report the bare facts of the case. Now for the first time Paul Cheston could give his readers a full account as it emerged at the Old Bailey.

I did not know Cheston, who had been the *Standard*'s courts correspondent for the past four years. Something of a barrister manqué, he had achieved his ambition of becoming a courtroom specialist after years of general reporting. Now he found it a bit of a drug, moving from Crown Court to High Court to cover the most interesting cases of the day.

We met, long after the Korkolis trial was over, in the Fleet Street branch of El Vino's, once the haunt of journalists but now, since the diaspora of the newspapers from EC4, overwhelmed by lawyers.

Cheston has attended hundreds of jury trials and reported on some very odd behaviour by juries. But he still believed strongly that serious crimes, libels, and what he called in the jargon of our trade 'human interest' cases should be heard by juries. Like so many other regular court attenders whom I have spoken to, he made an exception for big City frauds. In such cases, he thought, some sort of tribunal system was long overdue. 'As you know,' he said, 'anyone with any brains, finding himself on a jury panel of a hundred and fifty, told that this is a complicated City fraud trial and likely to last between six months and a year, will get off. There are so many get-out clauses you can pull one out of a hat. You end up with a jury consisting of the twelve people who haven't been able to think of an excuse.'

There was another problem here, a version of the Stockholm Syndrome, where jurors listening to a long-running case in the Chichester Rents (the dreary Old Bailey annexe in Chancery Lane specialising in frauds) begin to sympathise with the only other person in court who is banged up there day after day against his will, i.e. the defendant.

Paul Cheston long ago gave up trying to predict which way a jury would jump. He was so often wrong. The police always said that if the deliberations dragged on for any length of time, it was a bad sign for the prosecution, but that was not always true either. Overall he thought juries reached understandable, if not invariably the 'right' verdicts. Although he had never sat on a jury himself, he imagined that the 'beyond reasonable doubt' requirement could sometimes prevent jurors from seeing the wood for the trees. He was also keen on the idea that the defence should be required to be more forthcoming about the line it was going to take at an early stage in the trial. Apart from making the jury's job easier, it would be tremendously helpful to accurate court reporting.

Cheston covered the 'Jury from Hell' case in a memorable report for the *Evening Standard* in 1996. The jury was trying a man called Ray Lee for the killing of a young police constable in Ilford. 'For four days of fruitless deliberations,' Cheston wrote, 'the jury drove barristers to anger and frustration, caused untold anguish to PC Walters' parents, left an usher in tears and the tax-payer with a £250,000 bill.' The jury, who appeared to be unusually young and immature, squabbled over the question of smoking, sent notes complaining about each other to the judge, demanded a change of hotel to one with a gym thirty miles away, turned up late one morning because some of them had been working out, and were also hit by illness. Two of the jurors had spent their breaks canoodling in the corridor outside the court. Eventually, when they failed to reach a verdict, the judge dismissed them and ordered a re-trial.

He also reported on the infamous case of a double murderer convicted twice in the same year, 1994. The first guilty verdict had been quashed after it was revealed that some members of the jury had tried to contact the dead murder victims with an ouija board.

There was a trial at Snaresbrook Crown Court in 1993 where a jury had had to be dismissed when, after three hours' deliberating over a robbery case, they had sent the judge a note asking: 'Is it a question of whether we have to decide whether the person is guilty or not guilty?'

Despite such occasional horror stories, Cheston's faith in the system remained unshaken. In practice he thought the most urgent improvement could be brought about by making it harder for well-qualified people to dodge the draft – exactly the sort of people who might have pulled the Ray

Lee jury back from the brink of hell, tossed the ouija board in the bin and told the Snaresbrook jurors what they were supposed to be doing.

MEMBERS OF THE JURY

I have talked to numbers of people who have done jury service. Only one or two complained that their faith in the system had been shaken by the experience. On the whole ex-jurors say they found it absorbing and worthwhile.

My sister-in-law was the foreman of a jury in Sydney which tried a man facing nine charges of rape – a crime notoriously difficult for juries because of the absence of third-party witnesses. When they found him guilty, they had not only the intense satisfaction of learning that he had a string of previous convictions but the glee (her word) of knowing that they had rid the city of the odious 'Executive Rapist': this was what the newspapers called him because the victims he stalked and raped were all professional women. The problem for the jury was that these women were so composed and articulate that they did not come across as vulnerable in the witness box. Some of the jurors took a good deal of convincing that they had been violated in a most horrible way and not simply inconvenienced by a smooth talker. He was sentenced to seventeen years. (And paroled, to the jurors' fury, after six.)

The writer Drusilla Beyfus had a quite different experience as a juror on a London theft case. Her jury felt in their hearts that the accused man was guilty, but found the prosecution evidence so thin that they acquitted. Many years later, Miss Beyfus still remembers the trial vividly, and thinks that the jury's behaviour was a tremendous vindication of the system: the jurors determinedly put aside their gut instincts and stuck to their oath to try the accused 'according to the evidence'.

Middle-class people often say they were impressed by the conscientiousness of their fellow jurors. Their own prejudices about the prejudices of others were shaken: taxi drivers are not necessarily right-wing; blacks can be harder on blacks than whites; women are often tougher on women than men; the well-educated may be less clear-sighted than the ignoramuses; the old can be more broad-minded than the young. TV producer Jenny Barraclough told me that when she was on a jury trying a man on a grievous bodily harm charge, she had been completely taken in by his mother, who testified very touchingly that her son was a good boy at heart. The other jurors, all East Enders, were much more cynical. They quickly – and correctly – put her right.

The keenest supporters of juries are usually those who have served on one. I have a lawyer friend who is distinctly iffy: he has never been a juror. His wife is an ardent supporter: she has.

A publisher, Sue Bradbury, wrote to me to say that her jury service in East Croydon had given her faith 'in the ability of twelve perfectly ordinary people to deliver a just verdict, in spite of the woman who thought everything was a frame-up by the police and the old man who confessed to being a "chronic bad judge of character" ... It was some time ago now, but I remember it as an experience both humbling and heartening which I thought everyone ought to have.'

She added a reflection which would have pleased Sir Stephen Tumim. Her jury had been trying a shoplifting case. 'At one point,' she wrote, 'the judge addressed us and said we were probably wondering about the financial wisdom of taking up the precious time of twelve busy people to debate a packet of prawns worth £2.73. "May I remind you," he said, "that the packet of prawns represents this man's honour, his good name." He'd paid nearly £30 for everything else in his trolley and walked out of

Tesco's with a soggy packet of prawns hidden by a plastic bag . . .'

Even a juror who had been on a long fraud trial, a fate most jury panellists move heaven and earth to avoid, told me she found the experience fascinating. A kind of hostage mentality had held the jury together through six months of nerve-jangling boredom. Yet they would have been livid had the judge cut the trial short and told them to acquit, which at one point they had feared he would. They were so involved they desperately wanted to see it through to the end. Which they did. The let-down was that after the emotionally demanding experience of deciding to convict, the defendants were given piffling sentences. 'One of them got just six months,' Rachel Halliburton said. 'That was no more than our own "sentence" had been.'

Sometimes a juror's enthusiasm gets out of hand. A woman member of the jury that was discharged after failing to reach a verdict in the first 'soccer bungs' trial involving footballers Bruce Grobbelaar and John Fashanu in 1997 turned up for the re-trial at Winchester Crown Court. She wanted to 'champion the case for the defence'. She offered to reveal details of how the first jury had split. The judge had to silence her by threatening her with imprisonment.

Being on a jury is not pure fun. Everyone who has done it moans about the tedium and the time-wasting. Many find the deliberating process draining. In some cases the experience can be profoundly distressing. Jurors in a murder trial may have to listen to accounts of appalling violence and depravity. They may be told to look at close-up pictures of a dead child or a mutilated woman. Nauseating exhibits are passed around the jury in a rape case. The jury in the trial of Peter Sutcliffe, the Yorkshire Ripper, had to look at scores of stomach-turning photographs and handle murder weapons that made them shudder with loathing. Bruce Houlder QC has had to put many juries through this sort of ordeal. He told me he always takes great care to steel jurors before showing them such horrors.

The jurors trying the murderer of Harry and Nicola Fuller at the Old Bailey in 1994 had to listen to a tape of Mrs Fuller trying to call the police for help while the telephone receiver filled with blood from her shattered jaw. They then heard the shot that finally killed her. 'You cannot believe the shock that runs through you,' said one of the jurors who had had to hear the tape. 'The fear when you know this is what happened.'

In a *Daily Mail* article in 1996 headlined 'Can jury service damage your health?' Angela Neustatter quoted cases of jurors being physically sick, having panic attacks and suffering acute depressions. One does not like to think what the Rosemary West trial jury had to go through. It is small comfort to know there were counsellors at hand.

There was no counsellor to help Ann Routley after her scarring experience as a juror in 1993. Four years later she was still deeply troubled by her belief that she had helped to send an innocent teenager to prison for manslaughter.

Seventeen-year-old Paul Esslemont was accused of killing a baby boy by battering him to death with a golf club. Ann Routley, a musician then in her late thirties, was on the jury at Birmingham Crown Court. She had never done jury service before. And she would never do it again, she told Gill Martin for an article in the *Evening Standard* in June 1997.

Any murder case must be distressing for the jury. This one was particularly so. The judge warned them that they would have to look at photographs, but that the face of the dead baby boy, Carl Kennedy, would be masked. 'I didn't sleep the night before we saw the pictures,' Ann Routley recalled. 'In the jury room we had the choice to see pictures without the masking tape. I decided to look at these. There was a sense that all this had happened and had to be faced.'

She described the trapped feeling many jurors must

experience: 'You are pulled off the street, which is the value of the jury system, and given the most horrendous responsibility and not allowed to get out of it.' The judge had said, 'If you say he is guilty when he is innocent there's a killer on the loose – and if you say he is innocent when he is guilty there's a killer on the loose.'

A devout Christian, Ann felt the burden of what she had to do dreadfully. She had been sorry for the young boy in the dock and had smiled at him every day 'to reassure him that we were there to give him a fair hearing, and that we wanted to believe the best of him'.

Despite her own doubts about the prosecution evidence, the jury of five men and seven women found him guilty of manslaughter by a ten-to-two majority. 'When the verdict was announced all of us were crying,' Ann remembered. 'One woman juror threw up. I can't describe how awful it is to stand there and hear the foreman say "Guilty".'

Her misery continued after the trial, compounded by the fact that she felt she could not talk about it to a solitary soul because of the contempt laws. Convinced of Esslemont's innocence, she finally screwed up the nerve to go and see his barrister. 'He had never met a juror before me,' she says, 'and it had never occurred to him what it costs people to do their civic duty.' She started a scrapbook. She wrote the boy letters. Eventually she went to see him at the Feltham detention centre for young offenders. And when his first appeal failed, she prompted the BBC to make a *Rough Justice* programme about the case. Other television appearances followed. There was a second appeal. This one was successful. When Paul Esslemont was finally released, on 4 July 1997 ('Independence Day!' Ann told me delightedly on the telephone), he gave a public thank-you to the juror who had worked so hard on his behalf.

Living with the fear that one has contributed to a miscarriage of justice must be appalling. Lord Devlin wrote that 'the sleep of the final verdict is disturbed by the nightmare of miscarriage'. In fact most such errors of judgement are less the jury's fault than the result of inadequate or false evidence. Ann Routley told me that even though they were divided, she still felt her jury had reached the right decision, given what they had to go on. 'Despite my belief that Paul Esslemont was unjustly convicted, I still have faith in the system,' she said.

After all, there may be something to be said for the proposition that if a mistake is made, it is preferable that it should have been made by twelve disinterested people acting in good faith and representing the community rather than a solitary judge representing only the law. Or as Lord Shawcross once observed, 'It is better to risk a bad jury making a mistake in a single case than to have a bad judge able, if not checked by a jury, to make mistakes throughout his judicial career.'

Ann Routley's experience was not typical. However, in extreme form it not only underlines the seriousness of the jury's task but demonstrates the conscientiousness it can inspire in those called on to perform it. And looking back, she says, she did find it stimulating as well as harrowing. 'After all, *Twelve Angry Men* is my father's favourite film.'

THE AMERICAN EXPERIENCE

Nowhere is the jury system more highly revered than in the United States, where *Twelve Angry Men* virtually has the status of a sacred text. And nowhere are its shortcomings more cruelly exposed. The reverence dates back to pre-revolutionary times, when the English jury system, by a nice irony, provided a legal means of subverting the English colonial power. The shortcomings go back a good way, too: at the start of this century Mark Twain wrote the scathing words quoted at the beginning of this book: 'The jury system puts a ban upon intelligence and honesty, and a premium upon ignorance, stupidity, and perjury.'

Of course, that is the sort of thing a non-admirer might have said about juries anywhere any time. The real problems with the American legal system are of more recent vintage. One thinks of the trial of the four Los Angeles policemen, acquitted of assaulting Rodney King despite a video showing them doing exactly that; of the first O.J. Simpson trial; and of the hung juries which failed to agree that Lyle and Erik Menendez had (or hadn't) murdered their parents in cold blood. No one suggested that these juries failed to act according to their consciences. But there was something distinctly unsettling about how they were chosen and why they acted the way they did. Some British people would want to include the Louise Woodward jury in this catalogue but, as I have said before, it seems to me it was the defence lawyers, not the jurors, who got it wrong in that instance, and the judge evidently agreed.

During the same decade that these criminal cases hit the headlines, there was a growing number of eye-watering jury awards in commercial law suits, personal injury claims, discrimination cases and the like. It was a trend that was already well under way in the 1980s. By 1992 the annual cost of civil liability cases tried by juries was estimated to have reached an astounding three hundred billion dollars a year.

The upshot is that there have been outbreaks of serious concern in the US about the jury system. It was persuasively expressed by Stephen Adler in *The Jury: Disorder in the Court*, which begins like this:

We love the idea of the jury but hate the way it works. We celebrate the jurors' democratic power but no longer trust the decisions they reach. We say we have the best system in the world, but when called to serve, most of us do everything we can to duck out.

I certainly endorse that last complaint, since it applies here too. But as to the others, it is with relief that one reads some of Adler's more hair-raising passages and realises that the worst excesses he is describing could not happen here. For one thing, British juries are no longer involved in civil trials other than libel cases: even there, the freedom which they used to have to dish out the kind of damages that froze the blood of newspaper editors has been curtailed. Whereas in some of the civil trials that Adler is able to reconstruct, one is torn between sympathy and distaste for the jurors whom he talked to (quite legally) about their deliberations: sympathy for their anxiety at being incapable of grasping abstruse points of commercial law, for example, or at the lack of guidance in trying to put a money value on an Aids sufferer's suffering; distaste at the spirit of materialism and vengefulness with which they dream up their multi-million-dollar damages. The rule of thumb seems to be: the bigger the corporation, the more noughts you add.

Another difficulty we are largely spared in England and Wales is the hung jury, thanks to the introduction of majority verdicts under Roy Jenkins's Home Secretaryship. In most states in the US, verdicts still have to be unanimous. This leads to mis-trials, delays, stress for the defendants and costly re-trials – sometimes because just one 'holdout' juror, perhaps overcome by moral scruples, has stood out against the rest. In Washington DC and Los Angeles, for example, the hung-jury rate is about 13 per cent of criminal trials.

In New Zealand there have been similar problems. By 1997 the hung-jury ratio had risen above 10 per cent and there were mounting calls to introduce majority verdicts as in Australia and the UK. But Stephen Adler tells me there is no such pressure in the US. 'The twelve people on a jury are seen as one decision-maker.'

I wonder whether a subconscious reason why the unanimity rule still holds sway may be because of capital punishment, which is on the statute books in thirty-six states. Jurors in a case where a guilty verdict might lead to the electric chair or a lethal injection are closely questioned by the court to ensure that they are 'death-qualified', i.e. not opposed in principle to the ultimate penalty. If that sounds grisly to our ears (and also appears to give the jury selection a somewhat retributionist bias), at least all twelve jurors must be of one mind. In most states it is their job not only to reach the verdict but also to decide whether the death penalty should be imposed. So perhaps it would be argued that if a murderer gets the benefit of a unanimous jury, the bank robber and the child molester should have the same protection.

Stephen Adler's book highlights another bizarre development which again has no direct relevance here but which serves to underline a real merit of the English jury system. The way we select our juries is not completely random, because so many well-qualified people are exempt, can be excused or find it easy to get off. But we no longer have peremptory challenges. Broadly speaking, the jury you get is the jury you are stuck with. In the US, by contrast, the opportunities for jury challenges are not only generous but have become such a key part of the trial process that it can take weeks or even months to find a dozen people who meet with the lawyers' approval.

On the back of this there has grown up an extraordinarily lucrative business, that of the jury consultants. These are specialists in assessing jury panellists in terms of their likely inclinations to condemn or acquit in any given case. They are retained by lawyers in big cases to help decide how to exercise peremptory challenges. They are aided by pre-trial questionnaires which each panellist must fill in, relating to background, religious beliefs, prejudices etc, and an interview with each potential juror conducted by the judge and counsel, known as a '*voir dire*'. They may even resort to using private investigators, if John Grisham's chilling portrayal of juror selection in *The Runaway Jury* is halfway true to life. In 1989, these people earned an estimated two hundred million dollars for their services. The figure must be vastly greater now.

In the old days American lawyers prided themselves on being able to handle this sort of thing on their own. Adler quotes from an article by the famous defence lawyer Clarence Darrow, writing in 1936 in *Esquire* magazine. His chief targets for a peremptory challenge were Presbyterians ('cold as the grave') and Scandinavians ('almost always sure to convict'). Other attorneys have their own pet theories: Adler mentions one who thinks Irish-Americans are prone to side with the police and that blacks tend to sympathise with the accused. Men are less censorious than women. The old are more understanding than the young. The young are more anti-authoritarian than the old. And so on. There is even a flourishing trade in DIY books on jury selection, which teach the tyro defence lawyer 'how to assemble your winning jury, step-by-step'. The unsuccessful prosecution lawyer in the O.J. Simpson trial thought she had a particular rapport with middle-aged black women jurors, according to a fascinating article in the *New Yorker*. It did not help on that occasion.

What a Pandora's Box is opened here. In a commentary in March 1997 the *New Yorker* magazine angrily denounced the systematic use of peremptory challenges 'to distort jury demographics'. In the name of swearing-in an unprejudiced jury, every kind of prejudice is sanctioned: racism, ageism, sexism, anti-intellectualism.

Stephen Adler was alarmed by much of what he discovered

in his researches. He suggested the American courts should look to England to redress some of the problems, notably the abuse of peremptory challenges. For a time his prize-winning book sparked some support. There were loud rumblings and enthusiastic conferences following the Menendez and O. J. Simpson trials. But the momentum petered out: the power of the US Trial Bar is simply too great to fight, he told me. When it comes to reforming or even abolishing the peremptory challenge process, too many lawyers have invested too much energy in becoming expert jury selectors – and made too much money in consequence – to abandon the status quo.

What is heartening about this book is what it reveals about the attitude of jurors. Because the author was free to interview them about what went on in the jury room, he was able to follow the verdict-reaching process in great detail and a wide variety of cases, from a double murder in Dallas to the fraud trial of Imelda Marcos in 1990. In some of these cases the jury did its job in model fashion. In others, they were shockingly hampered by complexities which they were incapable of fathoming. But what was common to all of them was the seriousness with which they approached their task. Greater intelligence on the part of some of the jurors, clearer presentation on the part of some of the lawyers, more understanding from some of the judges might have produced 'better' verdicts. But they would not have been more honest ones.

I like to think that if the same sort of scrutiny were applied in this country it would, in that respect, lead to a similar conclusion.

TRIMMING THE LAMP

MAJOR ADJUSTMENTS

No one would claim that the jury is a precision instrument for discovering the truth. As the 12th Juror says in Ann Routley's father's favourite film, 'This isn't an exact science.' Juries are clumsy, expensive, fallible and slow. But the jury is not only an administrative device. It also has a symbolic and political function. It is Lord Devlin's 'lamp that shows that freedom lives'. It is Sir William Blackstone's 'sacred bulwark of the nation'. It is de Tocqueville's 'peerless teacher of citizenship'. It is Lord Bingham's 'safety valve'. It is the rope by which the great hot-air balloon of the law is tethered to terra firma. It is a prodigious breeder of metaphors.

The question is whether the lofty claims made for the jury system as a democratic and historic institution are being undermined by its practical imperfections. Sir Louis Blom-Cooper thinks they are: costs alone will bring it down one day unless it is reformed, he predicts. But no British government would want to be seen cheering on the process too eagerly. Certainly not this one, you would think. Any Prime Minister who refers to The People as often as Tony Blair does ought to approach the jury box on bended knee.

Yet as we have seen, the jury is certainly not immune from reform at Labour's hands. Less than two years after the Tories shied away from the Runciman Report's controversial proposal to curtail a defendant's right to opt for trial by jury in 'either-way' cases, the new government was blithely following in Michael Howard's footsteps.

Likewise on the matter of complex fraud trials, I would bet a lunch at El Vino's against an Old Bailey coffee that the Roskill Committee's 1986 report will be back on the table before the new millennium is very old. The Solicitor-General, Lord Falconer, has already set the ball rolling in his Denning Lecture in October 1997. The subject was raised again at a well-attended seminar at Gray's Inn two months later, presided over by the Lord Chief Justice. The Lord Chancellor, Lord Irvine of Lairg, has also signalled his approval for a re-examination of trial by jury in certain kinds of fraud case. And in February 1998 the Home Office joined in what was beginning to look like a concerted effort by issuing a consultation document.

Roskill recommended that in complex fraud trials 'falling within certain guidelines' the jury should be replaced by a tribunal, consisting of a judge and two lay members. This was not acted upon by the Conservative government. One counter-argument was that it would be the thin end of the wedge, opening the way for juries to be removed from other complicated cases. Another was that it would be seen as unfair to withdraw a defendant's right to jury trial for just one kind of criminal offence.

I can only offer a layman's observations on this subject. One is that as far as I can tell the general public would not give a fig if difficult fraud cases were tried without juries. This is not the kind of crime that concerns them much, with the odd exception such as the Maxwell case. Potential jurors live in terror of being empanelled for a long fraud trial – terror of boredom, first, and inadequacy, second.

Can justice really be done in such circumstances? The answer from Rachel Halliburton, the ex-fraud-trial juror I mentioned earlier, a Cambridge classics graduate in her twenties, is that it can. Her trial at the Old Bailey lasted six months. Her fellow-jurors were unusually young and had no knowledge of high finance. At times they were driven close to screaming point by boredom and frustration. But they fastened on to the human rather than the book-keeping aspects of the trial and, after two days' deliberation, reached a unanimous guilty verdict. In other words they coped.

However, Rachel Halliburton considered that the way her jury had come together as a team was exceptional: she was not confident that other juries would have been as competent. On reflection, despite her evident pride in her own jury's achievement, she thought Roskill was right. From her experience, she agreed that a jury on a big fraud trial can be an invitation for the defence to bombard it with paper and bamboozle it with figures until it rolls over on its back and says *pax*: not guilty. She and her juror friends were sharp enough to realise they were being made the targets of precisely such treatment. The defence counsel 'meandered' endlessly, she said. But the fact that they overcame this strategy in their own case does not mean it is not a serious problem in others.

The former chairman of the Criminal Bar Association, Roy Amlot QC, has argued that 'All complex issues can be made simple . . . That is the task of the judge and advocate.' The question is: are these learned worthies always up to that task?

One further point in reconsidering the conduct of fraud trials is that a Roskill-style tribunal is not the only alternative to a jury. The danger with this solution is that if some fat-cat financier were acquitted on a fraud charge by a judge and two City types sitting as lay assessors it could all too easily look like an establishment stitch-up. My own preference would be to retain juries in such cases, for the sake of public confidence, but to allow that the jurors should be specially qualified, either by education or work experience or both.

As for curtailing the right of defendants to opt for trial by jury in 'either-way' cases, should the Runciman proposals come to be implemented, I have these self-contradictory observations. First, there seems to be a fairly widespread prejudice that defendants who take such cases to the higher court are often guilty, but banking on a brain-dead jury to let them off. No doubt this is monstrously cynical, but it does happen to be true that nine out of ten of those who elect trial by jury have previous convictions. Second, since defendants refused trial by jury will have the right to appeal against the magistrates' decision, the savings in time and money may well not be very great. And third, one must never forget Judge Tumim's observation that 'a box of chocolates can be a serious matter if you are an elderly clergyman'.

Meantime, there are some much less controversial reforms which might help to trim Lord Devlin's lamp by enhancing both the fairness and efficiency of the jury system.

MODEST PROPOSALS

Exemptions and excuses

The single most effective way of bolstering the jury's credibility would be to revise the rules that govern its selection. Before the property qualification for jurors was abolished in 1972 and the lower age limit dropped to 18, juries were widely seen as 'middle-aged, middle-minded and middle-class' (Lord Devlin again). Now they are widely seen as being not nearly middling enough. As it happens, that is not borne out by such statistics as there are. But as always in matters of justice, which as we know must be seen to be done, the perception is all-important. And the perception is that juries have been dumbed down to a worrying degree.

The way things look, there is a nod-and-a-wink conspiracy between the courts and the professional classes to allow the best-qualified members of the public to get off doing jury service. That not only seems unfair to those who cannot avoid it. It might also seem unfair to a defendant, who expects to be judged by his peers. It might seem unfair to the police, whose hard work comes to nothing when a jury is outwitted by a clever defence counsel. It might seem equally unfair to a clever defence counsel, if she happens to be someone like Helena Kennedy who also feels unhappy with a 'lumpen' jury.

All in all, it would be better if things did not look the way they do.

First, the long list of exemptions from jury service should be reviewed. The reason for excluding clergymen and prison medical officers, to take just two categories, escapes me. But it is the host of people who, whether by self-interested lobbying or establishment diktat, 'have the right to be excused' that really needs drastic pruning. MPs, peers, nurses, vets, chemists, soldiers, sailors . . . These are all people who find it possible to take their summer holidays without putting constituents, patients, pets or the defence of the realm at risk. There is no reason on earth why they could not arrange to do a fortnight's jury service once in their lifetimes. As it is, the jury system is deprived of their expertise and special knowledge of the world: its representativeness is reduced and its randomness is diminished. That is a shame.

(I think MPs and senior civil servants should serve on juries not once in their lives but once every five years or so. It ought to be a condition of office. It would help them to keep in touch with the world they make laws for and administer. In *Democracy in America* Alexis de Tocqueville wrote that jury service makes people 'feel the duties which they are bound to discharge towards society . . . [and] rubs off that private selfishness which is the rust of society'. Forget the health farm. A stint in the jury box is what our rulers need.)

Almost as irritating as the official excusees are the quantities of people who manage to get off by pleading hardship or a pre-booked holiday. As I have mentioned before, the preponderance of the well-qualified and well-educated among their number is striking. Off they skip, having made their excuses, leaving the rest feeling like mugs, as though their time were considered less valuable than the escapers'. It is not quite the scandal it is in America, where more than half those summoned for jury service either don't show up at all or plead 'extreme inconvenience' to get off. But New York's clampdown on middle-class jury-dodgers would be a good model for New Labour too.

DC Ian Slade had the right idea here: give people advance notice that they will be summoned for jury service within a certain period, say a year or eighteen months; then let them select the dates that suit them best. Once they were committed to a given fortnight, the penalty for non-attendance would be tough.

The idea that only little people do jury service has got about. It is bad for justice, bad for democracy, and bad for the long-term future of trial by jury. It ought to be changed.

Volunteers

One way to upgrade juries would be to welcome volunteer jurors. Of course, I can see the objections. All kinds of martinets and busybodies would be inclined to put their hands up. But exactly the same objections apply to lay magistrates. A simple screening process could deal with the problem. And a limit of, say, two or three stints could avoid the risk of case-hardening. Meanwhile, there are thousands of people eager and well-qualified to do jury service – particularly among the retired – who never get the chance. It is a great waste of untapped civic energy.

The age limit

I have serious doubts about jurors as young as 18 being allowed to sit on juries. What can they know of the world at that age? Beyond bringing comfort to a youthful defendant there is no virtue in this genuflection towards the young. Being one of twelve on a jury that could decide a man's future for years to come is a much weightier matter than being one of millions allowed to vote at election time. Twenty-one would be more acceptable. If magistrates must be 27 before they are regarded as eligible, shouldn't similar albeit less stringent considerations apply to jurors, who generally speaking are trying much more serious cases?

The challenge

The abolition of the peremptory challenge in 1988 was arguably regrettable. The upside for the juror is that he or she won't be turned away for having a red face or wearing pearls, as might once have happened and sometimes did. The downside for the accused is obviously more serious. The defendant may now find himself being tried by a jury containing no one he recognises as a peer and maybe several people whose appearance he finds objectionable. Race, sex, class and age all come into this.

In 1989 the Court of Appeal decided that judges had no power to order a new jury panel if they thought it would be fairer to have a different racial or sexual balance. In *Freedom, the Individual and the Law*, Geoffrey Robertson argues that it 'is plainly necessary to give judges by statute this very power'. The Runciman Commission made the same recommendation, though only for cases with a 'racial dimension'.

I don't know. We should be very careful. This way all sorts of madnesses lie, as America knows better than we do: there they are well aware of the danger of challenges that look as though they are made on a purely racial basis, which of course they often are. In any case, black people are not the only minorities. Should homosexual defendants be entitled to some token gays in the jury box? Should a Moonie be allowed some fellow Moonies? Could an Old Harrovian insist on there being at least one ex-public schoolboy among his judges? Just over a century ago, Constantinos Korkolis would have been entitled to a jury '*de medietate linguae*', which could have included a few fellow-countrymen. Why not now?

This matter is bound to resurface sooner or later, the way our grievance-driven, discrimination-conscious society is going. One way to deal with it would be simply to restore the right to three (or maybe fewer) peremptory challenges. That would be a sop to fairness, though not a guarantee of it. Another, as we have seen, would be to allow judges to pressurise the prosecution into exercising its stand-by right in instances where the composition of the jury seemed inappropriate. That would have the merit of being a good old-fashioned compromise. It would require no legislation, merely a directive from the Lord Chief Justice. The problem would be what to do if counsel for the prosecution refused to play ball . . . Discuss.

Juror education

Most courts make some sort of attempt at letting jurors know what they are in for and how to go about it. Even so, nothing can quite prepare them for the emotional impact of sitting through a trial and then having to reach a verdict which might mean a defendant's ending up in prison. One proposal put forward by Sean Enright and James Morton in *Taking Liberties* would be to ensure that potential jurors watch part or all of a trial before they sit for the first time.

This would not only settle their nerves. It would also, the authors suggest, help to deal with the 'new juror' syndrome: 'Simply stated, this means that jurors on their first trial (for reasons that are easy to understand) are notoriously prone to acquit.'

This seems to me an excellent notion. I also agree with them that 'better education of our children about the responsibility of citizenship (including jury service) might have a beneficial effect'.

The Thirteenth Juror

As Helena Kennedy explained to me, this is a very straight-forward, unobjectionable device, used widely in the United States. It amounts to this: that for long cases one or more extra jurors should be sworn in, who would hear the trial alongside the dozen in the jury box. In the event of one of them having to drop out, a replacement juror would drop in and the trial would proceed smoothly. This way the risk of the jury's shrinking below the majority-verdict quorum would be avoided and there would be no costly re-trial.

In Russia, the jury system is being enthusiastically revived on largely English lines (thanks to the efforts of proselytisers such as Robin Grey QC, chairman of the international committee of the Criminal Bar Association, who has made numerous trips there). However, the Russians do like the American idea of replacement jurors, and mean to adopt it.

The invisible jury

If one were designing a courtroom today, one would not site the jury box in full view of the public gallery. The authorities do their best to stage terrorist cases and organised crime trials in suitable venues, but it is not always possible. Jurors should be made to feel that their security is a top priority. They are treated as cannon fodder anyway. To put them literally in danger is unacceptable if enough courts could be re-designed so as to minimise the risk.

Note-taking

Despite the Old Bailey's introductory video and helpful pamphlets, jurors are often uncertain about note-taking. In the US nearly 40 per cent of judges are against the idea. They say jurors writing in longhand fall behind. But even that is better than having to rely solely on one's memory. In a reader's letter in the *Independent* in May 1997 an ex-juror claimed that, as the only one taking notes on his jury, the record he had kept had been vital to their reaching a sensible verdict.

Judges should spend a moment at the beginning of a trial urging the jury to jot down at least a word or two every few minutes, without frightening them into making them feel they have to. The risk of a note-taker getting something wrong and its then being treated as gospel simply because it has been written down would be diminished if the other jurors were taking notes too.

Questions

Judges should make quite clear the procedure for the jury to send questions up to the bench. Some ex-jurors have told me they were unaware they could even do this. (In the US, a majority of judges are against juries asking any questions at all. Some in this country feel the same.) In our own case, it took the jury quite a while to get up the courage to put a query. After that, individual jurors became so keen to catch the usher's eye with their own piercingly perceptive questions that proceedings kept grinding to a halt. Had we been allowed to carry on we might have ended up, like some medieval juries, trying to run the trial ourselves. As it was, the judge reined us in by saying he would only take questions if they were put by the jury as a whole.

Instructions

By tradition, the judge instructs the jury on the law as it relates to a case at the very end of the trial. It had not occurred to me that there was anything odd about this until I read an American judge's comment that this was like 'telling jurors to watch a baseball game and decide who won without telling them what the rules are until the end of the game'. Another senior federal judge, writing in the *American Bar Association Journal* in 1960, had this to say:

> What manner of mind can go back over a stream of conflicting statements of alleged facts, recall the intonations, the demeanour, or even the existence of the witnesses, and retrospectively fit all these recollections into a pattern of evaluation and judgement given him for the first time after the events?

Stephen Adler commends the approach of some judges who give their juries preliminary instructions on the law at the beginning of a case as well as a fuller version at the end. This sounds like good sense, though it would have to be managed so as not to increase the opportunities for an appeal on grounds of misdirection.

What makes even better sense to me is the suggestion from my fellow juror Sophie that defence barristers should also do a bit of preliminary instructing before introducing their examinations-in-chief of a witness – maybe even their cross-examinations, too. That way jurors would have a better idea what they were supposed to be listening out for and counsel would find it harder to go on exasperating 'fishing expeditions'.

Language

The language of the courtroom veers between the obscure when lawyers address each other, to the commonplace when they address the jury. Apart from the occasional sense that one is being talked down to, I don't think jurors have much to complain about. However, there are two crucial bits of legal terminology that recur in both scenarios. They are 'the burden of proof' and 'beyond reasonable doubt'. Judges and barristers address these words to juries as though their meaning were self-evident. I am not certain it is.

Does 'beyond reasonable doubt' mean 'beyond a shadow of a doubt' or is it closer to 'almost certainly'? How reasonable does reasonable have to be? As that contemporary philosopher Eric Cantona might put it, if a drop of black paint lands on a white wall, is it still a white wall?

If lawyers think this is quibbling, consider the standard definition of 'reasonable doubt' given to juries in the State of California:

> It is not a mere possible doubt; because everything relating to human affairs, and depending on moral evidence, is open to some possible or imaginary doubt. It is that state of the case which, after the entire comparison and consideration of all the evidence, leaves the minds of the jurors in that condition that they cannot say they feel an abiding conviction, to a moral certainty, of the truth of the charge.

The constitutionality of this impenetrable definition was upheld by the US Supreme Court in 1994.

Mr Justice Popplewell agreed that this was a difficulty.

He himself used to explain to juries that what was meant was 'a doubt for which you can give a reason', but much preferred present practice which is for judges not to use the phrase at all. Instead they say, 'You must be satisfied so that you are sure.' Defence lawyers, however, still adhere to reasonable doubt – which should tell us something about which side it might be thought to favour.

Perhaps judges could explain such terms more fully to their juries. Or a little glossary could be included in the new juror's introductory bumf. 'Admissible evidence' might be added to the list, along with some other courtroom favourites such as 'infer', 'indictment', 'hearsay', 'deposition' – although the line would have to be drawn somewhere: I was told of a jury which had sent a note up to the judge asking him for a definition of 'common sense'.

Research

The Runciman Commission recommended that Section 8 of the Contempt of Court Act 1981 should be amended 'so that informed debate can take place rather than an argument based only on surmise and anecdote'. Nothing has so far happened, save for a nod and a wink from the Solicitor-General in October 1997 that the Government might consider reviewing Section 8. The purpose of such a relaxation would be to collect material 'which may be of assistance in determining whether there are certain trials which are wholly inappropriate for juries'. (It was clear he had complicated fraud cases in mind.) It was followed by similar hints from the Lord Chancellor and the Lord Chief Justice.

I am in two minds about all this. My journalistic instincts are on the side of inquisitiveness. I sympathise with Geoffrey Robertson's view that the present restrictions pose a 'formidable obstacle to any rational understanding of the corner-stone of the criminal justice system'. On the other hand I would be nervous that too close a scrutiny would show up merely the flaws in the institution while doing nothing to explain its strengths.

We would discover that the 'wrong' people go about reaching their verdicts in the 'wrong' way for the 'wrong' reasons and forget that by any measure they still mostly come to the 'right' decisions.

All the same I do not like to think that the reason juries are shrouded in secrecy is because there is so much to hide. There ought to be a way for academic researchers to open the jury-room door a crack without its occupants rushing past them on to the courthouse steps to sell their stories to the Sunday papers. There must be scope for research that guarded anonymity, did not name cases and stuck to agreed guidelines. But it would have to be conducted with extreme care. As A.P. Herbert wrote: 'The Common Law of England has been laboriously built about a mythical figure – the figure of "The Reasonable Man".'

Faith in that figure is what keeps the jury system going.

JURY SERVICE:
A SURVIVAL GUIDE

The summons

Sod's Law dictates that if you are one of those people who is longing to do jury service, you will never get a summons. If you belong to the other half and fear the buff envelope because you are too busy, too timid or too grand to spend a fortnight rubbing up against real life, the chances are you will get one.

When it arrives, my advice is: don't panic. You may be mad or on probation, in which case you are disqualified. Or you may fall into one of those categories, such as midwives and MPs, where you can ask to be excused from jury service. If the former, too bad. If the latter, think twice before exercising your right to be let off. Ask yourself whether that is an honourable thing to do – especially if you are one of those who thinks juries these days are dominated by anti-social morons.

If you are at least 18 years old, under 70 and belong to none of these categories you will have to turn up at the appointed court at the appointed time (though the over- 65s can ask to be excused). You may still get a deferral if you can give a good reason, but I am not encouraging you to do so. If you are a good citizen you should do jury service anyway. If you are not it may help turn you into one.

The first day

If you are determined to duck out, there is usually an early opportunity to approach the jury bailiff and make your excuses.

If you stay put, then different courts have different arrangements, but there will generally be some form of instruction as to your jury duties and how to go about them.

For many jurors, sitting around doing nothing dominates their fortnight's jury service. This is highly regrettable but should be approached in a positive spirit. Readers will find it bliss, provided they come well-equipped with a good big book. Card-players, knitters, crossword-puzzlers and Scrabblers should likewise kit themselves out as though for a summer holiday in Wales.

Once you have sampled the canteen you can decide whether you need to bring in your own coffee and sandwiches thenceforward. Weigh your pockets down with chewing gum, cough sweets, cigarettes and aspirin. You may not need all of these things yourself but they are a good way of making friends and cementing jury solidarity. A sewing kit, a calculator and some blank birthday cards can also come in handy.

Eventually you will be called, along with fifteen or so others, and led into a courtroom by an usher. The clerk of the court will then shuffle some cards and read out the names on them one by one until twelve people have taken their places in the jury box. Occasionally this process may be disrupted. For example, if it is going to be a long case, the judge may give potential jurors an extra chance to excuse themselves: they will have to approach the bench and explain why. In some cases where there are to be a lot of documents, jurors with reading difficulties will be asked to withdraw. There are other special instances in which jurors with particular connections – say to Eire or Northern Ireland in the case of terrorist trials – may have the option to step down. When this happens, the next name on the cards is read out until the jury box is full.

The jury must now be sworn. This is straightforward if you are happy to take your oath on the Testament. But it is sometimes not pointed out to jurors that not only may they swear on another holy book such as the Koran; they may also simply affirm. If that is what you want to do, just tell the usher.

The courtroom

The courts I have been in, apart from Number I Court at the Old Bailey, have seemed much smaller than they look on television. The jury is only feet away from some of the principal players, which can be unnerving.

Courts have different layouts, but it is usually obvious which the bench is and which the dock. In front of the judge sits the clerk of the court. Close by will be the court shorthand-taker and the usher.

The barristers are in the front row of the stalls, so to speak, facing the bench. In a serious case there will usually be two barristers for the Crown – a Queen's Counsel, who is very experienced and very expensive, and a junior barrister. The same kind of Batman and Robin set-up will apply to each defendant. In a more modest case, one barrister each will do. But in a big trial with several people in the dock, there will be enough wig-hair in court to stuff a double mattress.

The men and women behind the barristers, not wearing gowns and wigs, are the solicitors for the defendants and for the Crown Prosecution Service. Solicitors do not normally speak in court. Their job is to take instructions from their clients, brief the barristers and do the day-to-day work involved in preparing the case.

In the dock will be the defendant and a prison officer. If he has two prison officers with him it is a safe deduction that he is regarded as a security risk – though of course whether he is or not is really the jury's job to decide.

Elsewhere in the courtroom there will be the policeman in charge of the case, possibly with an exhibits officer by his side. And if it is an important trial, the press will be clustered together with their pens poised and notebooks open.

Finally there is the public gallery, whose comings and goings can sometimes offer richer entertainment than what is going on in the well of the court. It takes a typical tourist couple five minutes to settle in their places and fold their anoraks, another ten to realise they haven't the faintest notion what is going on and a further quarter of an hour to get up the courage to creep out, looking as guilty as if they were walking out of a first night at the National Theatre.

Rather more alarming is the sight of the same person in the gallery day after day, staring down unsmilingly and fixing the jury with a glare from time to time. Perhaps he is the defendant's cousin.

The trial

The trial is now ready to begin. Do not be concerned if you are not present to hear the defendant plead guilty or not guilty to the indictment. That often happens in the jury's absence. What you can be sure of is that the person or persons in the dock is/are pleading not guilty to the charges that the clerk of the court now reads out. Otherwise there would be no need for you to be there.

The judge then says 'Yes, Mr (or Miss or Mrs) So-and-so . . .' and prosecuting counsel opens the case, explaining what it is about and what the Crown will seek to prove. Then the first witness will be called. The thing to remember here is that the barristers are not giving evidence. They are merely eliciting it and commenting on it. The witnesses' evidence is what is important, not the spin-doctoring – which lawyers invented long before politicians gave a name to it. Each witness, whether for the Crown or for the defence, undergoes an examination-in-chief first, conducted by the side for which he or she is appearing, then a cross-examination by the opposition, followed by a re-examination at the hands of the original inquisitor. You will soon get used to the pattern.

Fog will set in quite quickly. New evidence will start to jostle out the old. Take notes. If you are not an experienced note-taker, simply concentrate on jotting down the date of each day's sitting, who is in the witness box and a few headlines that will jog your memory later: anything that strikes you as remarkable or unexpected.

The jury can ask any question it likes, more or less whenever it likes. The inquisitive jury is frowned upon by some judges, but effectively the court must be prepared to do what it can to help a jury in its task.

It is best if a question is put by the jury as a whole, perhaps after discussion during a break. You might wish to clarify something a witness has said, or you might want the witness to be asked something which counsel seems to have overlooked. In the latter case, it is a good idea to wait until the examination-in-chief and cross-examinations are completed, as nine times out of ten the question you are burning to ask will be put by one of the barristers. However, take care: don't leave your question until after the witness has been released as it is unlikely he or she will be recalled to the stand just for your sake.

When you have agreed your question, it should be written down on a bit of paper: 'My Lord/Your Honour: The jury would like to know etc etc.' Back in court, catch the usher's attention and hand him the note. The usher will pass it to the judge. Proceedings will halt and the judge will then decide how to deal with your query, making sure that all counsel get a look at it.

This is also the procedure for asking for any special information the jury thinks could be helpful. For example, there might be video evidence that you would like to be shown, or you might want to visit the scene of the crime. This will be up to the judge, but if the jury favours some such an expedition, it is best to get the request in fairly early as these things take a while to organise.

A note to the judge is also the way to deal with emergencies arising from foolhardy lunchtime pints. The individual concerned will suffer some embarrassment but that cannot be helped. 'My Lord, could the jury have a short break?' is the usual formula. All the same, take care not to behave flippantly. A London judge once halted a trial after a juror had sent him a note brazenly saying: 'When is it dinnertime?'

Closing speeches

When the last witness has departed, prosecuting counsel addresses the jury for the final time. Throughout the trial, the Crown's job has been to present evidence to prove that the accused is guilty as charged. This closing speech is the opportunity to remind the jury of what the evidence was, explain why it is so damning and heap scorn on the defence's attempts to discredit it.

When the prosecution has sat down, the defence counsel gets up. If there are several defendants, each barrister will speak in turn. Obviously their task is to persuade you that the prosecution evidence was flawed, that the defence's own evidence was much more credible and that the Crown has not proved its case. Defence barristers in their closing speeches are liable to remind you repeatedly that the burden of proof falls on the prosecution and it is not the defence's job to prove the defendant innocent. They will also remind you more than once, with solemn looks and wagging fingers, that to reach a guilty verdict you must be sure 'beyond reasonable doubt' – a phrase which will come back to haunt you.

In his workmanlike book *Jury Service: A Practical Guide* (Hale, 1983) Alan Jones, a retired barrister himself, offers some tips as to how to interpret a defence counsel's closing speech:

> Ask yourself, is he dealing with the evidence or does he restrict himself to criticising prosecuting counsel's speech or talk in generalities such as the burden of proof, the wonderful legal system we have, how the jury system is admired worldwide ... does he speak a long time ... about miscarriages of justice?

These are all signs that he cannot think of anything to say on the facts, says Alan Jones: 'In other words he thinks the defence case is hopeless.'

Hopeless or otherwise, the defence has one great advantage: it has the last word. Only the judge's impartial summing-up remains to be heard.

The summing-up

The summing-up will usually address first the law, then the evidence. You will be reminded of exactly what the indictment means, what the prosecution needs to have proved to win its case, and what the defence needs to have done for you to be persuaded to acquit. Then the judge will probably go back over those bits of the evidence which seem to him important or which were most hotly disputed. He or she may be succinct, or ramble on for hours or even days. What seems important to Your Honour or My Lord may not seem so important to you. 'But then, members of the jury, that is a matter entirely for you to decide . . .'

The judge will tell you to elect a foreman, if you have not done so already. He will tell you to reach a unanimous verdict. If after a certain time (which is not spelt out, though it will depend on the length and complexity of the case) you fail to do so, he will be prepared to consider a majority verdict. In that case you will be recalled to court for further instructions . . . Then the ushers take an oath to keep you in a 'private and convenient place' and off you go.

The deliberation

The usher has seen you to your jury room, told you how to summon food and drink, confiscated any mobile phones, wished you luck and – click – shut the door behind him. You are on your own. Panic. What happens now?

In cases that are going to run for several days, some judges suggest to juries that they elect a foreman early in the trial, which is an excellent idea. Any jury can do this off its own bat, without being encouraged to. If you have not got a foreman, however, now is the time to get one. There are no rules as to how to go about it. The most straightforward approach might be to let candidates volunteer, then have a secret ballot. Alan Jones makes the valuable point that one should not necessarily support the strongest personality: a chairman, not a leader, is what is wanted.

From then on, it is up to the foreman and the rest of the jury to decide how to proceed. In a short case with an open-and-shut feel about it, an immediate show of hands might be in order. Anything more complicated, however, should be approached with greater caution. Common sense tells you that forcing people to take an early stand could be dangerous: they might feel they had to defend it not out of conviction but for reasons of *amour propre*, or because they felt solidarity with others who had taken the same view.

My guess is that many jurors at the beginning of their deliberations feel more comfortable retaining an open mind for as long as possible. Listening to others – and more important, to themselves – is a good way of discovering what they really think. Strong opinions expressed too eagerly and too early will put backs up and probably lead to a resistance movement.

The longer the trial has been, the longer jurors will feel they should take to make up their minds. My advice is to take things easy, ramble over the evidence for a while, send for an exhibit or two. Then agree on a half-dozen key points and home in on them. Once there is a measure of agreement there, then one might move on to the charges themselves.

Inevitably if there is a split vote with a small dissenting minority there will be a temptation for the many to turn on the few. I don't see how this can be avoided, but it is obviously desirable that there should be no bullying, which might be counter-productive anyway. The best person to win over someone who is holding out is less likely to be the most formidable debater than someone who herself or himself has converted from that view.

Sometimes a deliberating jury will want something clarified

– a point of law, or the exact words a witness said. Don't hesitate about sending a note to the judge, who will usually call the jury back into court and answer the question in front of counsel and the defendants. When jurors are at loggerheads on a particular issue, this may be a good way of ending the tension, if only by releasing them from their fetid jury room for a short while.

If no unanimous verdict has been reached on all counts in the indictment(s) after several hours – or maybe days in a longer case – the jury will be brought into court and the judge will say that he is prepared to accept a majority verdict of ten to two.

At this point a jury that is already split ten-two or eleven-one might very well put its feet up for a few minutes just for the sake of decorum and then call the usher to announce that it has reached a majority verdict. That would be perfectly OK, but it is not very satisfying for the jury (nor possibly for the defendant, judge, barristers, police etc). A jury that has worked well together will want to be unanimous. So unless it is a Friday afternoon and everyone is yearning to get off to the pub, a conscientious jury might suggest a time limit within which to try to achieve unanimity.

The final round-the-table gathering of verdicts is a grave business if the jury is going to convict; less so I imagine in the case of an acquittal. One does not even care to speculate about the prevailing atmosphere in the event of a hung jury.

The verdict

The jurors' duty is now almost done. It only remains for the foreman to deliver the verdicts in response to the clerk of the court's questions. This can be a nerve-racking experience when a jury is finding someone guilty, even if it is only for a relatively minor offence. You are condemning this person on society's behalf, marking him as a criminal, probably sending him to prison. There may no longer be a death penalty for the most serious crime of all, but a jury convicting a young man or woman of murder will know very well what is at stake.

The sentence

The jury does not have to be present for the sentencing, but in the event of a guilty verdict it would be an odd jury that did not want to be, even if it were held over to another day. Prior to the judge's deciding what the sentence should be, prosecuting counsel and the police will disclose the prisoner's antecedents. More often than not they will reveal a history of criminal behaviour and a string of prior convictions. This is a sweet moment for a jury that has agonised over finding a defendant guilty. The record suggests you have done the right thing after all.

After hearing the sentence, the jurymen and women in such a case will retire to the pub content that they have done their duty, but grumbling about why it all had to be so complicated, why the truth was arrived at in such a crablike fashion, why they could not have been told the man was a crook from the beginning.

No one will bother to explain to you that what you have been doing is upholding two great beliefs: the first is that anyone, whatever his character, must be held to be innocent until proved guilty; the second is that as a general rule in this country no court can put someone behind bars for longer than six months unless the defendant's fellow-citizens have found him guilty.

You were the fellow-citizens. You found him guilty. Justice was done.

INDEX

A NOTE ON THE AUTHOR

Trevor Grove grew up in Argentina but was educated mainly in England. After Oxford University he became a journalist, working for the *Spectator*, the London *Evening Standard*, the *Observer* and the *Daily Telegraph*, and was editor of the *Sunday Telegraph*. He lives in London.